HOME COMFORT

A HISTORY OF
DOMESTIC ARRANGEMENTS

IN ASSOCIATION WITH
THE NATIONAL TRUST

CHRISTINA HARDYMENT

VIKING
IN ASSOCIATION WITH
THE NATIONAL TRUST

VIKING

Published by the Penguin Group
Penguin Books Ltd, 27 Wrights Lane, London W8 5TZ, England
Viking Penguin, 375 Hudson Street, New York, New York 10014, USA
Penguin Books Australia Ltd, Ringwood, Victoria, Australia
Penguin Books Canada Ltd, 10 Alcorn Avenue, Toronto, Ontario, Canada, Canada M4V 3BZ
Penguin Books (NZ) Ltd, 182–190 Wairau Road, Auckland 10, New Zealand

Penguin Books Ltd, Registered Offices: Harmondsworth, Middlesex, England

First published in Great Britain by Viking 1992

10 9 8 7 6 5 4 3 2 1

Filmset in 11 on 14pt Monophoto Bembo

Printed in Great Britain by Butler & Tanner Ltd, Frome and London

A CIP catalogue record for this book is available from the British Library

ISBN 0–670–823651

In the well-regulated household, which it is the ambition of all housewives to maintain, the smooth running of the domestic machinery must depend on the efficiency of those offices which, hidden away behind the baize-covered doors of the service passage, are not visible to the eyes of the visitor. The drawing-room may be upholstered and furnished in the very best of taste; the rooms may be all, or even more, than the neighbours can boast, and yet excite ridicule rather than envy, if not backed up by the more solid qualities of a businesslike disposition of these offices, which stand in the same relation to the house as the heart does to the body.

Laurence Weaver, *The House and its Equipment*, 1912

On the south side of the house there is a large woodyard and necessary buildings of dairies, washing, brewing and baking, a pigeon house, and on the south side thereof, and of the court before the house, are several orchards of cherries, pears, plums, others of apples, and also good kitchen gardens with two fishponds all incompassed with a wall. On the west side of the house there is a large voyd court sett with rowes of trees in order, of elmes and walnuttes leading to the stables, barns and stalles and other large buildings for servants, granaries and other necessary uses, where are also several fish ponds and also a hop garden of an acre and a half...

Survey of Montacute, 1667

A place for everything, and everything in its place.

Samuel Smiles, *Thrift*, 1875

To Sarah Dancy

Contents

CONTENTS

PREFACE

As we move round our houses, switching on lights, reaching for food from the refrigerator, running a bath, it is easy to ignore the long history behind the facility with which we now make ourselves comfortable. We drive to the supermarket when we need groceries, forgetting hundreds of years of expertise in the preservation and storage of food. We cook and wash up at the flick of a switch, eliminating memories of the full-time jobs of cooks and scullions. We buy clothes in shops and toss their easy-care fabrics into automatic washer-dryers without a thought for the seamstresses and laundresses who once slaved to make, wash and mend durable garments that lasted the wearer a lifetime and beyond. Lights? Fires? Only the nostalgically minded need do more than plug in to electricity or turn on the gas.

But nostalgia is a powerful force. Every year it takes millions of visitors round the many and various properties owned by the National Trust. That this book was commissioned at all reflects a change in the National Trust's approach to presenting the houses in its care. For many years visitors to Britain's stately homes have been admitted at the front door as if they were guests. As they strolled round salons and dining-rooms, libraries and state bedchambers, they stayed on the smart side of a barrier which had been carefully erected between them and the serious business of managing the house. Occasionally, for those who had eyes to see, there were clues – a bell-pull beside an elaborate marble fireplace, a concealed door in the wainscot panelling, a hand-pumped fire-engine standing forlorn in the corner of a courtyard.

In recent years, however, it has become evident that there is much robust interest in the household offices regarded by Laurence Weaver and other informed commentators as the 'heart' of the house. (They used the term pragmatically, of course: an essential pump, rather than a romantic focus.) After the highly successful experiment of making the servants' quarters the official entrance to Erddig, in Clwyd, the National Trust has begun to open wider the heavy doors that divide formal apartments from domestic offices. In such houses as Shugborough, Uppark and Dunham Massey reconstructed arrangements of the larders, pantries, and housekeeping rooms convey their original uses. Visitors linger in the laundries and dally in the dairies, murmuring of days gone by and exclaiming in delighted recognition that they, or their parents or grandparents, had one 'just like that'. Questions recur time and again:

Townend, Cumbria: servants' stairs wind away to a hidden world. Even in this relatively modest yeoman's house arrangements were made for the family and its servants to live parallel, separate lives.

'How on earth did they manage to cook on that range? To do the washing in those funny wooden tubs? To brew their own beer and make their own bread? To keep everything CLEAN?'

In the attempt to answer those and other questions thoroughly I have spent the last three years engaged upon what is best described as domestic archaeology. I have visited well over a hundred houses of all shapes and sizes, groping through cellars and dilapidated service passages, clambering over ice houses and into dovecotes, poking up chimneys and down drains. It has been both enormously interesting and physically exhausting. 'I must frankly own that, if I had known beforehand the labour which this book has entailed, I should never have been courageous enough to commence it'; so runs the first line of *Mrs Beeton's Book of Household Management*, and so perhaps should run the first line of *Home Comfort*.

My own interest in the history of domesticity began in 1970 in a sewing-machine repair shop on Herne Hill in south London. I was collecting my uninspiring but efficient electric sewing-machine after a service when I spotted a curious G-shaped metal object under the counter. It turned out to be a machine traded in by a previous customer, totally useless as far as the shop owner was concerned. He was happy to take a fiver for it. That Wilcox and Gibbs chain-stitch machine became the basis of a collection that eventually ranged from a massive shoemaker's Singer to a tiny table-edge Moldacot Pocket Seamstress. In time the collection extended to mangles and mincers, marmalade slicers, foot-pumped vacuum cleaners and a small library of old manuals of household management. Reading in these of nursery management, as befitted the mother of four I was in process of becoming, led to a book about the history of baby-care theories (*Dream Babies*, Cape, 1983). The collection itself inspired *Mangle to Microwave* (Polity, 1989), a history of domestic technology since the Great Exhibition.

I was then offered the opportunity to apply my antique housewifely expertise to practical use and to reconstruct, from surviving examples of domestic quarters owned by the National Trust, how and where practical housekeeping actually happened. Confining the scope of the book to National Trust properties has had several advantages. One is that, since most of the houses mentioned are open to the public, I have felt able to describe exact details of, say, the sinks in a housemaid's cupboard or the arrangements of the bins in a wine cellar, in the knowledge that readers will be able, if sufficiently interested, to inspect them for themselves. Another is the convenient boundaries thus set around an enormous and inexhaustible subject. Even so, I am aware that any one of the chapters in this book could have been extended into a book in its own right. Thirdly, thanks to the freedom with which I could use the National Trust archives and exploit the memories of owners and curators, the book is well endowed with anecdotes of particular places and particular people.

One house in particular deserves special mention in this context. At Shugborough, which is run partly by the National Trust and partly by the Staffordshire County Council, there are exceptionally interesting reconstructed working displays to be enjoyed both on the home farm and in such domestic offices as the laundry, the brewery and the kitchen. This is largely because of the initiative and research of Pamela Sambrook, who has collected together reminiscences from former servants in the house, domestic relics of all kinds and all sort of other evidence. She now has a great deal of invaluable practical domestic experience with, for example, washing dollies, box mangles, kitchen-range dampers and brewing tuns.

Otherwise the written history of the layout and workings of domestic offices is patchy and scattered. I have had to glean it from guidebooks, housecraft manuals, treatises on dairies, glossy company histories of brewing and handwritten household inventories. Some authorities became like good and trusted friends. I can recommend Gervase Markham and Thomas Tusser to anyone who wants to forget fast food and

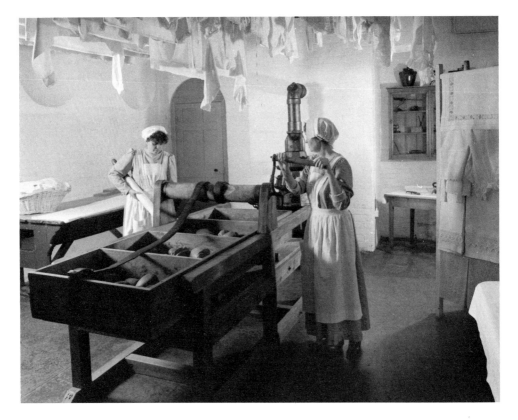

The faithfully restored laundry at Shugborough Hall, Staffs., where clothes are still washed, ironed and mangled. Until the 1930s there were usually three laundresses working six days a week here.

to step back into the golden days of brewing Candlemas Ale and distilling rose-water. Husband and wife teams have considerable charm – one day I will write a little thesis called 'Blinkers and Tentacles' on their differences of approach. Those consulted most frequently are John (an architect and garden designer) and Jane (who wrote novels in her spare time) Loudon, Samuel and Sarah Adams ('fifty years servants in different families'), William and Anne Cobbett, rural radicals to the last, and Isabella and Sam Beeton (few people realize that most of the legendary Mrs Beeton's published wisdom was written by her husband in the three decades after her untimely death). Another extraordinarily useful source has been the complete *Oxford English Dictionary*, which offers leisurely explanations and useful references for such obscure items as brattices and limbecks, incorporators and worm tubs. Only once, in the wine cellar, did I find it at a loss, faced with 'corking-boot'.

Because of the scale of public interest, many National Trust houses have plans to open more of their servants' quarters than were on display when I visited them. I have made the gazetteer at the back of the book as informative and up-to-date as possible concerning items and places of especial domestic interest. The gazetteer will also, I hope, lessen the reader's possible sense of confusion in the face of brief references to so many different houses. On the first occasion of mentioning a house, I have characterized it briefly, or at least said where it is. The effect is to make the first chapter or two of the book clumsy with geographical parenthesis, as overweighted with introductions as the first half-hour of a party, and I apologize for this. Matters should improve as you read on, and the gazetteer and index can be used for cross-references.

Finally, a word about Uppark, badly damaged by fire in 1989, and at present closed for rebuilding. It has extremely interesting servants' quarters, which I had visited before the fire. After some thought, I decided to include descriptions of them as they were, in the hope that it will not be long before they are restored and can be visited once again.

Oxford, 1991

ACKNOWLEDGEMENTS

So many people have been helpful and informative that I cannot list them all. The volunteers who staff the rooms of Trust houses all over the country have been a mine of information – this book should really be dedicated to them. Administrators and historic-building representatives have also been patient and painstaking with suggestions and corrections; many of them gave me personal hospitality. As usual, I am indebted to the two libraries I use most – Oxford's Bodleian Library and the London Library in St James's Square. Pat Eaton of the National Trust Picture Library has spent a great deal of time rootling out pictures. Pamela Sambrook, Gervase Jackson-Stops, Simone Sekers and Sara Paston-Williams read the manuscript and gave useful advice; Margaret Willes, the Trust's Publisher, knows the debt I owe her. Finally Eleo Gordon's unstoppable energy has overcome all the inevitable hitches that a complex project of this sort comes up against.

CHAPTER ONE
THE DOMESTIC PLAN

Houses are built to live in, and not to look upon; therefore
let use be preferred before uniformity, except when both
may be had.

Francis Bacon, 'Of Building', *Essays*, 1625

In 1800 guests jolting inside a carriage as it made its way up the meandering drive
to Florence Court in County Fermanagh would have been impressed – as they were
meant to be – by the calm order of the façade: the long windows promising elegant
reception rooms behind and comfortable bedrooms above, the arcades in which they
could take the air despite the all-too-frequent Irish rain, the sweeping lawns leading
to small summer-houses and woody glades. It probably didn't cross their minds that
they saw only a tiny fraction of the reality of Florence Court; indeed it would be a
reflection of the success of their visit if they remained unaware of the sixty or more
separate departments that provided the hospitality they enjoyed.

Florence Court, built by the Coles of Enniskillen in 1770, has altered very little
over the years. It still conveys the clarity of the eighteenth-century balance between
two separate but connected domestic worlds. Three hundred years earlier, in a
medieval house like Speke Hall, near Liverpool, the physical boundaries between the
occupants were much less distinct. Its black timbers and white plasterwork straggle
around a communal central courtyard, a lay cloister which was a focus of domestic
business for everybody. Such a house was built for one community, not two. Senior
servants were gentlefolk, possibly related to, certainly part of, the family. At the
other extreme, in the nineteenth-century mansion of Cragside, in Northumberland,
the family might just as well have lived on a different planet from the domestic staff,
who served them literally by remote control, through bell systems, house telephones
and a hierarchy of intermediaries.

The bulk of this book will examine in detail the different domestic departments
that provided food, warmth, light and cleanliness in the home, from medieval times
to the beginning of this century. In order to give, as it were, a long shot of the whole
before zooming in to a practical examination of the parts, and to provide a brief

explanation of changes in household management over time, this introduction will contrast the domestic arrangements of these three houses, Speke Hall, Florence Court and Cragside, when they were first built. The different systems can be loosely defined as organic, rational and scientific. Each has a major prophet, as well as a host of minor apologists. Thomas Tusser, the sixteenth-century author of *Five Hundred Points of Good Husbandrie* and its significantly shorter coda, *The Points of Huswiferie*, wrote his invaluable advice on every aspect of house, farm and garden management in easily memorized rhyming couplets. The successive editions of John Loudon's *Cottage . . . and Villa Architecture* between 1796 and 1847 outlined a very different world: all rules and plans, lists and firm order. Finally, Hermann Muthesius, a German architect who was more eloquent than any Englishman on our traditions of home comfort, completed a three-volume celebration of the technological triumphs of *The English House* in 1904.

THE ORGANIC TRADITION: SPEKE HALL

Of all other doings house-keeping is cheefe,
For daily it helpeth the poore with releefe;
The neighbour, the stranger, and all that have neede,
Which causeth thy doings the better to speede.

Thomas Tusser, 1573

The word 'housekeeping' has shifted its meaning over the years. When Shakespeare described Henry VI as a good housekeeper, he was referring to his reputation for liberal hospitality. Feudal obligations, and an acknowledgement of the physical difficulties of travelling in an age when a man could drown in a pothole in the road, meant that charity to all comers was expected. There were no inns or hotels, although the monasteries and convents undertook to provide for travellers in need. The great hall was arranged so that another seat could always be fitted in at the long tables that ran its length. After all, before the days of postal services and telephones there was no reliable way of warning your host that you were about to arrive.

The Willoughby Household Orders of 1572 for Wollaton, in Northamptonshire, directed the usher to make sure 'that no stranger be suffered to pass without offering him to drink'. After dinner, he was to put 'the remainder of the meat . . . into the almes table, which is always by him to be kept safely locked, to be distributed among the poor on the dayes appointed'.

The general arrangement of a medieval manor-house was to put the great hall and the chambers on two sides of a quadrangle and the servants' quarters on the remaining two sides. At Speke Hall, built in the sixteenth century, the main rooms of the house,

*The inner courtyard of Speke Hall, Merseyside, built in the sixteenth century, formed
a communal lay cloister which was the focus for domestic busy-ness. On a fine day,
washing, vegetable preparation and even cooking took place outside.*

as well as the kitchen, dairy and scullery, were all placed around one central courtyard.
Just outside this, but linked to the scullery by storerooms and larders, was the laundry.
The dairy was separated from the kitchen by a passageway; its scullery had an external
door so that milk did not have to be carried through the central court. The great
hall was serviced by the buttery and the pantry, and these, with the beer and wine
cellars, were arranged between it and the kitchen. The present servants' hall was

3

originally the house's private chapel – there was no need for a servants' hall when servants and family lived and ate together in the Great Hall itself.

In a house like Speke Hall, there was no distinct topographical division between masters and servants. It is important to realize that a good position in a noble household was a creditable profession in itself. Upper 'servants' such as stewards, ushers and ladies-in-waiting are better thought of as courtiers than inferiors ('Your servant, sir,' was a polite form of address among upper-class equals until well into the nineteenth century). There were also a number of able-bodied men known as retainers attached more or less closely to the household who were in effect bodyguards. When they were in residence, they might carry out household chores as part of their daily duties. From as young as ten years old, children went to the houses of relations and friends (a word often used with the connotation of powerful connections and patronage) to learn to wait at table and make themselves cultured and civilized. 'This child here waiting at the table, whosoever shall live to see it, will

Speke Hall: plan of the ground floor with the room names used in 1917.

prove a marvellous man,' commented Cardinal Morton of a small page of his called Thomas More (William Roper, *Vitae Thomae Mori*, 1716). It was also a way of matchmaking. The renowned Bess of Hardwick, one of the wealthiest women in Elizabethan England, started her remarkably lucrative marital career in this way. Although her family was a good one, it was impoverished in 1528 when her father died leaving her (aged one) and her sisters only £26 13s 4d each. In her teens she went into service in the household of a neighbouring Derbyshire family, the substantial household of Sir John and Lady Zouche of Cadnor Castle, where she met Robert Barlow, the first of the four husbands she outlived.

Such manuals of manners as the fifteenth-century *Babees Book* or Hollybrand's lively Elizabethan *Dialogues* gave these children instructions which are full of illuminating details of everyday life.

Why have you not covered with the table-cloth & napkins of damask? You have not plate trenchers enough. Set at every trencher plate a knife, a spoon and a silver forke. Take away the saltsellers cover. Are the silver plates upon the Cup-board? Go fetch another basin and Ewer for these two be too few for us all to wash in and see that every basin has its towell ... Is the pepper boxe on the table? See that the little silver bottle be full of Vinegar of Roses.

Servants at a humbler level than these gentle retainers tended to be permanent fixtures, inheriting their job from their parents or siblings, and being trained up to spend a lifetime at it. The names of the staff at Knole, in Kent, in 1613 are redolent of rural byways: Diggory Dyer, Marfidy Snipt, Clement Doory, Solomon, birdcatcher, Goodwife Small and (sudden exoticism) 'John Morockoe, a Black-amoor'. They were described as part of the family in the larger sense of the word – a meaning which, like that of 'good house-keeping' in the sense of hospitality, we have now lost. In some ways they were treated very similarly to children, disciplined and fined for bad behaviour in a way which would have been unthinkable to the status-conscious high-Victorian servant class.

This literal 'familiarity' was reflected in the fact that there were no hard and fast lines drawn between the accommodation of servants and of the family. Personal servants slept on truckle beds kept under the four-posters, or stretched out in passages and on window-seats. There were also far more men than women in large establishments, a reflection on the fact that servants were useful for defence as well as service. Only the laundry, dairy, poultry-yard and nursery were staffed by women; the kitchens, the buttery and the pantry were male preserves. In the 1624 Catalogue of the Household at Knole under Lady Dorset, there were three ladies-in-waiting and a trio of housemaids, but men outnumbered women in the household by roughly four to one – there were ninety-five men and twenty-four women altogether.

At my Lord's Table

My Lord	My Lady
My Lady Margaret	My Lady Isabella
Mr Sackville	Mr Frost
John Musgrave	Thomas Garret

At the Parlour Table

Mrs Field	Mr Duck, Page
Mrs Grimsditch	Mr Josiah Cooper, Page
Mrs Fletcher	Mr John Belgrave, Page
Mr Dupper, chaplain	Mr Billingsley
Mr Matthew Caldicott	Mr Graverner, Gentleman Usher
Mr Edward Legge, steward	Mr Marshall, Auditor
Mr Peter Basket, gentleman of the horse	Mr Edwards, Secretary
Mr Marsh, attendant on My Lady	Mr Drake, Attendant
Mr Wooldridge	Mrs Willoughby
Mr Cheyney	Mrs Stewkley
	Mrs Wood

At the Clerks' Table in the Hall

Edward Fulks & John Edwards, Clerks of the Kitchen	Thomas Vinson, Cook
Edward Care, Master Cook	John Elnor, Cook
William Smith, Yeoman of the Buttery	Ralph Hussie, Cook
Henry Keble, Yeoman of the Pantry	John Avery, Usher of the Hall
Robert Elnor, Slaughterman	Richard Wickling, Gardener
Ben Staples, Groom of the Great Chamber	Thomas Clements, Under Brewer
Thomas Petley, Brewer	Samuel Vans, Caterer
William Turner, Baker	Edward Small, Groom of the Wardrobe
Francis Steeling, Gardener	Samuel Southern, Under Baker
John Mitchell, Pastryman	Lowry, a French Boy

The Nursery

Nurse Carpenter	Widow Ben
Jane Sisley	Dorothy Pickenden

At the Long Table in the Hall

Robert Care, Attendant on my Lord	Mr Adam Bradford, Barber
Mr Gray, Attendant Likewise	Mr John Guy, Groom of my Lord's Bedchamber
Mr Roger Cook, Attendant on Lady Margaret	Walter Comestone, Attendant on my Lady

Edward Lane, Scrivener
Mr Thomas Poor, Yeoman of the
    Wardrobe
Mr Thomas Leonard, Master Huntsman
Mr Woodgate, Yeoman of the Great
    Chamber
John Hall, Falconer
James Flennel, Yeoman of the Granary
Rawlinson, Armourer
Moses Shonk, Coachman
Anthony Ashley, Groom of the Great
    Horse
Griffin Edwards, Groom of my Lady's
    Horse
Francis Turner, Groom of the Great Horse
William Grynes, Groom of the Great
    Horse
Acton Curvett, Chief Footman
James Loveall, Footman
Sampson Ashley, Footman
William Petley, Footman
Nicholas James, Footman
Paschal Beard, Footman
Elias Thomas, Footman

Henry Spencer, Farrier
Edward Goodsall
John Sant, the Steward's Man
Ralph Wise, Groom of the Stables
Thomas Petley, Under Farrier
John Stephens, the Chaplain's Man
John Haite, Groom of the Stranger's
    Horse
Thomas Giles, Groom of the Stables
Richard Thomas, Groom of the Hall
Christopher Wood, Groom of the Pantry
George Owen, Huntsman
George Vigeon, Huntsman
Thomas Grittan, Groom of the Buttery
Solomon, the Bird-Catcher
Richard Thornton, the Coachman's Man
Richard Pickendon, Postilion
William Roberts, Groom
The Armourer's Man
Ralph Wise, his servant
John Swift, Porter's Man
John Atkins
Clement Doory

The Laundry Maids' Table

Mrs Judith Simpton
Mrs Grace Simpton
Penelope Tutty, Lady Margaret's Maid
Anne Mills, Dairy-Maid
Prudence Butcher
Anne Howse

Faith Husband
Elinor Thompson
Goodwife Burton
Grace Robinson, a Blackamoor
Goodwife Small
William Lewis, a Porter

Kitchen and Scullery

Diggory Dyer
Marfidy Snipt
John Watson

Thomas Harman
Thomas Johnson
John Morockoe, a Blackamoor

At this time, as the occupations of the long roll-calls of male servants (falconers, huntsmen, brewers, bakers, gardeners, slaughtermen, etc.) attest, self-sufficiency was a highly rated domestic virtue. The ideal was to provide for the household and its guests from the estate itself. Medieval manors were not far removed from the farmyard, the orchard, the fish-ponds and the gardens. Speke Hall once had a moat, which was stocked with carp and perch. There was also a lake to the north, and what appears to be a poultry-yard with a duck pond beyond the stable block to the east. An account book of 1710–19 mentions a considerable amount of gardening activity: references to 'weeding in Garden Courts', 'mowing ye squares' and 'dressing ye squares when mown'. There were nut and fruit orchards, kitchen gardens for soft fruits and vegetables and mention of 'Gardiners' hott bed glasses'. A hopyard provided hops for the brewhouse.

Since transport and communications were unreliable at best, an estate such as Speke expected to provide and keep in store the necessaries of life, growing its own corn, baking bread, brewing beer and slaughtering its own cattle. The granary, bakehouse, brewery, slaughterhouse and a capacious larder all had to be accessible from the kitchen. There would also originally have been a wealth of storage rooms known by their contents (trenchers, pewters, brushes and spiceries), a bolting house (where grain was sieved and stored) and a meat house.

RATIONAL ORGANIZATION: FLORENCE COURT

> The work of the house is performed as if by magic, but it is the magic of system . . . The whole goes on like well-oiled clockwork, where there is no noise nor jarring in its operations.
>
> Washington Irving, *Bracebridge Hall*, 1822

The most satisfying aspect of the great eighteenth-century mansions was the lucid logic of their domestic arrangements. Speke Hall seems almost to have grown, rather than being deliberately designed, and to have been added to as convenience dictated until a comfortable conclusion was reached. Houses like Florence Court, on the other hand, were carefully planned. This was the age of the gentleman architect, and the first theorists of how domestic life should be lived. Details for a small villa laid down by John Loudon shows how carefully ordered arrangements had replaced the piecemeal development of earlier centuries.

The door to the rear of the hall completely divides the offices from the superior part of the house. The pantry is near the dining-room and commands the porch. The servants' hall is beyond the door leading to the yard, and has the effect of being detached from the house, though really within it. The kitchen is arranged with the same advantages; the door opposite the pantry is only in use for the service of dinner. The scullery is wholly removed from the house. The laundry and wash-house are yet more retired, and immediately under the inspection of the housekeeper, who, in this arrangement, is considered as cook also. The knife and shoe room adjoins the servants' hall. The larder and dairy are farther removed from the inhabited parts; and the offices on this side are approachable by a trellis colonnade, so that at all seasons they are accessible with safety. The minor staircase leads to the chamber landings and to the cellars; there is a stair to the cellar also, from the colonnade. The chambers contain three apartments for the men, three for the maidservants and a room for stores.

Notice the clear separation between the 'superior parts of the house' and the domestic offices. Concealing their existence completely became increasingly fashionable, with tunnels running out to servants' courtyards discreetly hidden in the trees or disguised by pretty pavilion fronts. At Castle Ward, County Down, doors to service corridors are hidden in the panelling and the butler could enter Lord Bangor's library through false bookcases at each side of the fireplace. One 'bookcase' gives conveniently direct access to the cellars, while the other leads out to the green baize door to the pantry which is tucked away behind the main staircase.

But a close connection remained between the practical and the polite parts of the house. This is reflected in the decorative aspects of any of the household offices in which the mistress or master of the house maintained an interest. At Florence Court the dairy, game larder and ice house were all designed to be visited and enjoyed by the Coles and their guests. In contemporary literature, the romantic idea of the country seat as a little island safe from the increasingly busy world was often articulated. The text of the times was Daniel Defoe's *Robinson Crusoe*. Lord of all he surveys, completely independent, he could also be hospitable when the occasion arose. In *The Spectator* (no. 15, 1711) we read of a family 'under so regular an Œconomy . . . that it looks like a little Common-wealth within itself'. Their happiness is due to Aurelia and her husband's 'retired self-sufficiency' which is contrasted with the fashionable townee Fulvia's 'baseless self-importance, which demands perpetual motion of Body and restlessness of thought, and condemns her to a continual sense of incompleteness'.

Change was in the air. As the old tradition of household service declined, the men who had once been content to be ushers or gentlemen in waiting looked for a different type of opportunity in business, trade or colonial conquest. Estates became less self-sufficient as roads and waterways improved and such luxuries as Canary wine, bohea tea and curiosities from all over the world became indispensable attributes of a gentleman's life. The old tradition of hospitality without strings was on the wane. *The Guardian* (no. 9, 1713) described a Mr Sharwell's destruction of the good large old house that needed 'a hundred in Family' to keep it up. By now, servants were no longer referred to as 'family'. At Florence Court they slept in attic or basement bedrooms, strictly segregated into male and female domains. A German visitor,

Erddig, Clwyd: servant's bedroom. A servant's bedstead is tucked into the eaves of an attic. Bed curtains were a practical necessity in a draughty age when privacy was hard to come by.

Prince Pückler-Muskau, remarked on the fact, evidently a novelty to a Continental, that

[The English] have the good taste to wait on themselves rather than have an attendant spirit always at their heels. The servants live in a large room in a remote part of the house, generally on the ground-floor, where all, male and female, eat together, and where the bells of the whole house are placed. They are suspended in a row on the wall, numbered so that it is immediately seen in what room any one has rung; a sort of pendulum is attached to each, which continues to vibrate for ten minutes after the sound has ceased to remind the sluggish of their duty.

We do not know the architect of the central block of Florence Court, but it was clearly inspired by the Italian architect Palladio. The basic Palladian theme was the villa, originally a working farmhouse, flanked by attendant barns and stables, themselves often housed in elegant pavilions. This arrangement might involve all of the domestic offices being banished to basements or to separate courtyards, but serious thought was given to making them both convenient and picturesque.

Although guests winding up the carefully landscaped drive to Florence Court saw only a calm façade, tradesmen, who took a more direct route to the back of the house, found a very different world – noisier and larger, more down to earth but highly ordered. A crescent of outbuildings frames the two wings that seem to prop up the main house: one for the stables and the home farm, the other for the dairy, laundry, hen-house, brewhouse and bakehouse, and a capacious barn for storing wood and coal. In the centre of the laundry courtyard was a drying green and a well, and behind the dairy there are traces of a horse-wheel, a primitive source of rotary power for raising water and for other purposes.

This was just the outer ring of household offices. In the basement underneath the reception rooms there is a maze of rooms from which the immediate needs of William Willoughby Cole, Earl of Enniskillen, his family and their guests were once unobtrusively furnished. Every task had its setting and its allotted officer. Secondary staircases gave discreet access to the different floors of the house, hidden service lifts carried up food, coals and hot water. In effect, the Coles were wrapped in a cocoon of care.

The servants' hall is at the heart of the house's well-planned and still remarkably complete inner core of household offices. Although at the front of the house these offices appear to be in the basement, behind it the hillside was excavated so that they are on the same level as the courtyards to the rear. Around the hall, separate areas

Behind and underneath the calm façade of Florence Court, Co. Fermanagh, sixty or more separate departments catered for the needs of the family. (This photograph was taken in the 1860s.)

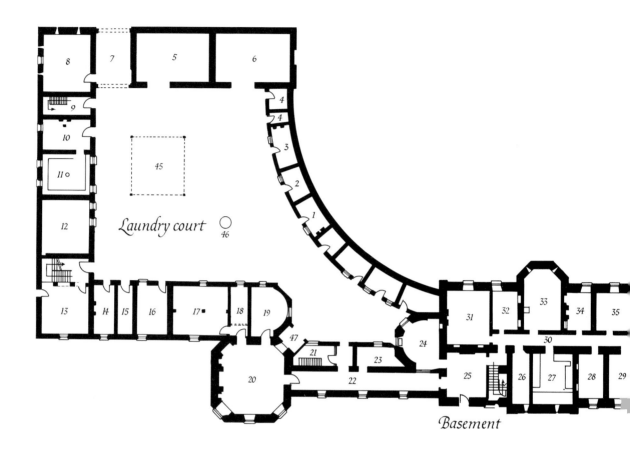

Florence Court: plan of the basement.

were set aside for every aspect of household management. The butler had his pantry, from which he organized the serving of meals and where he cared for the silver and glass in his charge. He also oversaw the running of the boot room (originally just off the pantry to the west, but demolished in 1964), the lamp room and the plate room. The post room was not only a sorting point for mail but the place where the butler and the housekeeper did the household accounts. There was a large beer cellar (now a boiler-room) with a platform for barrels of beer, and some provision for wine, perhaps home-made. A pump in the corridor drew water from the well in the stable yard. The wine cellar had enough bins to hold some three thousand bottles.

North of this was the housekeeper's domain. Opposite the housekeeper's own sitting-room was the china store, still-room, where tea was prepared and fancy baking and preserves concocted, and housemaids' room, home of all the household

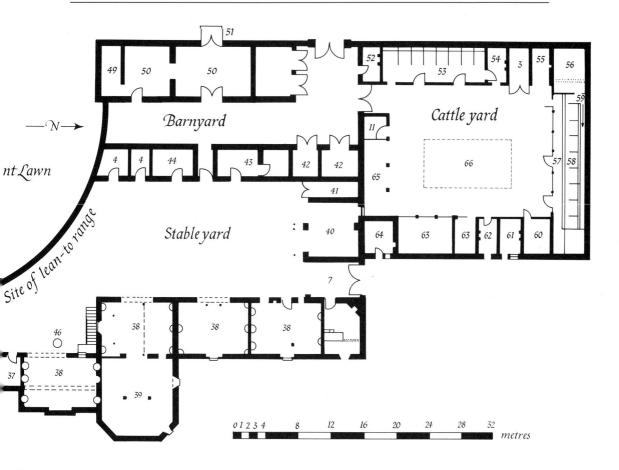

KEY

1 Hamper house
2 Hens
3 Store
4 WC
5 Stick house 1
6 Stick house 2
7 Archway
8 Potato house
9 Men's way
10 Ironing room
11 Dairy
12 Drying Room
13 Implements shed
14 Tea shed
15 Coal
16 Washroom
17 Scullery

18 Coal house
19 Cook's pantry
20 Old kitchen
21 Jam house
22 Corridor
23 Former stairway
24 Butler's pantry
25 Lamp room
26 Silver chest
27 Wine cellar
28 China store
29 Maid's store
30 Spine passage
31 Servant's hall
32 Postman's room
33 Boiler–room
34 Butler's bedroom

35 Housekeeper's
    room
36 Still–room
37 Bakery
38 Stables
39 Old stables
40 Coach–houses
41 Coach–house
42 Hay barn
43 Storage
44 Livery room
45 Washing line
46 Well (site of)
47 Rubbish
48 Oil drum
49 Oil room
50 Workshop

51 Loading ramp
52 Steward's office
53 Stalls (horses)
54 Saddle room
55 Boiling house
56 Food preparation
    room
57 Dunging passage
58 Stalls (cows)
59 Feeding passage
60 Bull house
61 Bedroom
62 Living–room
63 Stalls (pigs)
64 Oil house
65 Carts
66 Demolished piggery

brushes, pails and cleaning materials. Beyond the still-room was a bakehouse. From beside the still-room, a flight of stairs once led up to two long rectangular linen rooms which occupied the first part of the north wing above the still-room and the bakehouse. On the other side of the wall to the east an open arcade leads from the front hall of the house to the 'Colonel's room', the engine house of the estate's management. The wall is windowless, a symbol of the clear line drawn between the two worlds.

At the end of the south wing are the kitchen and its offices. In the scullery, crockery was washed and vegetables cleaned and prepared for cooking. Beside it is a coal store, which originally could be filled from the laundry yard outside. Next to this is the cook's pantry, part larder, part a place where pastry could be made away from the heat of the kitchen fire. Provisions were also stored next door to the pantry in the 'jam house', a makeshift cupboard at the foot of a small staircase which went up to the attic corridor of servants' bedrooms – they balanced the linen rooms in the attics on the other side. A window from the kitchen looks out into a shelter at one side of the laundry yard, a relic of the old charitable traditions. Through the window, soup was handed through bars to the needy, some perhaps sick or elderly tenants on the estate, others passing travellers who called by to ask for odd jobs.

SCIENTIFIC MANAGEMENT: CRAGSIDE

> Houses now became veritable networks of pipes, supply-pipes and waste-pipes, pipes of every kind, for hot water, heating, electric light, for the news service, so that they resembled complex organisms with arteries, veins and nerves like the human body. The most important consequence was that the aesthetic beauty of the earlier ideals was necessarily relegated to the background. But in time perhaps, it will be replaced by an entirely new type of beauty, that of a spiritualized practical intention.
>
> Hermann Muthesius, *The English House*, 1904

By the nineteenth century, domestic independence was increasingly replaced by reliance on tradesmen and towns. Necessities were bought rather than made, and the supportive offices of brewhouse, bakehouse, dairy and laundry were replaced by commercial firms in nearby towns. Young ladies began to be educated less in the old, essentially productive, household skills and more in decorative accomplishments. Housekeeping became an indoor affair, the business of domestic professionals, and quite separate from concerns of farm and garden.

In the great country houses a plentiful supply of servants was still taken for granted, and the prestige of an establishment increased in proportion to their numbers. The basic preconceptions underlying the planning of servants' quarters were inherited from the eighteenth century, but they were elaborated *ad absurdum*. A new servants' wing added to Arlington Court, Devon, in 1864–5 doubled the size of the house. Rooms in each department were grouped together. According to Robert Kerr, author of the influential *The Gentleman's House* (1864), 'Every servant, every operation, every utensil, every fixture should have a right place and no right place but one.' Perhaps the ultimate in specialization was reached at Kinmel, where one room was set aside entirely for ironing newspapers.

By the 1870s there had been an absolute fall in the numbers of male indoor servants, despite a population rise. The number of women servants increased, but only by 11 per cent at a time when the population as whole rose by 49 per cent. The bulk of that population rise was among the non-servant-keeping classes. I suspect that what was actually happening was a replacement of male servants by women.

In 1880 J. J. Stevenson wrote in *House Architecture* that the most striking characteristic of the planning of modern English houses was 'its multifariousness'.

Keeping pace with our more complicated ways of living, we have not only increased the number of rooms in ordinary houses, but have assigned to each a special use. Instead of the hall and single chamber of the middle ages, with which even kings were content, every ordinary house must have a number of separate bedrooms, at least three public rooms, and a complicated arrangement of servants' offices.

Stevenson heralded a growing reaction to the maze of purpose-built rooms for every possible household task. 'All these places, with the interminable passages connecting them, have to be kept in order; and, if they increase the facility of doing the work, they increase the labour of the house, and necessitate a greater number of servants.' Although the Victorian domestic offices of the seventeenth-century Cornish mansion of Lanhydrock, extensively rebuilt after a fire in 1881, still had strings of small rooms for every task in just this manner, it was houses like Cragside, home of the inventor and armaments millionaire Sir William Armstrong, that pointed the way into the future.

Cragside was converted from a humble shooting lodge by the famous architect Norman Shaw between 1870 and 1885. Its domestic offices have none of the picturesqueness of Speke Hall or the elegance of Florence Court. It is a shock even now to leave the opulence of the panelled and papered hall for the barely furnished and clumsily proportioned butler's pantry. Because of its advanced technology and the no-nonsense pragmatism of its creator, the house made do with far fewer separate service rooms than other contemporary houses of substance. It had no dairy, brewhouse or bakehouse. All these services were located in the nearby town of Rothbury. The laundry block (now derelict) once housed supplementary domestic offices, but electric power, telephone communications and highly efficient planning meant that a relatively small complement of staff could do a great deal with a minimum of effort. New virtuosity in heating and water supply meant that bathrooms and boiler-rooms were installed; even the bedroom washstands had hot water on tap.

Technologically, Cragside is extraordinary: a contemporary described it as 'the Palace of a Modern Magician'. Armstrong was an innovative hydraulics engineer (a

Cragside, Northumberland: plan of the ground floor.

Portrait of Lord Armstrong by H. H. Emmerson. 'William has water on the brain,' joked the family of the armaments millionaire who used hydroelectricity to turn a humble Northumberland shooting lodge into the 'Palace of a Modern Magician'. His favourite inglenook was made more comfortable by Cragside's excellent central heating; hot air rises through grilles in the floor beside his chair.

family joke ran 'William has water on the brain'), and he harnessed power from artificial lakes around the house not only to create electricity but to drive everything from the service lifts to the rotating pots for orange trees in the hothouses.

The kitchen is hygienically tiled and well lit, with roomy table tops and all the latest small gadgets for food preparation. A service lift links it with a basement scullery, which contained sinks, an auxiliary gas-cooker and larders. The capacious kitchen range is framed by an hydraulically operated spit mechanism. A primitive dish-washing machine juts into the room, conveniently close to the china closets. An electric gong summoned diners, and throughout the house ostentatiously elaborate light brackets remind the visitor that Cragside was the first country house in the world to be lit by electricity.

By the end of the century, the domestic mood was defensive and introverted. Beleaguered by the busy-ness of the world about it, the Englishman's home was becoming his castle in practice as well as in law. Theodor Fontane, having toured England and Scotland in the late 1890s, commented rather bitterly on the change which had taken place in his lifetime.

Old England's hospitality is now no more than a phrase, at best an exception. It lives in the old statutes, but has died in the hearts. The country is open, but the homes are closed. From time to time I receive letters in which the phrase 'our English hospitality' occurs in every other line; but the otherwise doubtful assurance of this hospitality is always accompanied by regrets that, for one reason or another, it is impossible for the writer to entertain his friends ... The hospitality of Old England is dead, and he has double cause to regret it, who, like myself, in former years, had the privilege of coming to know in its fullest bloom this charming trait in the national character of the English.

Aus England und Schottland, Berlin, 1900

Behind the closed doors, the organization of comfort reached an apogee of intricacy bordering on the obsessional. 'Getting and spending we lay waste our powers,' Wordsworth, the poet laureate, had lamented early on. Or was it all a matter of climate? A novel but none the less thought-provoking theory that the weather was at the root of Britain's excessive obsession with the technology of domesticity was offered in 1896 by a Portuguese visitor called Oliveira Martins. Depressed by a nasty touch of Thames fog while holed up in a substantial country house, he wrote:

The dark weather that came over explained to me the English preoccupation with home, and their science of domestic comfort, whence comes the interior psychology of their genius. They gather themselves up within themselves, they roll themselves up like snails in their shells, constructing an artificial world with an infinity of indispensable things – complicated bathrooms; kitchens like laboratories; delicate apparel; lavatories bending under the weight of brushes, razors, scissors, mirrors, sponges, perfumes and creams ... All this makes life dreadfully complicated: all this completely absorbs time; and this complication and absorption, added to the money that so artificial a life costs, causes the genius of the people to sterilize itself in the indispensable necessity of earning much money.

Jacob Joseph, ed., *As Others See Us*

Whether or not we can attribute national decline to meteorological escapism, it is certainly true that the organization of servants' quarters reached a peak of comfort and efficiency towards the end of the nineteenth century and before the outbreak of war. Domestic offices at this time were proudly functional. In 1911 the architect C. H. B. Quennell compared the kitchen offices of a large house to 'a modern factory, so that from the moment the food is delivered like raw material at the tradesman's door it will pass along until it is delivered as the final product in the dining-room, and make steady progressions during its journey'.

As we all know, the days of great country houses with huge domestic staffs were numbered. Castle Drogo, in Devon, that dramatic masterpiece of the most domestically inspired of all architects, Edwin Lutyens, was obsolete almost as soon as it was finished. Striking and carefully thought-out as its domestic offices were, they were never occupied by more than a skeleton staff, and the house was only lived in as originally intended for twenty-five years or so. But this is not the place to tell of the decline of what Arthurian chroniclers might have called 'the high housekeeping'. That can wait to the end of the book. I want now to enter into the everyday practical details of how home comfort was brought about.

CHAPTER TWO

MEN AT THE TOP

Every man's first care is domestic.

Dr Johnson

Who actually ran the household? Who made sure the family and all its dependents were kept warm, clean and well-fed? Whether a household was large or small, there were certain pivots of power, crucial central control rooms from which the different domestic offices were organized.

In a large establishment, the original general of the domestic army was the steward. He was a proxy master of the house, right-hand-man to its mistress in the absence of her spouse. He hired and fired all domestic servants, took charge of any necessary marketing and kept the household accounts. He held the actual purse-strings, and the housekeeper sent all tradesmen's charges to him for approval. Alone among the servants, he did not wear a livery or uniform of any kind. Originally, like many members of medieval and Elizabethan households, he would have been of the same social class as his employer – Richard II's steward, for example, was Thomas Percy, Earl of Worcester.

The steward's role diminished in prestige and power as the mistress of the house took on more domestic responsibilities and more female servants were employed. In the eighteenth century the role of house steward and land steward became separate, and the former job was more that of a principal butler than anything else. Mark Girouard, in *Life in the English Country House*, records a Mr Drummond, related to the Earl of Perth, putting in for a job as steward and being rejected as 'too good for the job'. In Victorian times only very grand households had a steward, and if they did, they rarely had a butler as well.

If there was one, the steward's room was generally strategically located between the male preserves of smoking-room or library, and was the centre of domestic activities. It had to be both close to the master's office and to the tradesmen's entrance. Its secondary purpose was as a dining-room for the upper servants, in which they took lunch and dinner (breakfast and tea were served in the housekeeper's room).

Beneath the steward were the butler and the housekeeper, each with their own

Polesden Lacey, Surrey: butler and footmen. There was a time when armed retainers would take care of the housekeeping in the intervals of defending their territories (and attacking others). This formidable team of menservants looked game for anything as late as 1978.

territories, male and female respectively. Lower down the social scale such offices were combined. In the nineteenth century a cook-housekeeper could manage a modest country rectory with the help of a parlourmaid. A city clerk like Mr Pooter in George Grossmith's *Diary of a Nobody* (1892) made do with a 'general' and a great deal of self-help by both husband and wife.

The butler governed the men of the household, the housekeeper the women, and the two sides met in the servants' hall, 'the heart of the household', as Adeline Hartcup has described it. The twin hubs of domestic power, then, can be neatly symbolized by the butler's pantry and the housekeeper's sitting-room.

THE BUTLER'S PANTRY

The 'butler's pantry' was a composite domestic department. It combined the ancient offices of the yeoman of the buttery (*botellarium*), who was responsible for providing wine and beer, and the yeoman of the pantry (*panetarium*), who oversaw the deliveries of bread, butter, cheese and other basic pantry provisions, assayed them (for correct weight and purity) and arranged it on the table. The two rooms normally flanked the passage to the kitchen from the great hall of a medieval house. The bustle of service at the business end of the hall was customarily hidden by a great screen, with three doorways set in it and a musicians' gallery above. This arrangement, still in everyday use in such medieval foundations as Oxford and Cambridge colleges, can be seen in miniature in Bradley Manor, Devon, and on a grand scale in Hardwick Hall, Derbyshire. At both these houses, the rooms are still described as butteries. The mixture of lime and ash traditionally used to make a particularly hard-wearing floor has survived at Bradley – there is even a worn path across it, showing the route the servants once took to get from the kitchen to the great hall.

A third office was also gradually assumed by the butler – that of the sewer, or server, the servant responsible for arranging and serving at table. Old inventories show that by the fifteenth century plate and articles for service of the table were kept in the buttery. In Sir John Fastolfe's buttery in 1455 there were 'certayns pecys of napre[table linen]'; a variety of knives – 'ij kerving knyves, iij kneyves in a schethe, the haftys of every [ivory], with naylys [nails] gilt'; about a dozen bottles of different kinds – 'ij gret and hoge botellis, iiij galon pottis of lether, I grete tankard; xiiij candylokys of laton [brass, candlesticks]'. There was also an impressive collection of silver plates and vessels – chargers, platters, dishes 'enameled with violetts and dayseys', pots, salt-cellars and a great basin 'of silver, percyll gylte, with a dowble rose, his armis enamelid in the bottom, between his helme and his crest'.

Household orders for the old manor-house of Wollaton in 1572 give useful details of what was expected of the butler and his staff.

Penne being appointed for the buttery, his office is ever to keep clean and sweet his buttery, and likewise his plate and cups, making sure every day to have fresh and clean water, and for the most part twice a day to wash the same withal. His jacks [jugs] appointed for the hall are to be kept from furring and unsweet savour. His office with th'aid of an under-butler is to keep the great chamber clean, to make the fires there, and to provide for lights in due season, and to cover the boards and cupboards there, having very good regard to the cleanness of his linen, and likewise to provide for cards and dice, whereof he is to have the profit.

The buttery was evidently the place from which food and drink were dispensed at agreed mealtimes. Like a modern office canteen, it closed down in between these times.

The pantry became progressively more separated from the dining hall. The excellently detailed 1710 inventory of the contents of Dyrham Park, Avon, show that there was then a pantry but no buttery. The list below suggests that it was still more or less a servery rather than an approximation of a butler's pantry as it was understood a hundred years or so later.

Dyrham Park 1710 Inventory: In the Pantry

15 white handled knives and forks
12 dark color'd handle knives tipt and three forks
7 black handle knives & 2 large drinking muggs
3 Tables 2 Leather Chairs 1 byrd cage a Fire Grate
2 Copper cisterns 1 large crystall decanter
2 Crewetts 7 water botles & 9 glass tumblers
31 glasses 1 Incorporator
11 high Brass and 11 hand candlesticks
7 pr snuffers 4 extinguishers
2 baskets for glasses a basket for knives
a basket for table linen a basket for foul plates
a Rasp for Bread
a hand bell to ring at Dinner Time
a Hammar, a hand saw and 2 chissells

This seems a relatively small amount of cutlery, and very few forks. Perhaps few people used them, or perhaps silver cutlery was locked away securely in a plate safe. At this period, a knife and fork for personal use was still part of a well-bred traveller's hand-luggage. The incorporator was a vessel for mixing such popular hot alcoholic nightcaps as negus, bishop and punch. The small tools are an interesting item – they may have been useful for minor household emergencies or for handling the casks of beer and wine. The bird cage remains obscure. Were its occupants pets, or part of the living larder?

During a visit to the great Georgian house of Saltram, in Devon, in 1811, the Revd Thomas Talbot noted, as if it was something of an innovation, that 'there is a sort of second gradation of Domestic between the Steward's Room and Servants' Hall – the under Butler has a sort of Room and Butlery to himself and seems to have a great Charge on him'. His observation reflected the rise of the butler to his nineteenth-century eminence, and the corresponding decline of the steward.

If Robert Adam, who restyled several of the rooms of Saltram thirty years before, had had his way, the butler's department at Saltram would have been even more extensive. A fire in the kitchen court which destroyed the laundry and brewhouse in 1778 made some sort of domestic rearrangement necessary. The plans Adam drew up in 1779 show three rooms for the butler, and a symmetrically arranged set of domestic quarters that would have impressed even late Victorian architects with their consideration for servants' convenience. But it was not to be. Lord Boringdon, a widower with mounting debts, employed Stockman, the estate carpenter, and Parlby, a naval architect from Portsmouth, to build a new kitchen on the site of the old laundry and brewhouse, and rebuild the laundry and brewhouse in a separate block to the north of the house. The staff at Saltram continued to muddle along in the 'picturesque anarchy' of the house's sixteenth-century core.

By the nineteenth century, it was usual to provide an entire suite of rooms for the butler, in some cases including a plate room (often fortified by iron doors or in a brick vault of its own), a bedroom, a parlour, possibly a pantry scullery, and a tail of smaller workrooms for filling lamps, cleaning boots, polishing knives and brushing clothes. At Lanhydrock, the butler's suite was a parlour and a pantry with a bedroom and strongroom between them. There was a similar set-up at Cragside, where the butler's bedroom can still be seen. Separated from the pantry by the kitchen and tucked behind the main lift shaft, it is simply furnished with a brass bedstead and *fin de siècle* furniture.

At seventeenth-century Uppark, in West Sussex, the spacious pantry is arranged to show the varied range of duties carried out by the butler and his staff: preparing and serving wines, cleaning silver, glassware and cutlery, polishing knives (in the neighbouring knife room), providing lamps, receiving visitors, attending to gentlemen's wardrobes (ironing and brushing equipment on a side-table), guarding valuables (a strongroom for plate leads off the pantry) and keeping the house itself secure (a mobile fire-pump). There are some over-enthusiastic touches: the hip-bath and the sugar-nippers, for example, but it is a satisfyingly busy display.

At one end of the room are cupboards in which the dining-room china and glass currently in use would have been arranged. Corridors were also used to accommodate china and glass cupboards in many houses. The pantry sink is deep and wide enough to hold two wooden washing bowls to protect fragile china and glass from breakage. There is a supply of lead shot for cleaning inside decanters, and a variety of soaps and scouring agents, most of them once home-made. At right-angles to it is a shallow lead-lined draining sink. Cloths were spread in this and glasses placed upside-down on them to drain before being polished with a clean soft cloth, or, if they were made of cut glass, with a soft brush. A pipe from the cold-water supply runs to a filter for drinking water.

Keeping the silver clean was a constant occupation for butlers – many early engravings show him in a capacious apron with a few forks in one hand and a cloth in the other. The best method for cleaning plate, advised Anne Cobbett, was to have ready two leathers and a soft plate brush for crevices: 'The plate being washed clean, rub over it, with a piece of flannel, a mixture of levigated hartshorn and spirits of turpentine; rub this off with one of the leathers, and then polish with the other one.' Cutlery was cleaned with rouge, a paste made from powdered rust which smoothed out scratches in the silver and gave it an unmistakable rosy glow.

THE KNIFE ROOM

Knives and other cutlery made from stainful steel and with ivory or bone handles required special treatment and much elbow grease. 'It is next to impossible for a woman to clean them well.' The blades had to be rubbed with bathbrick (a block of powdered limestone), or, better, against a knife-board. 'A good kind of knife-board,' wrote Anne Cobbett, 'is made as follows: take a perfectly smooth board, and cover it with a thick buff leather, which must be pulled tight, and nailed on the under side; then spread over it, the thickness of a shilling, a paste made of one fourth part of emery powder, and three parts of crocus, mixed well with lard.' Both knives and forks were the sweeter for being plunged into fresh fine earth for ten minutes. As a substitute, an oyster barrel of fine sand, mixed with a little hay or moss, could be kept for this purpose. When not in use, knives had to be greased with a little mutton fat and rolled in brown paper.

Knife-cleaning was a major chore before the invention of stainless steel, and a special room like the small closet off the pantry at Uppark was often put aside for the purpose. In the ghostly basement of eighteenth-century Wimpole Hall, Cambridgeshire, unchanged since the service quarters were moved out in the nineteenth century, there is still a door labelled 'Knife Room'. Machines were also invented to take the labour out of polishing rust and stains off the knives. The best known of these was William Kent's broad wooden canister on its elegant cast-iron stand. It was originally shown at the Great Exhibition in 1851, and was still being recommended as 'exceptionally good' in 1902. The knives were pushed into its sides, and emery boards and brushes were rotated against them by a handle. The result was 'a mirror-like finish'. The machine also sharpened the knives slightly, but occasionally a grindstone had to be used. Many of the old shallow stone sinks once fitted in pantries and sculleries have a worn semicircle at the front that shows where the knives were sharpened.

THE PLATE ROOM

When the plate was very valuable, a fireproof walk-in safe was built in – there are examples of these at Uppark and Erddig. Where the safe was placed would again depend on the size of the establishment. Kerr felt that it should lead off the butler's bedroom, this being placed next door to the pantry, and Lutyens adopted this arrangement at Castle Drogo, as did Richard Coad, the architect who rebuilt Lanhydrock. Another expedient was to install a closet bedstead – an ingenious piece of gadgetry that folded into a cupboard when not in use. This was not generally for the butler himself, but for a trusted subordinate to sleep on. There is one on display in the butler's pantry at Uppark, and both a 'mess bedstead' and a 'leather bed' were kept in the butler's pantry at Erddig, according to the 1833 inventory.

THE LAMP ROOM

To looking after the candlesticks, as in Sir John Fastolfe's buttery, the nineteenth-century butler had to add care of the lamps. The labour of cleaning, filling and delivering the dozens of oil lamps required by a large household was work for at least one footman or hall boy, and in this situation a lamp room would be necessary. At Florence Court, one of the few houses still to have a lamp room, it is a large one, sensibly positioned at the foot of the servants' stairs. There will also be a lamp room among the range of small service rooms at Calke Abbey in Derbyshire when they are eventually restored. Once domestic electricity was introduced at the end of the nineteenth century, lamp rooms were often appropriately used to house the formidable array of fuse-boxes required by early electricity-generating systems.

BRUSHING ROOM

In a medium-sized household, the butler might have undertaken such valeting duties as ironing top hats, whitening riding breeches, brushing pink coats and washing and stretching gloves. In larger households, a separate room was provided for valets. A 'brushing room' close to the entrance of the servants' courtyard is marked on a floor plan of Dunham Massey, in Cheshire. Cragside has a glassed-in lobby on an upper landing which displays all the paraphernalia of valeting: boot trees, hatboxes, stiff, soft and wire brushes, polishes and mothballs, wall hooks for hats, riding crops and military trappings.

THE WINE CELLAR

Cellars, and the wine and beer stored in them, were originally looked after by a household official called the *cellarius*. His duties were taken over by the butler, originally more of a 'front-man' as far as drink was concerned. It was an ordinary morning duty for the butler to fetch the wine of the day from the cellar, and prepare it: standing it on the dresser in his pantry to reach room temperature if it was red; bedding it in ice if it was white. Sherry, port and vintage wine would be decanted well before they were required, and champagne and dessert wines chilled. Wine-coolers designed to be kept in the dining-room were often very decorative items: disguised as elaborate urns, and roomy enough both to be insulated with a charcoal lining and to hold ice. A fine pair stand on a sideboard of the dining-room of Dunster

Castle, in Somerset. Beer too would be brought up, both for the domestic staff and any members of the family who required it.

The butler was also responsible for the cellar book, which provided a vital inventory of wine and beer. Part of his duty was to advise his employer when stocks were running low, and many butlers took a connoisseur's interest in the quality of the contents of the cellar.

Cellar books are interesting evidence of changing fashions in drinking. Gladys Scott Thomson has pointed out that neither champagne nor port figures significantly in English cellar books until after the king came into his own again in the second half of the seventeenth century – 'Champagne and the Restoration,' she comments, 'were not unfitly closely connected.' Until then the staple fortified wines were sack, sherry, Malaga and Canary. Claret, burgundy, and Rhine wines were also imported, but until the invention of the cylindrical bottle with its tightly fitted cork, vintage wines were unknown – all wine was perforce new wine, drawn from the cask and drunk from bulbous bottles that stood upright, corked relatively loosely with a conical cork. Wine was neither exported in bottles nor stored in them for any length of time until Louis Pasteur discovered the effect of oxygen on wine in 1863. After this date, brick bins for bottles were built in many cellars to replace the old racks for casks.

David Conyngham of Springhill, County Londonderry, left a stylishly stocked cellar in 1789: the cellar book records '1 Cagg of Rum (16$\frac{1}{2}$ gallons), 8 gallons of vinegar [presumably home-made], 1 hogshead of port wine, and another half full; 1 hogshead of Clarrett in bottles; 5 dozen of Sherry; 10 dozen French Clarret in bottles; 2 and a half dozen of Frontiniac'. On a more heroic scale, the Attingham Park cellar book could boast, among many other wines, 400 bottles of sherry, 300 of port, and 140 of Madeira. In 1833 Erddig's cellar held '79 doz port, 1 doz champ, 3 doz claret, 6 doz sherry, 2 doz madeira, 2 doz raisin, two doz ginger, two doz elder' – a reasonably moderate quantity, except for that port. Perhaps there had been a run of fine years. Perhaps the Yorkes were just partial to the stuff.

A good cellar needed to be dry and of an even temperature. It was best built under the house, on the north side, and well away from the drains if possible. The floor would be of beaten earth, cobbled or paved. A charcoal stove was sometimes kept alight in it in very cold weather. Other requisites were a rope to lower down wine casks, or a plank on which to roll them down the stairs, if the cellar was below the level of the other offices, a spade, a rake and a birch broom to lay and level the sawdust that was often spread over the floor.

A receiving cellar was recommended, with space for unpacking, washing bottles, stowing hampers and so on, and with a window for light. A good example of this can be seen in what is called the crypt at Dunster Castle. Here the fact that the service wing is built on a slope gives the cellars the unusual advantages of being under the house, well-lit and easily approached by a roadway. There is a sink for washing bottles, and some racks and bins for temporary storage.

Beyond is what was known as a 'wine-in-wood' cellar, where wine could be stored in the pipe and where there was space to bottle it. Various tools were required for piercing casks, inserting and drawing bungs, tightening their hoops and drawing corks. There would also need to be space to store wooden and copper funnels, flannel and linen bags for straining wine into the bottles and a mallet for driving home the corks. In 1861 Mrs Beeton's wine-bottling directions mention a gadget which seems to have vanished from history entirely (it does not rate a mention in the new *OED*): a bottling or corking boot.

Having thoroughly washed and dried the bottles, supposing they have been before used for the same kind of wine, provide corks, which will be improved by being slightly boiled, or at least steeped in hot water, a wooden hammer or mallet, a bottling boot, and a squeezer for corks. Bore a hole in the lower part of the cask with a gimlet, receiving the liquid stream which follows in the bottle and filterer, which is placed in a tub or basin. This operation is best performed by two persons, one to draw the wine, the other to cork the bottles. The drawer is to see that the bottles are up to the mark, but not too full, the bottle being placed in a clean tub to avoid waste. The corking boot is buckled by a strap to the knee, the bottle placed in it, and the cork, after being squeezed in the press, driven in by a flat wooden mallet.

This contortionist method, besides bruising a great many kneecaps, must have been the predecessor of the lever-operated corking machine, an example of which can be seen in the butler's pantry at Erddig.

There is an excellent range of cellars on view at Tatton Park, a Cheshire mansion which is one of the most domestically interesting and complete of National Trust houses. A flight of stairs just outside the butler's pantry leads to a receiving cellar and an inner cellar, each lined with bins. Wine bins were generally 24 or 30 inches square on the face and 22 inches deep, so as to take two bottles laid neck to neck. Their size was governed by the number of bottles that could be filled from the 'pipe' (about 5 or 6 ft long and almost a yard in diameter), in which port or burgundy was purchased. Each bin was thus devoted to one particular year of one particular wine with ease. In 1868 J.J. Stevenson suggested that 'smaller bins holding a few dozen would better suit our modern custom of drinking many different kinds of wine. They may easily be formed out of the ordinary large bins by wooden divisions.' The atmospheric cellar of Castle Ward, County Down, is arranged on this principle, and the labels for different types of wine still hang beside each bin.

Further along the corridor at Tatton Park is the butler's cellar (not on view). Stevenson suggested that this should hold wine for immediate use, 'in the charge of the butler, leaving the general stock under the key of the master'. This was perhaps a sensible precaution; it also saved daily groping around in large and probably unlit wine cellars. At Erddig, where the entrance to the wine cellar is in the pantry itself, racks of wine for current use were kept in the lamp room. At Cotehele a brick-built vault fitted with miniature wine bins was constructed in late Georgian times in the punch room, enabling the butler to be dispensed with altogether at the informal and convivial parties for which this cosy offshoot of the dining-room was intended.

THE SERVERY

The servery, or serving room was an important link between the kitchen offices and the dining-room. Originally, of course, the buttery and pantry had fulfilled its function, but once the kitchen was removed, either to the basement or to a separate pavilion in the grounds, there had to be a staging post where covers could be removed and the final touches given to the food before it was presented at table. In small houses, of course, the butler's pantry, if conveniently situated, was an adequate servery, but in large establishments, as the butler's pantry became a rather specialized province, a separate serving room became necessary. At Calke Abbey a lift brings food up from the basement to the first-floor servery next door to the dining-room. At the seventeenth-century 'doll's house' mansion of Belton, in Lincolnshire, there is a railway (not at present on view) underneath the kitchen courtyard along which food was pushed on a trolley before being carried upstairs to the servery. A similar, more modern railway is on view at Tatton Park, where service trolleys can be pushed along the long basement passages. At corridor junctions, there are turntables, so that the trolleys turn corners with ease.

One of the most striking of serveries was provided by Repton at Uppark. At one end there is a stained-glass window, lit by lamps put in by climbing a ladder in the kitchen below. That kitchen was originally used only for small-scale family cookery and still-room work. On formal occasions food was brought over from the kitchen pavilion some two hundred yards away. Repton designed underground tunnels along which charcoal-heated hot-cupboards could be trundled, but two sets of stairs still had to be negotiated. It is hardly surprising that the distant kitchen fell into disuse during the long, reclusive reign of Mary Ellen and her sister Frances Bullock. After Frances died in 1895, their successor, Colonel Turnour, arranged the present kitchen.

Blickling, in Norfolk, a house noted for almost incessant alterations of its domestic offices, none of them very satisfactory, has a good serving room with a wooden cover to extend setting-down surfaces over the sinks. There are shelves all around, a butler's tray on a folding stand (these could be taken from room to room, enabling impromptu meals to be eaten wherever there happened to be a fire), a clock on the wall. In 1793 it was called 'the confectioner's room' and hung with portraits. It was converted to a servery during the alterations of 1864, when a staircase down to the service tunnel from the western range was built, and a sink, dresser and hot cabinet installed.

At Dunham Massey there is an exceptionally fine servery, as well as a very complete butler's suite (not all of it open to the public). Doors opposite the dining-room conceal what was formerly the butler's sitting-room, bedroom, and a strongroom built within the bedroom. The sitting-room may have been the original butler's pantry, but in 1892 William Grey, the 9th Earl of Stamford, turned up at Dunham Massey with all the freshness of eye that unexpected inheritance can supply. Either consideration for the servants or a desire for hot food made him decide in 1903 to make a new dining-room close to the service wing. He employed Compton Hall to convert the redundant steward's room and the housemaid's sitting-room into a panelled and parqueted dining-room. At great expense, the floor was excavated and the windows lengthened so that although guests came down a short flight of steps into the dining-room, there was a level approach to the splendid new quarters for the business side of the butler's duties.

A handsome mahogany portal, with a double door to lessen the danger of noise and smells from the kitchen quarters, opens directly into the servery. This was fitted out by Jeakes of Great Russell Street with cast-iron cupboards heated by hot-water pipes from the kitchen range. These are flanked by oak side tables, with perfectly fitting drawers, which line the rest of the room. Presumably they were tailor-made for it by the estate carpenter. Otherwise, the room is perfectly bare: ready to receive first food from the kitchens and finally detritus from the table.

Changes in the design of cooking ranges in the nineteenth century closed the old wide chimney flues and made the invasion of kitchen smells into the reception rooms of the house far more of a problem. One solution was to increase the distance between kitchen and dining-room, a development which made serving hot food something of a challenge. During a meal that was particularly unsuccessful in this respect, Disraeli is reported as muttering when the champagne was poured: 'Thank God for something warm' (quoted in Jill Franklin, *The Gentleman's Country House and its Plan*). Serveries began to be equipped not just to keep food warm but to reheat it. Calke Abbey has a small range in the servery, just beside the lift in which food was hoisted after its long journey through meandering basement passages from the kitchen. A Jeakes hot cupboard was installed at Lanhydrock. At Tatton Park, capacious and well-insulated electrically heated trolleys solved the problem.

SUMMONED BY BELLS

It was also the butler's job to respond to a knock at the door and to answer the bell. Perhaps the most familiar image that comes to mind when people think about the servants' quarters of a high Victorian house of any size is that of a line of bells, numbered or labelled to show from which room in the house the summons had come. Sophisticated systems, as at Castle Ward, even sounded different notes so that any but the tone deaf could know without looking whether they were required in drawing-room or dining-room, bedroom or nursery. Mark Girouard goes so far as to suggest that the invention of such bell networks made it possible to remove the servants' offices from the basement and resite them in an adjacent wing of the house. Whether this was the cause or the effect of a growing preference for privacy is difficult to ascertain. Certainly it could have contributed to the discontent of servants.

Little is known about the history of the common household bell. The three-inch high legend 'RING *THE BELL*' is engraved next to a well-polished brass knob beside the front door of the great Restoration mansion of Sudbury Hall in Derbyshire. This was presumably a necessary hint when such technology was novel. The Dyrham Park Inventory of 1710 refers to a 'Pulley Bell' for summoning servants – not from a distance, but from an ante-room near by. Its numerous references to pallet beds, often in workrooms and even employers' bedrooms, confirm that personal servants slept all over the place, even in corridors, in order to be on call quickly if they were needed.

By the end of the eighteenth century, bell wires could be elaborately plumbed around the house. Plumbers or chimney-sweeps often combined their trade with that of bell-hanger, and in 1802 a Mr Phair wrote a useful treatise on bell-wires and chimneys for their information. Loudon explains how such wires were installed. The wires rose perpendicularly in tubes from the different rooms to a concealed passage in the attic storey and then descended in one tube or trunk to the bells themselves, which were usually hung in a service passage in the basement.

At Belton the reception rooms are furnished with pairs of bell-pulls – marked 'upstairs' on one side of fireplace, and 'downstairs' on the other. There seem to have been at least two indicator boards, one in the servery, and another upstairs, perhaps in the maids' sitting-room or bedroom. Ivory tags hang on heavy tasselled ropes in the Chinese bedroom; neat black on white enamelled handles serve the boudoir.

At Uppark the long line of bells in the basement passage serves fourteen different rooms. The wire tension system is a common late-eighteenth-century feature, but the wooden indicator board is unusual. Wires on it release small wooden flaps to show which room has sent a signal. The board is strategically placed at the foot of

*Bell wires were elaborately plumbed all over Tatton Park, Cheshire, by the end of
the eighteenth century. Different notes signalled the room in which service was required.
Underneath the bell a pendulum remained swinging for several minutes after it was
rung, perhaps for the sake of the tone deaf.*

the stairs so that it can be seen from the ground floor as well as from the basement.
The names of the rooms painted on the board suggest that it dates from around
1840.

Convenient as a bell system of this kind might be for those who rang them, they
must have been tiresome in the extreme for those expected to respond. In a little
sketch in an 1843 issue of the *Family Economiser*, mercilessly yanked pulley bells frame
'the model maid-of-all-work', a far more familiar character in most Victorian families
than the great staffs of country houses. 'She gets £6 a-year and is expected to wait
on about twenty persons, to do the work of five servants, to love all the children in
the house, and to be honest for the money.' An extract in the same year from *Punch*
described to such a servant how her new mistress would 'show you the bells, and
tell you which is the house bell, which the parlour bell, which the drawing-room
bell, and which are the bells of the different bedrooms; but she will not tell you how
you are to answer them when they are all ringing at once'.

From the 1840s, speaking tubes were available. These had the advantage of saving
a servant's legs, but the disadvantage of allowing background conversations to be
heard, both from above and below. One of what was originally a pair of speaking

tubes can still be seen *in situ* beside the dining-room fireplace at Canons Ashby, Northamptonshire. A hinged lid closed over the tube when not in use; a whistle was used to attract attention. There was evidently no shortage of communication in this particular dining-room: two bell handles are fixed just below the tube, and a bell-pull hangs down above.

Pneumatic bells and electric bells were developed at about the same time. They were an improvement on the old bell system, which often broke down, either through its wires being stretched or through its cranks and levers being clogged with dust in obscure recesses. Crown Point had electric bells in 1865, Rousdon pneumatic ones in 1872. There remained some risk of the india rubber tubing immediately under the pneumatic bell's button getting punctured, and in S. F. Murphy's *Our Homes* (1883), battery-powered electric bells were felt to be the most efficient of all. Names of the rooms on the electric-bell indicator at Castle Coole conjure up a European world we have lost: Leghorn, Petrograd, Stockholm, Palermo and St Omer. There is also a separate valet's indicator and maid's indicator.

Our Homes also discussed the likelihood of increased use of that novel invention, the telephone, already much more widely used in the United States than in Britain. The first person to transmit recognizable speech was Alexander Graham Bell in 1876. His profession was teaching the deaf, and he used to experiment in his spare time with sending musical notes by telegraphy. Thomas Edison's slightly different invention was patented shortly after Bell's, and in 1880 the two companies amalgamated, opening the United Telephone Company in London's Queen Victoria Street. In the long run, the public telephone system would have a profound effect on domestic management, making it possible to arrange commercial deliveries, summon a taxi, invite a friend to dinner, and so on, all without troubling a servant.

After the invention of the telephone, house telephones, powered by batteries, increased in popularity very rapidly. In 1911 they were referred to as 'one of the most usual conveniences to be found in a country house'. They made use of the old wiring tubes and bell-pushes of the pulley systems. An electric bellboard and a telephone exchange were regarded as essential internal installations for Castle Drogo when it was fully staffed. Forty-eight connections were provided, ranging from the obviously necessary ones at entrances in reception rooms and to less predictable sites – the maidservant's bathroom and the hall lavatory. The house telephone exchange was in the butler's pantry, complete with switchboard to connect callers in different parts of the house. In 1915 the first external telephone link was established. External calls could be directed via the pantry switchboard to any part of the house.

The butler was the domestic kingpin, and his personality affected the atmosphere of the house profoundly. Viola Bankes, who grew up at the seventeenth-century Dorset seat of the Bankes family, Kingston Lacy, in the early years of this century, has painted a vivid description of Mr Cooper, 'the keystone of Kingston Lacy'. Tall and dignified, with the same aristocratic profile as Lord Morley, he was always dressed in black and never lost his composure, although 'his whole body respectfully conveyed shocked disapproval at the familiarity of Canon Sowter, who insisted on shaking hands with him at the front door'. As a boy, Cooper had been page to the Duchess of Teck, Queen Mary's mother. He was an authority on wines, and especially proud of the pipes of port and the champagne laid down on the birth of the heir, Ralph Bankes, in 1902. He wielded his authority firmly but kindly, pausing as he cleaned the plate on a hot day to hand bottles of beer through the window to the gardeners labouring in the rose beds outside. He slept, as all good butlers did, close to the plate cellar and the muniment room, a long, inlaid ivory revolver close by his side. 'Nothing ever went wrong with the smooth running of the household during the time Cooper was our butler,' wrote Viola Bankes. 'He was as solid and reliable as the Bank of England and made Kingston Lacy seem just as secure.'

By this time, men in domestic service were few and far between, and the butler was sometimes the only male servant in the house. Indeed, as Kerr makes clear, many

House telephones were described in 1911 as 'one of the most usual conveniences to be found in a country house'. The telephone exchange switchboard at Dunham Massey, Cheshire, can still be seen in the butler's pantry. This extension in Lady Stamford's parlour had direct lines to five other rooms, accessed by moving the lever to the appropriate dial and pressing the button on the base of the receiver.

Roomy teak sinks for washing glass and silver in the window of Lutyens's beautifully finished butler's pantry at Castle Drogo, Devon.

so-called butler's pantries were actually the province of a housemaid rather than a manservant of any sort:

A small butler's pantry, where perhaps no manservant is kept, is to be contrived on the same principles; the service of wine, linen and plate is the object as before, and the fittings are therefore similar.

Anne Cobbett, too, whose *English Housekeeper* is addressed to more humble households than Kerr's rather grandiose *Gentleman's House*, remarks that

what is commonly called the *Butler's Pantry* does not of necessity imply the presence of a butler; not does it require to be spacious when the china and glass not in daily use is kept in the storeroom. Where women servants are kept, the care of the pantry belongs either to the parlour-maid or the housemaid, and the same servants usually perform the office of laying the cloth, and waiting at table; which is always done better by women.

Nevertheless, Edwin Lutyens still designed a spacious and confidently masculine pantry at Castle Drogo. Built by Dart and Francis in 1927, it remained in use until

1954. The glass-paned oak cupboards stand on slender pillars above a dresser shelf, with solid cupboards below. There are two roomy teak sinks in the bay window – butlers were privileged enough to be allowed sinks with a view. Everything is thought out, from the design of the soap tidies to the proud brass taps, including an extra one for drinking water. A door leads off into the butler's bedroom and the entrance to the plate safe. The telephone switchboard and the bellboard reflect the butler's role in arranging communications both with the outside world and between members of the household.

With the dignified exit of the butler, the last vestiges of the long tradition of masculine household service disappeared. Many of the butler's duties – seeing to the wine, carving the meat and locking up the household – did in fact devolve on to male heads of households. The steward's more influential role as chief household accountant, and hirer and firer of domestic personnel, had long been transferred to the housekeeper. This was the upper-class and middle-class manifestation of a very general shift from a sharing of domestic responsibility between husband and house-wife to a complete separation of spheres.

CHAPTER THREE

THE HOUSEKEEPER'S DOMAIN

'My first aim will be to *clean down* (do you comprehend the full force of the expression?) – *clean down* Moor House from chamber to cellar; my next to rub it up with beeswax, oil, and an indefinite number of cloths, till it glitters again; my third, to arrange every chair, table, bed, carpet, with mathematical precision . . .'

'I trust you will look a little higher than domestic endearments and household joys?'

'The best things the world has!' I interrupted.

Charlotte Brontë, *Jane Eyre*

If any one item symbolized the housekeeper, it was the large bunch of keys she carried at her waist. Everything, from spice-box to ice-box, had to be kept locked, and a conscientious housekeeper held herself accountable for every candle end and every slice off the Sunday joint. Thrift was her most important virtue.

Whether a housekeeper was a paid employee or the mistress of the household herself depended on the inclinations of the wife and the size and situation of the household. There were always mistresses who preferred to keep the reins in their own hands; others were too busy with charitable concerns, large families or socializing to take much active interest in domestic matters. But in a large rural establishment, one person, however diligently domestic, could not oversee everything. 'The mistress of a large family can neither afford the time, nor even have it in her power, to see what her servants are about, she must depend upon the Housekeeper to see all her orders are enforced and every rule kept up,' wrote Susanna Whatman in her *Housekeeping Book,* begun in 1776, and regularly amended. In 1782, when her children were eleven, eight and five years old, she engaged Hester Davis as housekeeper. The *Housekeeping Book,* with its amendments and additions over the years, was written in part for the benefit of Hester and her successors, in part for that of the next mistress of the household, and it is evident from its contents that Susanna herself continued to pay close attention to domestic affairs.

The heart of the housekeeper's domain was her own sitting-room, part workroom and office, part withdrawing-room. From here the female servants were governed and their domestic duties arranged. Close beside it were the still-room, the storeroom and the china closets. The housekeeper was also responsible for the organization of the linen closets and the housemaids' cupboards, where cleaning equipment was kept and from which clean hot water was supplied to the bedrooms. Perhaps the finest housekeeper's suite owned by the Trust is at Tatton Park. In the passage linking the housekeeper's sitting-room to the still-room are well-stocked linen and china closets. In the basement directly below are the china cellar, for storing less frequently used items, a dairy cellar and a housekeeper's cellar.

THE HOUSEKEEPER'S SITTING-ROOM

The housekeeper's sitting-room at Tatton meets almost exactly the detailed specification for such a room given by John Loudon: 'a spacious comfortable apartment. furnished as a respectable parlour, and situated so that the other offices are easily overlooked', offering 'all that is necessary for use and comfort in a rather plain way'. The floor is fitted with a jolly Brussels wall-to-wall carpet, rich in reds and blues;

A turn-of-the-century photograph of a housekeeper's room. One of the housekeeper's most important responsibilities was the maintenance of the family linen in apple-pie order. Sewing-machines, invented in the second half of the nineteenth century, made the task much easier.

the windows curtained in a chintz that had perhaps hung elsewhere in the freshness of youth. Cushions and a footstool make the fireside armchairs inviting, and six or seven upper servants could be accommodated for breakfast or tea at the round central table. A long table by the window was a convenient place for mending linen and doing the household accounts, and cupboards fitted with drawers flank the fireplace. There is a loyal little collection of photographs of the family on a side-table, a good clock on the mantelpiece and a few framed prints on the walls.

In 1825 Samuel and Sarah Adams's *Complete Servant* gave a good picture of the average housekeeper's daily round at the same period. She would not have to rise as early as the maids, perhaps making her first appearance in the still-room (of which more below) at 7.30, where she would oversee the putting out of china and table linen for breakfast. The still-room maid, if there was one, was in effect the house-keeper's personal servant. At eight o'clock the housekeeper took breakfast in her sitting-room with other senior servants, and checked the breakfast arrangements. Later she went to the storeroom to give out the stores for the day, then back to help the still-room maid wash up the china and put away the breakfast preserves.

During the morning she made a round of the bedrooms, checking the work of the housemaids and making sure that soap, candles, writing-paper and ink were attended to, and that drawers and wardrobes were dusted and freshly lined with paper. At one o'clock, she headed the servants' dining table, carving one of the joints (the butler carved the other); then she led the way to take pudding and cheese with the senior servants in her own room, irreverently nicknamed Pug's Parlour by the lower ranks. In the afternoon she arranged the dessert for dinner, prepared biscuits and cakes for five o'clock tea, and set out the tea and coffee which was sent up to the drawing-room after dinner.

This description errs on the side of simplification. A housekeeper also had to mediate between her employers and the lower servants, besides dealing with the myriad incidental details that make up the varied patchwork of domestic life. Mary Salisbury was housekeeper to the Yorkes of Erddig from 1798 to 1804, and the range of her concerns can be seen in the entries in her account books – 1s 4d to Mary Jones for sewing; 1s for 'The boys that found the Duck'; 3s for the washerwoman. On another day she paid 10s 6d for 'a Side of Venison' and 1s 6d for 'Musher Rooms', and gave 1s to the poor. She also gave the Yorke children their pocket money, and paid the harpsichord tuner and the chimney-sweep.

In a household without a mistress, such as the Warwickshire seat of the Lucy family, Charlecote, between 1744 and 1786, the housekeeper was peculiarly busy. Letters passed almost daily between George Lucy, the most eligible and elusive bachelor of his generation, and Philippa Hayes, the domestic treasure he employed from 1744 until 1768, when she became too ill to work. These letters, and her

Memorandum Book, written in smudged and blotted brown ink, are full of endearing domestic intimacies. They gossiped of courtships, criticized the state of the roads and deplored the weather. George sent bottles of Cheltenham water, instructing Mrs Hayes to dose the entire household with it. She in turn commissioned him to bring back groceries from London: tea from Thos. Twining (bohea and the finest green), powdered loaf sugar, Jordan almonds, French barley, Jamaican pepper, pistachio nuts, coffee beans, white paper for lining shelves, white starch and French brandy.

In 1755 George departed on a European tour, and a few months later asked her to send more clothes out to him in Rome ('people here dress much'). Obediently she packed off his best embroidered suit, a white Dresden waistcoat, two pairs of velvet breeches (one red, one black) and half a dozen fine ruffled shirts. None of them reached him – the ship was attacked by Moorish pirates. In 1758, George was home again, redesigning the gardens and re-equipping the house. He asked the young ladies he met in Bath for advice, visiting Petingals to choose new damask curtains. 'The hanging in festoons they say will certainly darken the rooms,' he wrote to Mrs Hayes. 'My only concern is to take nothing from, but to add as much light as I can, to your room.'

The handwriting in the Memorandum Book grows increasingly shaky as it records 'woodcock killed at Charlecote' and 'fish taken out of the great Bason in the Court for the master's dinner'. All the Lucys were partial to fish, in punning acknowledgement of their family crest perhaps: three 'lucies houriant' – a trio of pike coming up for air. To the end of his life George kept a taste for a tench boiled in ale and dressed in rosemary. In 1768 Mrs Hayes, increasingly feeble, retired. She died after a long illness, leaving George Lucy 'out of the great regard I have for him, my cornelian seal, and desire he will have my buff tabby to cover his easy chair'. The 'buff tabby' would have been a silk dress, no doubt with a quantity of usable material in its skirt.

Was it thrift or sentiment that suggested it should be used on that easy chair? Certainly, of all the servants, the housekeeper was closest to the family, and valued accordingly. Ideally, she was promoted from the lower ranks, and so knew the household well before taking over. Mary Webster, a canny widow, governed the affairs of Erddig for more than thirty years. A daguerreotype of 1852 shows her in a sober black afternoon gown with a bunch of keys hanging from her waist: the poem attached to the picture by the second Philip Yorke attested that she was quite as efficient as she looked.

> Upon the portly frame we look
> Of one who was our former Cook.
> No better keeper of our Store,

Mary Webster, a canny widow who governed the affairs of Erddig, Clwyd, for more than thirty years, was renowned for her thrift. Her most prominent badge of office was the ring of keys at her waist. (Daguerreotype of 1852.)

Did ever enter at our door.
She knew and pandered to our taste,
Allowed no want and yet no waste.

Not all housekeepers were as competent. At Uppark, the 'much-cupboarded, white-painted, chintz-brightened' housekeeper's room was described by H. G. Wells in *Tono-Bungay,* a novel which recreates the house's atmosphere in the 1880s. Wells spent his boyhood at Uppark, after his fifty-three-year-old mother Sarah, once a maid there, was summoned back in 1875 to become housekeeper to Frances Bullock Featherstonhaugh, the surviving sister of the dairymaid who had won the heart of the aged roué Sir Harry Featherstonhaugh (for more about this unlikely couple, turn to p. 73). But his mother was not at all like the efficient and dominant housekeeper he portrayed in his novel. 'Except that she was thoroughly honest, my mother was perhaps the worst housekeeper that was ever thought of,' he wrote in his *Autobiography.* 'She never had the slightest experience in housekeeping. She did not know how to plan work, control servants, buy stores or economize in any way. She did not know clearly what was wanted upstairs. She could not even add up her accounts

41

with assurance and kept me to do it for her.' Wells relates how his mother 'grew deafer and deafer, and she would not admit her deafness, but guessed at what was said to her, and made wild shots in reply'. In 1893 she was dismissed, though not ostensibly for inefficiency, but for gossip.

Wells remembered his mother's room vividly. 'There was an old peerage and a *Crockford* together with the books of recipes, the *Whitaker's Almanac*, the *Old Moore's Almanack,* and the eighteenth-century dictionary, on the little dresser that broke the cupboards on one side.' Until the disastrous fire of 1989, all this remained undisturbed at Uppark, conveying the strength of the superstitions, folk memory and ties with the past that permeated the traditions of domestic service there for so long. But after the long process of restoration is completed, it will once more convey the atmosphere of an afternoon in 1890, with tea table spread, kettle on the hob, sewing-machine at the ready, an iron for touching up linen, and of course Mrs Wells's indispensable ear trumpet.

THE STILL-ROOM

The still-room (still from distillery, rather than calmness) was originally the province of the housewife, a place where she could experiment with some of the most ancient arts of domesticity. The objects 'in Ye Still House' recorded in the 1710 inventory of Dyrham Park indicated the original functions of what is one of the most interesting of the ancillary domestic offices. The pewter limbeck (see below) was for distilling essential oils and spirituous cordials, the copper pot for boiling up the raw materials of cordials. The 'cold still' probably referred to the worm tub (see below) used to cool down vaporized infusions. There was a set of bellows to keep the little open cooking fire at full blast, and a pair of brass scales and weights to ensure the accuracy of the tiny quantities needed for patent medicines. There was a variety of containers: glass basins, tumblers and an old glass salver; and forty-four sweetmeat glasses and six syllabub glasses for delicate little puddings. Three dozen tin biscuit pans suggest there was a small baking oven or stove; the copper preserving pan was for making jams and jellies.

The portable still-room stove was a specialized piece of early equipment: a tall shallow cupboard with no doors. Its shelves were lined with tin or lead, on which crystallized, dried, candied and preserved fruits and flowers were laid. The stove was set fairly close to the cooking fire so that warm air circulated around the shelves and dried out the last of the moisture, preventing the confectionery from getting sticky. It could also be used for meringues and certain types of slow-cooking biscuits.

The variety and range of still-room products is indicated by the contents of *The Queen's Closet Open'd* (1696), a popular manual on the art of 'preserving, candying and cookery'. It included recipes for Melancholy Water and Candied Cowslips, Portugal Eggs (set in a sea of red jelly, and decorated with gilded laurel leaves) and Snail Water ('excellent for Consumption . . . Take a peck of snails with the shells on their backs . . .'). Leaving aside the attractions of Marmalott of Apricocks and Syrrop of Lemons, this recipe for 'Spirrit of Black Cherry' gives a representative method of distilling cordials.

Take Black Cherrys full and Ripe and beat them in a Stone Mortar be sure to break the stones put them in a wooden veysell that is some tub standing upright put to them Ale Yeast according to the quantity if 3 or 4 dozen of cherries a quart of yeast lett it stand eight Days Stirring them for 3 or 4 days twice a Day then lett them Stand until they have a Venomous Smell and have done rising then Still them off in a Limbeck.

A limbeck, or alembic, was a distilling apparatus. It was a gourd-shaped vessel, which came in several sizes. A household alembic might hold up to ten or twelve

The spacious still-room at Tatton Park, Cheshire, was re-equipped in the late nineteenth century. A brick-lined oven in the far wall was used for slow baking, and a small range (just out of sight to the right of the table) for boiling up preserves.

pints in the lower part (the cucurbit) which was three quarters filled with the infusion to be distilled and then heated. 'To obtain the essential oil of plants, you must distil with an open fire,' explained Jarrin's *Italian Confectioner* (1827). 'To distil spirits, the cucurbit must be put into a pan half full of water.' The vapour produced by heating the infusion rose into the head of the alembick (the capital) and from there was conducted into a spiral (worm) contained within a wooden tub (worm tub) filled with cold water. The cooling effect of the water turned the vapour back into liquid which collected at the base of the worm. Orange, wormwood, lavender, cinnamon, pennyroyal and strawberry water were all made by bruising the leaves of flowers and then infusing them in this fashion. Rose petals were steeped in salt, and made into an aromatic paste which was kept in a jar, added to daily, until enough was available to make rose water.

To make 'spirituous liquers' such as Hungary waters and ratafias, the ingredients were steeped in alcohol, only adding enough water to prevent a burnt flavour. The still-room was also used to make vinegars and pickles, jams and jellies, soap, cosmetics, medicines and even tallow and wax candles. And to experiment. At Springhill, a legend lingers about the making of blackcurrant whisky: the squeezed currants were thrown out in the yard where they were gulped down by the poultry in best *Danny the Champion of the World* style and the hens spent the rest of the afternoon reeling drunkenly around the policies.

Household polishes, soaps and waxes were also brewed up in the still-room. But as more and more commercially made products were available, its function became less interesting, an auxiliary office rather than a special sphere of operations in its own right. In 1904 Muthesius summed the situation up succinctly: 'It remained the province of the housewife until modern times, when the English housewife ceased to cross the threshold of the domestic quarters and it passed to the housekeeper.' In order to relieve the kitchen, the housekeeper prepared breakfast, afternoon tea and after-dinner beverages there with the help of the still-room maid. This change in use is reflected by John Loudon's list of the requirements of a nineteenth-century still-room:

A door in the housekeeper's room should open into the still-room, in which the housekeeper, assisted by the still-room maid, would make preserves. It should be furnished as a better kind of kitchen, containing a fireplace, with a boiler, a small oven, a range of charcoal stoves, with a cover; a small shut-up sink, with a water-pipe for a supply of water. A range of small closets for the maids, to keep their tea things, and tea and sugar, and things used at the housekeeper's table; a large table, with drawers in the centre of the room, and a smaller round table for work; and a dresser against the wall, to let down when not in use, would be convenient; shelves would also be useful for the pans, etc., used by the housekeeper. There should also be a round [roller] towel and a basin in the sink for washing hands; a small looking-glass might promote tidiness of person and a piece of common carpet would add to the comfort of the room. The chairs and stools should be neat and substantial, and a small case of well-chosen books should hang against the wall.

Under benevolent regimes, children might be allowed into the still-room to make toffee and ginger biscuits. The Egerton children had their own sets of wooden cutters and pastry cases stored in the capacious still-room at Tatton Park. Very completely equipped with a small sink and a large central work table, it has a cast-iron range fitted into one wall, and a brick baking oven (with an iron door) in another.

Traditions lingered at Longleat, where the Marchioness of Bath recalled the housekeeper

performing feats of Alchemy, distilling rose-water from dark damask roses, producing pot-pourri from an old family recipe, preserving fruits, making jam, candying peel, bottling morello cherries in brandy, drying lavender to keep the linen cupboard sweet, and forever harrying the still-room maids. The short spiral stair from the housekeeper's room to the still-room is forever haunted by the jingling sound of the keys she wore at her waistband and the smell of the old still-room itself – that delicious combination of hot bread, biscuits, coffee and herbs.

(*Longleat Kitchen and Recipe Book*, 1972)

THE HOUSEKEEPER'S STOREROOM

The business of provisioning large rural households before the age of motorized transport was no mean task. 'It is necessary to lay in larger stores of all the common articles of daily consumption than are ever required in town, where shops can be sent to in an emergency,' explained Jane Loudon. According to J. J. Stevenson, the contents of a storeroom were 'pretty much those of a grocer's shop – a chest of tea, a barrel of sugar, canisters of coffee, rice, sago, spices, preserves, condiments, soap, candles, etc.'

Groceries were best laid in only two or three times a year, taking advantage of the best seasonal prices. Starch, for example, was much cheaper after the wheat harvest. Anne Cobbett 'kept a quantity of rice more than three years by spreading a well-aired linen sheet in a box and folding it over the rice'. The sheet was lifted out on to the floor once every two or three months and the rice spread about on it for a day or two. 'This had the effect of keeping away the weevil' (*English Housekeeper*, 1842).

The storeroom was located as close to the kitchen as possible, preferably with a cellar underneath it to ensure that it was not damp. It could also be kept dry by running flues from the kitchen range through it – otherwise it might require a small fireplace of its own. Pickles and preserved fruit could be stored upside down. Battens

The early-nineteenth-century dry store at Tatton Park, Cheshire. Sugar and spice
and all things nice: the contents of the housekeeper's dry storeroom were 'pretty much
those of a grocer's shop'. It had to be capacious enough to hold several months' supplies
of such indispensables as tea, coffee, sugar, spices, dried fruit, rice and candles.

placed behind fitted cupboards protected groceries from damp walls. A cupboard
with folding doors like a wardrobe and a lock and key was useful for storing tea,
sugar and spices. Anne Cobbett suggested that there should be shelves in this,

on which should stand numerous tin canisters marked with the names of the different articles
they contain. In the upper part should be a shelf suspended by cords passing through holes
bored in the corners, for loaves of sugar, or any similar articles likely to be attacked by mice.
The common tea should be kept in a chest lined with lead, which may stand in the lower
part of the closet, and the finer kinds should be kept in canisters. A bag of raw coffee may
also stand on the lower shelf of the closet; but after the coffee is ground it should be kept in
a canister, and as far apart from the tea as possible, as, if it is near it, it will give the tea an
unpleasant taste.

A similar cupboard for soap and candles might have hooked nails driven into the
back to hang the candles from and 'a kind of bench or wooden stand for boxes of
mould candles, if you use any, though most people prefer the composition or stearine
candles as they do not require snuffing'. These candles, and those of wax or spermaceti,
would keep for a long time without injury if covered, but tallow candles could not

be kept for more than six years. Both candles and soap were best bought in the late summer and kept for some time before using.

Refined sugar was bought in large conical loaves, and cut up into lumps with sugar nippers, fiendish tools rather like those memorable scissors in *Strewelpeter*. Several examples of both cones and nippers are displayed on the kitchen table at Saltram. Susanna Whatman's storeroom closet had deep drawers, one for moist sugar and two for lump sugar. 'The pieces should be cut up as square as possible, and rather small,' she directed. 'The sugar that is powdered to fill the sugar castor should be kept in a basin in one of the drawers to prevent any insects getting into it, and be powdered *fine* in the mortar and kept ready for use.'

There would also be canisters for currants and other dried fruits; tins for cakes and puddings, boxes of almonds and raisins for dessert. Dried herbs were hung in muslin bags, and then rubbed into powder and stored in tins or glass jars. A little nest of drawers would be kept for medicinal articles, with proper weights and scales and graduated measures.

Although capacious fruit lofts were required for keeping large quantities of apples, pears, and so on, Anne Cobbett recommended wrapping apples and pears in soft paper, and then sealing them in large jars. Pears could be hung from their stalks along lines, as could bunches of grapes with six inches of stalk sealed with sealing wax. Nuts kept well in cemented jars in a dry cellar.

Every week stores had to be dispensed to the domestic staff in due proportion. A former housekeeper recalls the weekly storeroom routine at Shugborough in the 1930s vividly:

Friday was store day and it was a very busy morning. Everybody brought their cans to be filled and a list of what they wanted for working – soaps, Brasso for cleaning the brass, black lead for doing the grates, and all the general working stores as well as the food stores. Each one was allowed a quarter of a pound of butter per head per week. And they got so much jam – say a 2lb jar a week. Outside the stillroom is a pull-out table. It was pulled out on store day. And just to the left there was a cupboard that had all the soaps – all the bathroom soaps, toilet, large tablets and small tablets for the basins, and there were long yellow bars you had for scrubbing and washing clothes; the laundry maids got a couple of those every week. They used to get soap by the hundredweight. The best soaps they got from Harrods once a year.

THE LINEN CLOSET

Counting, marking, mending and keeping track of the linen as it circulated in use was an important part of any housekeeper's job. Fine linen was a measure of social status and prestige – heirlooms were handed down from generation to generation, in trust rather than merely useful. In 1824 Mary Elizabeth Lucy, mistress of Charlecote, gloated over the most useful connection of her accomplished (and female) cook, Sharp: 'She had an aunt who was housekeeper to the King and every third or seventh year (I forget which) she has as her perquisite all the Royal table linen. Through Sharp she offered us for £50 thirty of the finest Holland damask tablecloths very little the worse for wear. Of course we readily gave £50, there never was such a bargain!' (*Mistress of Charlecote*).

The grander the household, the greater the contents of the traditional 'bottom drawer' of linen which was part of a bride's dower. Ann Cook's *Plan of House-keeping* (1760) suggests 'four webs for sheets, 44 yards each, two fine and two coarse; also a web of Diaper and one of Hugaback for tablecloths' for a modest four-bedroomed house. The 1833 Erddig inventory of linen lists '23 diaper table cloths, thirty-seven damask ditto, forty-three damask dinner napkins, sixty diaper do, 34 huckaback cloths, 173 fringed towels, 10 doz plain do, 50 pillow cases, 16 common do, 12 pair large sheets, 18 smaller do, 18 fine crib do'. Another for Harewood house in 1836 mentions over 600 towels alone – each clearly marked for its destined place. Besides those for the family and guests, there were specific towels for the housekeeper, dairymaid, laundrymaid, still-room maid, and kitchen maids. Roller towels were used in kitchen, still-room, servants' hall, maids' hall, pantry and laundry, and by the groom, coachman and baker. There were also specialized cloths by the dozen – china cloths for the still-room, rubbers for the kitchen (rough scouring cloths), pocket cloths for the footman, glass-cloths for the butler and the stewards' room, lamp cloths for the pantry and the porter, dusters and china cloths for the housemaids, laundry and nursery, and horn cloths for the servants' hall.

Table linen in current use was kept in well-made cupboards in the housekeeper's own room (or in some cases by the butler), but large households would need at least one supplementary linen closet, either next door to the housekeeper's room or upstairs conveniently close to the bedrooms. Tatton Park's linen closet has sliding doors to maximize space, and an excellent display of linen. J.J. Stevenson suggested dividing the closet to form one part for bedlinen and one for table linen. The fitted cupboards or free-standing presses in which the linen was stored required divisions of about two feet, the size to which sheets and tablecloths were normally folded. They usually had shelves or sliding trays, and drawers. Some form of heating was desirable, perhaps by hot-water pipes running through the back of the cupboard. Ideally there was a long table arranged underneath a good light for folding and checking the linen. Mending was a major chore, although much alleviated by the invention of the sewing-machine in the 1850s.

The linen closet at Tatton Park is still filled with monogrammed sheets, towels, tablecloths and napkins. A substantial Victorian family might have as many as 600 towels alone. Everything had to be kept carefully sorted, marked and recorded in a linen book.

THE HOUSEMAID'S CLOSET

Besides being responsible for still-room, china and linen closets and storeroom, the housekeeper had to oversee the work of the housemaids and superintend the annual eruption of spring cleaning. To reduce the daily work of the housemaids, and to defend themselves against the twin enemies of light and dust, many houses spent most of the time in a perpetual twilight, wholly or partly wrapped in protective coverings for much of the year. Blinds were pulled down as soon as sunlight flooded in at windows, druggets covered carpets, loose holland covers masked upholstery, bags protected the bottoms of curtains and muslin wraps preserved the glitter of chandeliers. When Surtees's Mr Sponge set off on his sporting tour, 'he had the house put away in Brown Holland, the carpets rolled up, the pictures covered, the statues shrouded in muslin'.

The housemaids' routine varied from household to household, but this timetable,

49

regular as clockwork, which was suggested in *The Housekeeper's Oracle* (London, 1812), was a fairly representative one:

Rise at Six
Open shutters by a quarter past
Clean grates by Seven
Sweep rooms by half past
Dust and have downstairs rooms ready by Eight
Have your own breakfast till half past
Prepare all ready to go up Stairs by Nine
Turn down Beds and open windows by half past
Clear away things, empty slops and change water by Ten
Make beds by Eleven
Sweep bedrooms by half past
Dust and lay all smooth by One
Clean yourself ready for Needlework or whatever may be required by half past

The hub of cleaning operations was the housemaid's closet, home of all the pails, brooms, dusters and so on used in cleaning the house. John Loudon recommended that it be

light and roomy, with a plaster floor, with an inner closet for the bedroom night lights, or rushlight cases, etc., with drawers underneath for cloths and dusters. There should be pegs and shelves, on which to put anything out of the way. As warm water is very much used by the housemaid, their closet, in a large house, should contain a small copper, for heating water, and, if possible, it should be supplied with water by a leaden pipe, say from a cistern of rainwater from the roof; a sink-stone, connecting with a drain, would also be a great convenience. In large establishments, the labour of carrying up and down the stairs clean and dirty water is very great, so that a pipe supplying soft water and a sink for the slops is necessary in a place of this kind, which should also contain a large box in one corner, for a supply of coals to be used in the upper part of the house.

This description appeared in an edition of John Loudon dated 1846. Piped water was a fairly general convenience by then, and many houses would have hot water piped up from a kitchen boiler. Notice that a sewage drain was assumed to be a possibility — it is a widespread misapprehension to think that servants carried slops downstairs if they could possibly help it.

Many housemaid's closets were large enough to have been converted into bath-rooms in recent years, but at Dunham Massey a fine late-nineteenth-century closet with excellent plumbing is still on view. The heavy porcelain sink unit, set low with a battery of taps for hot, cold and drinking water, has two compartments. One is evidently intended for the disposal of slops from the bedroom commodes — a cistern above provides a flood of water to wash all down, and there is a resting-place for a

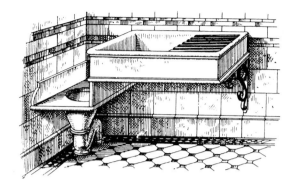

A housemaid's sink of the type fitted in Dunham Massey, Cheshire, in the late nineteenth century, with special provision for the emptying of slops from chamber-pots and washstand ewers.

lavatory brush beside it. At the other end of the closet are shelves for soaps, polishes and cloths, and space for brooms, brushes and mops.

A mind-boggling variety of brushes was listed by Mrs Beeton in 1883. Besides the basic scrubbing brushes and stiff bass broom, it is assumed that a house of any size will require curtain, or bed, brushes, a telescope brush (for high ceilings), carpet whisks, hand brushes, hearth brushes, single and double banister brushes, shoe brushes and stove brushes, plate brushes, oil brushes and dish brushes, bottle brushes, crumb brushes, closet brushes, dusting brushes, flue brushes, furniture brushes, feather dusters (one with a jointed pole), library brushes and velvet brushes.

But apart from the variations on this most basic of themes, the housemaids' equipment changed remarkably little over the centuries. In the 1780s, household bills received by Richard Colt Hoare of Stourhead, Wiltshire, mention whiting (for doorsteps), dry-rubbing, scrubbing and dusting brushes, and carpet, hearth, banister and long-hair brooms. A third bill a few years later mentions a long scrubber, mops, picture brushes and whisks. The contents of the housemaid's closet at Stourhead in 1915 were almost identical, with the addition of 'a patent carpet sweeper'.

Such carpet sweepers represented the first attempts to mechanize dust removal. They were inspired by horse-drawn street-sweeping machines, which used a chain-driven endless belt of brushes and were patented in 1842 by Joseph Whitworth. Drastically reduced in scale, this idea inspired the many patents for domestic sweeping machines registered in the 1850s. Perhaps the most successful was the series of machines developed by Melville Bissell, of Grand Rapids, Michigan, by the 1880s. Bissell could boast that his sweepers were 'in daily use in the households of HM The Queen and HRH The Princess of Wales'.

But it was the electric vacuum cleaner which revolutionized dust removal most completely. Instead of needing a specialized tool to approach every dusting task (a goose wing was recommended for cleaning the spines of books, for example), one greedy nozzle could suck almost anything off anywhere. It, more than any other single factor, made spring-cleaning unnecessary. Vacuum-cleaning was invented almost simultaneously on both sides of the Atlantic. In Britain it was patented by a fairground designer, H. C. Booth, in 1901. His first machine took the form of a large engine, horse-drawn and powered by steam, which was driven around London streets. Vacuum-cleaning tea parties were thrown to admire the smartly uniformed men from the 'BVC' at work.

Soon fixed-engine models were being installed in the basement of blocks of service flats. Minterne Magna in Dorset, built between 1903 and 1907, was probably the first country house to include such a machine in its fittings. The basement suction pump was connected by a series of tubes to the main rooms in the house. In these there were outlets in the skirting boards covered by brass flaps which housemaids could slide open to plug in hand-held hoses with broad dust-gulping nozzles. Sennowe Park in Norfolk, Eltham Palace in south-east London and Charters in Buckinghamshire were also fitted with such installations.

Small portable models had to wait for the development of a light electric motor, although many patents were taken out for hand- or foot-pumped vacuuming machines such as the 1906 Griffith or the 1910 Baby Daisy, both on view in the London Science Museum. The machine that was to become synonymous with vacuum-cleaning was patented in 1908 by an asthmatic school janitor in Ohio, James Spangler. He attached a pillowcase to a broom handle to catch the dust drawn up by a fan driven by a small electric motor. The reason why we are not all spangling our floors these days is that this invention was taken up and developed for the market by a relation of Spangler who was finding the effect of the automobile industry on his harness business disastrous. His name was W. H. Hoover.

Hoovers, sold in the USA on the credit system and from door to door, rapidly became an American institution. In Britain popular acceptance took longer. Fears of electrocution had to be allayed. 'There is one definite quality in all reputable makes of vacuum cleaner – the possibility of a shock being received while one is using them is so remote as to be non-existent for all practical purposes,' declared *Ideal Home*, not altogether reassuringly, in March 1930. But once electricity was not only a commonplace but generally available, vacuum cleaners – Goblins and Electroluxes as well as Hoovers – became indispensable. Regrettably perhaps, the visits from the BVC men became part of history. When housemaids exited in their thousands to take on more congenial office and factory work, their former mistresses were left to wield for themselves the nearest thing yet developed to an effective household robot.

CHAPTER FOUR

THE LIVING LARDER

No man need ever have an ill-provisioned house if there
be but attached to it a dovecot, a warren and a fishpond
wherein meat may be found as readily to hand as if it
were stored in a larder.

Olivier de Serres, 1603 (quoted by Dorothy Hartley, *Food
in England*)

Today we take it for granted that fresh meat, vegetables and dairy products, bread
and beer, are all items that have to be bought. But until the early nineteenth century,
when Britain was officially declared a nation of shopkeepers by both Adam Smith
and Napoleon, it was the ambition of any self-respecting household to be as self-
sufficient as possible. Daniel Defoe defined 'the English Gentleman' as having 'venison
perhaps in his park, sufficient for his own table at least, and rabbits in his own warren
adjoining, pigeons from a dove-house in the yard, fish in his own ponds or in some
small river adjoining and within his own royalty, and milk with all the needful
addenda to his kitchen, which a small dairy of four or five cows yields to him'.

John Loudon (who was something of a conservative) recommended in 1833 that
'every country gentleman ... be a farmer to a certain extent; the size of the farm to
be determined by the wants of his family'. To farm on a grand scale, he conceded,
involved too much anxiety – but a small farm was a means by which a gentleman
could stay in touch with tenants, understand the realities of country life, be realistic
as to what rents he might fairly expect, try out agricultural experiments and encourage
the dissemination of new ideas. It would also 'add to his weight and consequence'
locally and ensure 'a liberal style of housekeeping at prime cost'.

Under the system of management supposed, beside the ordinary provision supplied by the
farm, the estate generally would afford game and wildfowl; the park and the waters in it
would supply venison and freshwater fish of several kinds; and the gardens and orchards all
sorts of fruit and vegetables; so that there would be nothing to purchase for the house except
groceries and chandlery.

The next few chapters will describe how households provisioned themselves before the coming of the commercial food industry that now almost completely directs our eating habits.

THE HOME FARM

In medieval times, the manor was inseparable from the farmyard and often attached to it. At Bradley Manor in Devon and Trerice in Cornwall, farm buildings were virtually wings of the main house. Cotehele, another Cornish house, is probably the best surviving example of this arrangement – an 1830 engraving shows cows being milked under its windows. The great stone barn built by Sir Richard Edgcumbe in the 1480s still flanks the gatehouse, and the improvements to the much-neglected estate in the 1860s retained the farmyard atmosphere of the outbuildings. In Northern Ireland the connection between house and farm was similarly unbroken. Almost all the Irish houses owned by the Trust have a farm adjoining them or very close by – a reflection of the enduring importance of the agricultural economy in Ulster.

In England, more prosperous and mercantile, the architects of the Elizabethan 'great houses' shook off such unglamorous and pungent connections, and arranged their new mansions in splendid isolation. At Baddesley Clinton in Warwickshire, a litter of medieval farm buildings was cleared away to create a formal forecourt for the house in the seventeenth century – its uneven lawn is a relic of their former presence. The household's needs were supplied by local tenant farmers. With the eighteenth-century trend to 'emparkment', such tenant smallholdings were cleared. Rolling acres of deer park and carefully landscaped woodland became a setting for the house rather than being separated from it as had been the medieval custom. At Charlecote, for example, a ha-ha – a deep ditch with a fence concealed in it – was installed to give the illusion that deer could wander right up to the house. A substantial but quite separate 'home farm', often specially designed by an architect, catered for the household. Sometimes this was very close by, almost an extension of the house, as at Uppark or at Erddig. More often it was quite separate, offering a pleasant excursion for guests.

Go-ahead landlords saw the home farm as an opportunity to demonstrate new techniques to backward tenants and neighbours. In his *Management of Landed Estates* (1806) William Marshall described it as 'a seminary of improvements for the benefit and management of the estate at large'. At Petworth, West Sussex, the 3rd Earl of Egremont changed the medieval deer park into a home farm, and experimented with such novel crops as rhubarb. At Wimpole, Shugborough and Tatton Park, home farms of this sort are still operational, but their emphasis has changed from innovation to preservation: they offer a living history of agriculture.

Wimpole Home Farm (previously Park Farm) was rebuilt in 1794 to the designs of Sir John Soane, the architect of the Bank of England, who was employed by the 3rd Earl of Hardwicke to improve the mansion itself in 1791. The most important of the original buildings to survive is the Great Barn, 150 feet long, where corn, straw and other fodder were stored. There are also some unusual stag pens, and a large E-shaped cattle shed. Soane also designed a dairy, but the present dairy was built in the 1860s, as was the farmhouse. Wimpole specializes in rare breeds of cattle, sheep, pigs and poultry.

At Shugborough Park Farm, an extensive set of buildings was designed by Samuel Wyatt in 1805 for Thomas, 1st Viscount Anson, son-in-law of the legendary agricultural improver Coke of Holkham. It was described in 1817 by William Pitt in his *Topographical History of Staffordshire*:

Farming steward's house on one side; a range of buildings on another contains a brewhouse upon a large scale, a water corn mill for the use of the family and farm, and in which corn is ground for the neighbouring poor gratis, and also a malt-house. The opposite side and end are occupied by stalls for feeding cattle, store rooms, stables, and other appendages. In the middle of the yard is a very complete hoggery, built of large stones set edgewise and covered with slate.

The home farm was once closely linked to the manor-house. The seventeenth-century
Great Barn at East Riddlesden Hall, W. Yorks., houses a collection of traditional
agricultural machinery.

An 1835 description of the farm also mentions a dovecote, slaughterhouse, poultry houses and dairy. Today the farm is run as an agricultural museum by the Staffordshire County Council. Shire horses work the land, the corn mill produces flour for bread which is baked in a traditional brick oven. Milk from the dairy shorthorns is used to make butter and cheese, and farm workers' meals are prepared in the farmhouse kitchen. Pigs, of ancient lineage, are still reared in the farmyard's 'very complete hoggery': Gloucestershire Old Spots, Tamworths and even an 'Iron Age' sow (Henrietta). The Gloucestershire Old Spots used to be known as 'cottagers' or 'orchard pigs', because of their ability to survive and fatten on fallen apples. They were succeeded in popularity by 'Tamworths', pigs of a reddish colour with long noses and pricked ears. Excellent bacon pigs, they are descended from a well-known red boar kept near Tamworth in the nineteenth century.

Smaller country establishments maintained a more immediately domestic connection with farm produce. When The Argory, a delightful neoclassical gentleman's residence in County Armagh, was built in the 1820s, behind the formal block of the house the architect provided for a poultry yard, dairy, a fold yard for cows and sheep, bullock sheds, barn and piggeries, as well as coach-houses and stables.

Until the end of the nineteenth century, even cottagers kept a pig if they could. Neighbours took turns to slaughter their pigs, sharing the meat with each other. 'Now we have killed a porker, and Emma thinks of sending [Mrs and Miss Bates] a loin or a leg,' declared Jane Austen's Mr Woodhouse. Singed, scalded, salted down and smoked, pigs provided communal pork and bacon all the year round.

Snaring rabbits in the warren and catching small birds for the table were the duties of the gamekeeper and his assistants. Rabbits were introduced into Devon and Cornwall in the early thirteenth century. Special 'coning-earths' were made for them, mounds protected from predators by a ditch and a fence. Maintenance work on the Petworth warren is recorded in 1349. Palings and three gates were repaired, and tar bought to preserve the trunks of trees from rabbits nibbling the bark. There is still a bumpy area of Petworth Park known as Cony Park. A 'rabbit garden' existed at Fountains Abbey, in Yorkshire in 1457. Rabbit meat was originally regarded as a delicacy, and served up at banquets, but when the newcomers had bred with their legendary virtuosity, cony stew became common fare. The Charlecote cony warren was emparked in the early seventeenth century, and gamekeepers began to cull rabbits in landscaped gardens and parklands. But, as the thirty or so recipes offered by the 1884 edition of Mrs Beeton make clear, rabbits remained useful fare, particularly in winter.

Venison was also highly prized and necessary nourishment. Deer parks were a Norman innovation, as were fallow deer, much easier to keep in a park than red or roe deer. In the fourteenth century there were over three thousand deer parks in

England, all licensed by the Crown. Besides different types of deer, they also held wild pigs and wild cattle. One of the most renowned medieval deer parks was Lyme Park, in Cheshire, described as 'a fair park surrounded with a paling' in 1465. Every midsummer the stags were driven through a pond in front of the present stable block known as Stag Pool. In 1750 Dr Pococke described 'their horns moving like a wood along the water'. In the Stag Parlour, bas reliefs celebrate the pleasures of the chase at Lyme.

Charlecote too prides itself on the lineage of its deer herd: the fallow deer are traditionally claimed to be descended from the herd poached by a young Stratford tearaway called William Shakespeare. Shakespeare, caught red-handed (literally 'ensanguined' with the blood of the deer) revenged himself on the short-tempered magistrate and lord of Charlecote, Sir Thomas Lucy, notoriously proud of his ancient family crest of three pikes, by caricaturing him for eternity as the fussy foolish Justice Shallow ('the dozen white louses do become an old coat well') in *The Merry Wives of Windsor* and *Henry IV, Part 2*. 'You have beaten my men, killed my deer, and broken open my lodge,' complains Shallow to Falstaff, who more than once contemptuously refers to Shallow as 'the old pike'.

The division between outlying household offices, the concerns of the home farm and the business of the chase is something of an artificial one. The poultry yard, the dovecote, the fish-ponds and the dairy were often under the immediate care of the master and mistress of the house, both in a small household, where it was a necessary duty, and in a grand house, where it was an agreeable rural diversion. Occasionally, like the legendary Empress of Blandings, larger animals crossed the boundary that divided farm livestock from domestic pets. Faustina Gwynne, a remarkable cow, is commemorated with a gravestone at Rousham House in Oxfordshire; the Countess of Mount Edgcumbe erected an obelisk to her pet pig Cupid.

THE POULTRY YARD

Keeping poultry is thought by some to have been one of the many useful habits imported from the East by returning crusaders, but they may simply have brought back fresh breeds to add to native stocks. For many years, fowls scratched around in barnyards and gardens, haphazard layers and comparatively unmolested, although, as we can learn from the fairy tale 'Hansel and Gretel', fatting coops were accepted medieval practice. Gervase Markham gave detailed and reliable instructions on the management of the poultry house in his *Perfect Husbandry* (1615):

Your henne house would be large and spacious with some what a high roofe and walls strong and windowes upon the same rising; round about the inside of the walls upon the ground would be built large pens of 3 ft high for Geese, Ducks and Fowle to sit in.

Near to the eavings ... would be pearches ... on which should sit your cocks, Hennes, Capon and Turkies, each on severall pearches as they are disposed ... Let there be pins stucken into the walls so that your Poultry may clombe to their Pearches with ease, let the flore be ... of earth smooth and easie, let the small foule have a hole at one end of the house to come in and out at when they please ... this house would be placed near some Kitchen Brewhouse or else some Kilne where it may have some ayre of the fire and be perfumed with smoke which to pullen is delightful.

You shall gather up your eggs once a day and leave in the nest but the nest egge and no more, and that would ever be in the afternoone when you have seen every Henne come from the nest severally. Some Hennes will by the cackling tell you when they have layd, but some will lay mute, therefore you must let your owne eye be your instruction.

In the eighteenth century, agricultural theorists set their minds to a more scientific approach to poultry-keeping and began a search for better layers and plumper table birds. John Martin Robinson (*Georgian Model Farms*) feels that it was symptomatic of the seriousness with which farm buildings were treated in the late eighteenth century that even 'the august architect of the Bank of England did not consider the design of nesting boxes beneath his attention'. The meticulous attention to detail of Sir John Soane's designs for the poultry yard at Wimpole reveals that both the physical and the aesthetic well-being of its occupants was taken into consideration. His drawings offer a symmetrical classical composition of timber boxes with arched openings and neatly sketched nests. At Culzean Castle in Ayrshire, Robert Lugar designed a combined pheasantry, poultry house and dovecote for the 12th Earl of Cassilis in 1820. Another ornamental poultry yard was described in detail and sketched by John Loudon. Set against a sheltering wall, the two brick-built poultry houses provided accommodation and fatting coops for hens, ducks, geese and turkeys. Their upper storeys were green-painted lattice, which could be left open in summer and closed with shutters in winter.

Few eighteenth-century poultry yards survive today, although 'pop-holes' beside the one-time dairy cottage (now the ticket office) of Shugborough Park Farm betray its original use as a poultry house. However, the architect's drawings for what is now the laundry yard at The Argory show that this was originally a classically designed poultry yard in the best eighteenth-century tradition. What is now the washroom was originally the henwife's room, complete with copper for boiling up potato mash for the fowls. The northern building was divided into two spaces, one of which was the laying room. The small recesses for nests can still be seen. The centre of the yard had a pond in it, and the bowed wall to its east housed a pumping arm. As recommended by Markham, the yard is close to the former brewhouse.

The self-consciousness with which nineteenth-century writers apostrophized the poultry house, like the dairy, as a pleasant and improving place for ladies to pass the time has a hint of nostalgia about it which reflects, like Loudon's advice that a gentleman should dabble a little in farming, the fact that such things were no longer taken for granted. On his travels through England in the 1830s, Prince Pückler-Muskau experienced 'a pastoral sensibility' watching Fanny, the daughter of his host at Kinmel, feed the poultry with 'dainties in her apron'. The popular early-nineteenth-century novelist Mrs Bremer used this attractive rural image to telling effect in her domestic saga, *Strife and Peace* (1847):

Susanna approached the spring; and in her train came 'cock and hen, and chicken small'. Before her came waddling a troop of geese, gabbling noisily, and all white but one – a grey one. The grey goose walked with a timid, hesitating air, a little behind the others, compelled to retain this position by a tyrant in the white flock, who drove him back with outstretched neck and loud cry whenever he attempted to approach the rest. None of the other geese concerned themselves about their ill-used companion, but Susanna took it under her especial protection, and did all in her power to console it for the injustice of its kind. After the geese came the demure but clumsy ducks; the petulant turkey cock, with his awkward dames, one white, one black; and last, the turbulent race of chickens, with their stately pugnacious cocks. The prettiest of all the party were a flock of pigeons, who timidly, but confidently at the same time, now alighted on Susanna's shoulder and outstretched hand, and now rose in the air and flew in shining circles round her head; and then dropping to the earth, tripped on their little fringed feet, to drink at the spring; while the geese, with loud noise, plunged splashing into the river, and threw the water over the grass in a pearly shower.

What is interesting in this episode is the awareness of the individual character of the poultry. Considerable connoisseurship used to be exercised over the selection of the correct laying hen or table fowl for a particular size of house or region of the country. Such manuals as John Lawrence's *A Practical Treatise on ... Domestic Poultry* (1816) gave advice on the relative advantages of the many different available breeds. Anconas, the housewife was told, were active in habit, giving better laying results when allowed complete liberty. On the other hand Andalusians, 'capital layers of large white eggs', and the beautiful gold-laced Wyandottes were happy enough to be penned up. Deep-breasted White Dorkings were not suited to city grime; the pugnacious Old English Game with their incomparably tasty flesh had to be cropped of comb and spurs for their own protection. Polands, imported from Holland, with shiny black plumage and white-tipped heads, were 'plump and deep' in the flesh, and nicknamed everlasting layers. Bantams were 'valued most for their grotesque figures and delicate flesh'. The Malaysian Chittagong was a spectacular addition to the flock: 'largest of fowls, striated yellow and dark brown, long-necked, serpent-headed, and high upon the leg'. So too was the wonderful Indian cock with its blood-red crest, breast mottled with red and green, and tail of twelve large flaming feathers, resembling those of a peacock.

Gold-laced Wyandottes, a breed recommended for poultry yards, as they lay well even when penned.

Besides chickens of all varieties, a poultry yard would be incomplete without some ducks ('stimulating and savoury') and geese ('a food highly stimulant, its fat subtle, penetrating and resolvent'). A pair of turkeys fattened up in the Norfolk style with curds, buckwheat and chopped onions made excellent Michaelmas eating. Peacocks, once a common dish for the table, were not highly esteemed by John Lawrence, who condemned their flesh as 'coarse and ill-coloured' and advised that they be kept more for show than for eating. The swan, once a traditional 'dish of embellishment' was similarly dismissed: 'Only the cygnet is reckoned edible, and that after a peculiar preparation.' Bustards, by contrast, the largest land birds in Europe, were highly esteemed eating. Once found in flocks upon the heaths of East Anglia and Dorset, they were hunted with greyhounds and could be reared domestically on the same food as turkeys.

Idyllic as the vision of such variously feathered Gardens of Eden may seem, their management had its less attractive aspects. In an early-nineteenth-century pamphlet, Thomas Young advised dousing a hen in water, thrusting a feather through her nostrils, giving her half a glass of gin and swinging her round until seeming dead, then confining her in a pot during a day or two, leaving only a small breathing hole – all this amounting to an infallible way of forcing her to sit! Besides the old tradition of force-feeding, still preserved by the French in order to make *foie gras,* birds for the table were kept in fatting coops and geese might be plucked up to five times a year for their much prized feathers. 'Though the plucking of geese appears to be a barbaric custom, yet experience has proved that these birds, when properly stripped of their feathers, thrive better, and are more healthy than if they were permitted to drop them by moulting,' wrote one expert, a shade defensively. 'Geese should be thirteen or fourteen weeks old before they are subject to this operation, or they are liable to perish in cold summers.' The best feathers were plucked from the living birds, or from dead ones while still warm. The fact that 'neither the feathers nor the down of geese that have been dead for some time are fit for use' explains the urgency in the old ballad, 'Go tell Aunt Rhody the old grey goose is dead.'

Nor were limited quarters, paved floors and boiled food particularly conducive to healthy fowls. Jane Loudon's *Lady's Country Companion* (1845) offered a more informal layout for a yard, which she suggested should be at least half an acre in size: 'Fowls are never well unless they have an abundance of exercise.' At one end were the hen-houses, at the other a pond for the aquatic fowl. There was a tree for roosting in the centre, as both peafowl and guinea-fowl preferred roosting in the open air, and the whole was protected by a strong fence. Half the surface was of gravel and half of grass. The lively atmosphere of an informal poultry yard of this sort can be seen today at Saltram House, where the visitor enters via stables, flanked by a well-stocked duck pond, with nesting-houses arranged around its edge. At Wimpole, the home farm now has a large poultry-yard, run on modern free-range principles, with spacious pens for different sorts of poultry. Ardress and Tatton Park are also well-stocked with interesting breeds.

DOVECOTES

The keeping of pigeons in specially constructed houses has ancient origins, dating back perhaps four thousand years. The birds were valued for their flesh and their eggs, important winter variations on the monotonous diet of salted meat and fish that was necessary before improved winter fodder made it possible to stagger the slaughtering of cattle, sheep and pigs. The dung from dovecotes was a highly rated fertilizer; it was also used in the tanning industry to soften leather and in the manufacture of gunpowder. Pigeon down and feathers were used to fill pillows and beds, said to guarantee a ripe old age to the sleeper. For no very obvious reason, pigeons were prescribed by Pliny and later learned doctors as efficacious against dysentery (take an infusion of the dried and powdered stomach), bloodshot eyes (apply fresh pigeon blood) and the melancholy sadness (apply half a freshly killed pigeon to the head and the soles of the feet).

The Roman *columbarium* was succeeded by the medieval dovecote or culverhouse. In the Middle Ages, the building of a dovecote was a feudal privilege allowed only to the lord of the manor, and much complained of by the tenants, whose crops were regularly ravaged by 'these rapacious and insatiate vermin'. Four hundred birds was about average for a full-scale dovecote, but buildings housing up to 6,000 birds existed. Pigeon-keeping became less privileged and more general as time went on, but the equation of benefit to loss was often disputed. One of the demands of the 1539 Pilgrimage of Grace was that 'no man under the degree of knight or squire keep a dovehouse except it hath been an ancient custom'. By the late seventeenth century Britain had an estimated 26,000 dovecotes large and small, 'more than in any other kingdom in the world'. It was calculated that the grain eaten or destroyed by their 250,000 occupants could have provided bread for 100,000 people. Once winter feeds for cattle were developed by such eighteenth-century agricultural improvers as Turnip Townsend, large-scale pigeon-keeping declined.

The National Trust owns over twenty well-preserved dovecotes, several of them still tenanted. The buildings themselves offer a miniature reference chart of regional architecture and building materials: ranging from the dome of thin stone slabs squatting plumply in the grounds of Cotehele and the soaring half-timbered splendour of Hawford in Worcestershire to the tall stone turret of Springhill, the monumental landmark at Downhill and the dark-red brick octagon of Erddig. They sometimes stood alone, so that they would be easily distinguishable to the returning flocks, but were generally close enough to the house to deter intruders. 'Pigeons do well near dwellings, stables, bakehouse, brewhouses or such offices; or their proper place is the poultry court,' wrote Bonington Moubray in 1816. At Wichenford, in Worcestershire, it seems likely that the poultry yard was built around the dovecote, with the duck pond conveniently adjacent. At Calke and at Belton the dovecote forms the second storey of the stable, and the romantically battlemented nineteenth-century domestic improvements at Chirk Castle, on the Welsh borders, include a needle-slim dove tower near the stables. Snowshill, that 'old, very old' manor-house in Gloucestershire, has a late medieval dovecote built into the thickness of a wall, with niches for 380 birds – it still houses white doves.

'Pigeons are exceedingly fond of water,' noted Moubray, 'and, having a prescience of rain, will wait its coming until late in the evening, upon the house-top, spreading their wings to receive the refreshing shower.' A reliable supply of water was essential, and for this reason the cote was often built beside the fish-pond (as at Cotehele) or the duck pond. Besides assisting in the autumnal moult, baths helped to keep the birds free of vermin.

Dovecotes often have a fortress-like air, for good reason. The crowded sleepy birds were easy game for marauders – rats, mice and other vermin, stray cats and human prowlers. The earliest known designs are circular – some of these may just possibly be Roman in origin, although they are more likely survivals of or replacements for Norman buildings. A lantern or cupola at the peak of the roof of the building allowed birds to come and go; it was often equipped with landing ledges

Dovecotes had to repel such predators as rats, cats and hawks, and often had a fortress-like air. This sixteenth-century dovecote – built over the stables at Willington, in Bedfordshire – could house some 1,500 birds.

and sheltered perches so that the birds could take a view before they actually took flight. An internal trap could be wound up underneath the lantern to close the dovecote completely. Sometimes a series of external openings were arranged high up, with landing ledges underneath them, generally on the south side of the building. These could be closed with internal shutters. Dormer windows, also on the south side, were another variation. Again, they made it simple to close up the dovecote completely when cooping up new residents or culling an over-large flock.

Sixteenth- and seventeenth-century dovecotes were generally square or rectangular in design, with four-, or even six-gabled roofs. Many timber-framed black and white ('magpie') dovecotes of this period survive in Hereford and Worcestershire, notably those at Wichenford and Hawford Grange. The dovecote built in 1530 by Cardinal Wolsey's master of horse at Newton-le-Willows, in Nottinghamshire, was suitably gross in capacity: it could house nearly 3,000 birds in its 1,300 double nests. It has an unusual crow-stepped 'lectern' roof, of a design more common in Scotland and parts of France than in England. Another innovation of this period was the protruding stone string course round the outside of the building to prevent vermin from climbing up to the entrances.

In the eighteenth century, when the custom of breeding pigeons for table was in decline, dovecotes developed a distinctly ornamental aspect. Octagonal brickwork was much favoured, so too were classical details – dentil courses under the eaves, diaper-patterned brickwork and recessed panelling. The roof of the octagonal brick dovecote at Erddig is particularly attractive, with its four small dormer windows and decoratively arched cupola topped with a pigeon-shaped weathervane. Sometimes dovecotes were built on two, or even three storeys, the floors below being used for poultry, or even, as at Downhill, in County Londonderry, as an icehouse.

The dovecote at Felbrigg was probably built in around 1750, judging from the 'therm' windows (imitating those found in the baths of classical Rome) and the prominent cupola on its hipped roof. Inside it has niches for 2,000 stock doves. Left derelict after the First World War, it was restored by Robert Wyndham Ketton-Cremer in 1937 and is now well stocked with birds.

Standing inside an occupied dovecote is an extraordinary experience. As your eyes get used to the dimly lit interior, you see row upon row of nesting boxes, with glimpses of the birds inside and a marvellously soft noise made up of rustling feathers, gentle cooing and the occasional shrill squawks of the nestlings. Even an empty dovecote has a remarkable atmosphere. The nesting boxes could be arranged in a variety of fashions. They might be formed by the brickwork, a sheltered L-shaped niche hidden in the depth of the wall 'so that your bird sits dark and private'. Alternatively, wooden timbers with arched or circular entrances could be arranged. Landing ledges were essential. At Kinwarton, Warwickshire, they are formed by setting flat stones under the niches; at Wichenford wooden ledges run along under the nesting boxes. It was important not to start the ranges of nesting boxes too low, as predatory rats and other vermin were always eager to invade. At Hawford only the upper storey of the building was used as a dovecote; its capacious boxes, a little draughty perhaps, are formed from thin strips of wood. Cats were another answer to such a risk, but they could prove a mixed blessing. A cat of 'a known good breed' which had been brought up to be familiar with the birds could protect them, but an unreliable cat could depopulate the dovecote it was intended to protect.

To reach the nests, and to assist in cleaning, circular and octagonal dovecotes were provided with a potence (French for gallows), a central pole, fastened top and bottom on pivots, with two or three braced horizontal beams projecting from it. The outer edges supported ladders, which could be swung right round to give access to the whole of the inner wall of the dovecote. The potence at Dunster in Somerset is said to be over four hundred years old, and still moves smoothly at the push of a finger. There are also functioning potences at Erddig and Kinwarton. Square and rectangular dovecotes had an internal scaffolding of beams with ladders to give access to internal walkways.

During the initial period of stocking a new dovecote, the birds were often confined for a time, to give them a chance to mate and settle down, but once they had settled in, the birds' inborn homing instinct brought them reliably back to roost. Pigeons mate for life – the legendary faithfulness of the dove is well grounded in fact – and the hens produce two chicks at least eight times annually for about seven years. Moubray advises the provision of two nesting boxes for each pair of birds. Hens tended to give over a young brood to the cock while sitting on the next batch of eggs, and without two nests the eggs and the young risked being trampled on and destroyed.

The nestlings, known as 'squabs' or 'squeakers', were rated the best eating, and were culled from the nests before their pin feathers had developed and their flesh became toughened by flying. Adult birds were also culled to remove unproductive stock. In medieval times, they were used as quarry for falconry and more recently, until the advent of 'clay pigeons', large numbers were taken in nets to be set free as targets for shooting matches.

FISH-PONDS

Fish-ponds were another means of coping with a shortage of fresh meat, as well as providing a healthy substitute for it. Before the Reformation, all good Christians abstained from meat every Friday, as well as on other fast days and during the forty days of Lent. Dame Julians Barnes wrote one of the first treatises on angling (included in the *Boke of St Albans,* 1496), and medieval 'ordinances' of cookery are full of recipes for fish dishes, soups, stocks and preserves. In 1594 Queen Elizabeth passed laws to enforce observation of 'fish days' on Fridays and Saturdays, not from any religious motive but in order to ensure plenty of seadogs, fishermen being 'the chiefest nurse for mariners of this land'.

According to Thomas Tusser, part of the business of September husbandry was 'Thy ponds renew, put eeles in stew/To leeve till Lent, and then be spent.' 'Stews' were small tanks or ponds close to the house, often made into ornamental features of the kitchen garden and the flower garden. In them, fish could be kept and fattened up for the table. This was also a good way of separating predatory fish from the rest. Gervase Markham illustrated and described a fairly substantial set of such ponds in his *Cheap and Good Husbandry* (1614).

First drain your ground and bring all the water to one head or main reservoir. From this you form your canal to supply the pond. The sides of the canal are to be formed with piles, 6 feet long and 6 inches square, of oak, ash, or elm, to be driven in in rows and the earth well rammed behind them. You then form the sides of your pond with sloping banks covered with large sods of plot grass laid close and pinned down with small stakes. On one side you are to stake down bavens or faggots of brushwood for the fish to spawn in, and some sods piled up for the comfort of eels, and if you stick sharp sticks slantwise by every side of the pond that will keep thieves from robbing them.

His plan shows several different compartments, and the walks between the canals and ponds were to be planted with willows and fruit trees.

Very large establishments would have chains of small lakes in which fish were bred, as well as stews close by the house into which they were transferred to be fattened up and cleansed of their notoriously muddy flavour. In monasteries like Fountains, the fish-ponds were enormous, and were managed as carefully as are modern fish farms today. At Baddesley Clinton, Wednesdays and Saturdays, as well as Fridays, were kept as 'fish days' in the fifteenth century, hence the extensive chain of ponds linked by sluices that can still be seen there. They were originally dug in 1444, and it is clear from the names listed that teams of Welshmen did the navvying. Mention of stocking the pools is made in the bailiff's accounts for 1456–7. Most of the fish was brought from Eastcote and Berkwell, only a few miles away, but a barrel of roach, from 'Mill of Alstone', had to travel thirty miles. Two ten-gallon barrels with lids for transporting live fish cost 3s 6d.

A similar chain of medieval fish-ponds exists at Canons Ashby, although their straight edges were later blurred to make them look like lakes. Two large rectangular brick pools for the domestication of carp were built at Charlecote Park by Captain Thomas Lucy in the late 1670s, but these seemed to have been filled in, or else incorporated in the lake added to the landscape by George Lucy in the 1760s. Stew ponds close to a house supplied the household's immediate needs: in her Memorandum Book, Mrs Hayes, the housekeeper, recorded 'fish taken out of the Great Bason in the Court for the master's dinner'. At Felbrigg, William Windham I stocked the stew ponds to the south of the house with quantities of carp and tench; these ponds too were later enlarged into an ornamental lake in the 1750s. Wallington has a chain of fish-ponds in its woods, with sluices between them all, and an interesting 'siding' along which water could be diverted in winter to a shallow basin from which ice could conveniently be gathered for the nearby icehouse.

The Fish Pool Valley at Croft Castle in Herefordshire was landscaped in the eighteenth century. It is planted with a mixture of evergreen and deciduous trees, where extraordinary variety of texture, colour and outline is reflected in the series of pools that drop down towards the house. It embodies to perfection the theories of that great pundit of landscape gardening, Richard Payne Knight, who was a first cousin of Elizabeth Johnes of Croft. As Diana Uhlman has pointed out, these lines from his poem *The Landscape* (1794) could be a direct description of the little gorge with its tumbled foliage and shifting shadows.

> To show the clear reflection of the day
> And dart through hanging trees the refluent ray,
> And semi-lights and semi-shadows join
> And quivering play in harmony divine . . .

But the valley was still designed to be useful. Sluice gates between the lakes allowed for management of the various basins, which were kept well stocked with fish of all sorts.

Fish-ponds on this scale were often five or six acres in size, usually built in a natural hollow, and preferably fed from a river. Jane Loudon suggested that an island, and ornamental waterfowl, would add interest, as would a little decorative planting around the banks. Shoals near the side were desirable for the fish to sun themselves on, and lay their spawn. By varying the bottom, different varieties of fish could be encouraged to breed. Trout preferred gravel, carp and tench liked loam or clay, with plenty of waterweed, and eels throve in mud. Care had to be taken not to mix rapacious fish with gentler species. Carp and tench lived together in peace, but perch were so ravenous that they even ate their own spawn. Trout were not to be trusted in ponds, and the pike, 'the freshwater shark', was the most dangerous of all.

Such a pond needed to be drained every three or four years, in order to clear away excessive mud, reeds and weed, and to take out the smaller fish to stock other ponds. To make this easier, it was a good idea to divide the pond in two with an embankment, which was kept about two feet under water when the pond was full, and to have sluice gates in each half. By this means, half the pond could be cleared at a time, while the other half was used to store fish. Smaller ponds needed to be cleared out more frequently.

According to Merle's *Domestic Dictionary*, carp were the best fish for breeding, as they spawned several times in a year. Carp basins had to be supplied with a constantly running stream of water, with an outlet to carry off the excess, and 'artificial rocks with cavities for the fish to repose in' should be 'rather numerous'. Shelter of this sort stopped the fish from becoming 'shy or wild', which they tended to do if the water in the basin was transparent. Fish looked after in this way would often become so tame that they would come and feed out of the hand. Carp, tench and other fish in ponds were fed with boiled corn, or with fresh malt grains, preferably unbrewed.

The range of fish that was kept in the ponds and stews is evident from a glance at early recipe books. Cooks coped with roach, tench, bream, dace, perch, pike and of course trout. It was customary to flavour the fish with the plants that grew in the pools or streams in which they lived – watercress for perch, thyme for moorland trout or grayling. The books also make clear some of the drawbacks of pond fish. 'To remove the muddy flavour', a piece of bread was to be placed in 'the vacuum left after removing the stomach' and thrown away when the fish was cooked (quoted in Girouard's *The Country House Companion*). Carp, which Richard Bradley dismissed as 'an indifferent dish, being a fish full of crossbones' were sometimes kept alive out of the water, wrapped in wet moss and hung up in a net in a cool place. Suspended in limbo, the fish was fed bread and milk to improve the flavour of its flesh before it descended to the hell of a long copper fish-kettle.

At Charlecote, an eel trap can still be seen in the meadow to the south-east of the house. Eels slithered through the bars of the grating into a well of water, the level of which could be lowered by a sluice until it was lower than the grating. Then the eels could be netted and hoisted out. They were kept alive in the clear water of a fish tank for at least ten days before they were judged edible.

Ponds the size of lakes offered sport as well as sustenance. Just as the dairy and the poultry yard were a source of interest and pleasure to the master and mistress of the house, so were the fishing arrangements, and until the nineteenth century at least, angling was an acceptable sport for ladies as well as gentlemen. Richard Carew, poet of the pond, planned a small banqueting house, complete with kitchen to prepare 'fishing feasts', at Antony House in Cornwall in 1610, and celebrated his finny friends in verse:

> My fishful pond is my delight.
> There sucking mullet, swallowing bass,
> Side-walking crab, wry-mouthed fluke,
> And slip-fist eel, as evenings pass,
> For safe bait at due place do look,
> Bold to approach, quick to espy,
> Greedy to catch, ready to fly.

No doubt the catch from many pleasant fishing expeditions was cooked up in the little kitchen in the basement of the marvellous Mount Stewart banqueting house, the 'Tower of the Winds' which stands high on the hill overlooking Strangford Lough in County Down. 'Banqueting', incidentally, was originally more of a picnic than a specially grand occasion. On the lake at Kedleston Hall, in Derbyshire, there is a fishing room built to the design of Robert Adam in 1770–2. It lacks a kitchen, although it has a plunge bath in the basement and a pair of boat-houses flanking it from which enterprising guests could row out to fish. Roundels of putti mounted on sea monsters were carved by the stonemason George Moneypenny, and inside there are painted still lifes of fish, seascapes and anglers on the walls. A central arched Venetian window enabled ladies to cast their lines into the water while remaining protected from the weather – the sun was rightly regarded as dangerous to the complexion.

*Ladies tossed their lines from the windows of the elegant fishing pavilion on the
lakeside at Kedleston, Derbyshire. Designed by Robert Adam in the 1760s, it has
a plunge bath in the basement and boat-house at each side.*

In 1843 Jane Loudon wrote approvingly of 'very elegant dinners at a house in one
of the midland counties, where the table was supplied almost exclusively with home
produce. We had not, perhaps, a dish of seafood; but what we had was much better
than half-stale fish, procured from London at great expense, or from a neighbouring
town when it had been, perhaps, ten days out of the water; instead of this, we had
a dish of the finest carp or tench I ever met with, or probably a jack, or eels, each
taken from the stew ponds immediately before dinner, and thus eaten in the highest
perfection.' But as techniques of commercial refrigerated transport improved, delicately flavoured ocean fish and shellfish could be delivered by fishmongers even to
inland estates, and the old fish-ponds were filled in, or turned into ornamental pools
for goldfish and lilies.

Fishing was taken seriously on the great lakes constructed by Sir William Armstrong at Cragside, and in the challenging salmon rivers near by. In the north of

England and Scotland, so much salmon was caught that at the height of the fishing season it became a tedious diet, fitter for the servants' hall than the dining table.

Today, food production has become a specialized industry rather than part of ordinary domestic life. The dovecotes, dairies, breweries and poultry yards which furnished food for country kitchens have disappeared. Their products can be acquired in a half-hour visit to a supermarket. Self-sufficiency survives only in a few aggressively independent Celtic redoubts – and between the covers of books by such enthusiasts as John Seymour. The sales of such books in ratio to the numbers of practitioners suggests that the enduring attraction of the idea may be greatest when enjoyed vicariously from an armchair just after a trip to Sainsbury's.

CHAPTER FIVE

THE DAIRY

> From the show-dairy, with its painted glass windows,
> marble fountains and china bowls, to that of the common
> farmhouse, with its red brick floor, deal shelves, and
> brown milk pans, the dairy is always an object of interest,
> and is associated with every idea of real comfort, as well
> as of imaginary enjoyment, attendant upon a country life.
> But, it *must* be kept in proper order.

> Anne Cobbett, *The English Housekeeper*, 1842

Before the days of factory production of milk, dairy work was an essential element in domestic life. Cattle, once hunted only for their meat and hides, were first domesticated by the Celtic tribes of north and eastern Britain. The Celts also established the making of butter and simple cheeses developed from curdled milk. By Anglo-Saxon times, most cottagers had a milch cow if they could afford one. The self-sufficient medieval household ran a substantial dairy, usually attached to the home farm. Smaller establishments would use the back kitchen for dairy work, setting aside a corner of a larder for separating cream from milk, hanging up simple cream or cottage cheeses in muslin to drain, and storing home-churned butter. A cow might be rented from a local farmer, and returned to him when 'dry', and a goat kept to supplement lean periods.

Until the eighteenth century, dairy work was a seasonal business, as most cattle were slaughtered in the autumn for want of winter fodder. As Tusser put it:

> From April beginning, till Andrew [30 November] be past
> So long with good huswife her dairy doth last.

Although there were no machines to help the dairymaid, it was pleasant enough work according to Anne Cobbett – 'not attended with the disagreeables and vexations which so frequently occur in the occupation of a cookmaid'. First the cows had to be milked (an early painting of Uppark shows a dairymaid at work in the field to the left of the house). Then the pails of milk were taken into the dairy to be separated. The 1710 Dyrham Park inventory shows that the dairy was very simply furnished:

71

In ye Dairy:

a Table
a Butter Churn and Staff
1 wooden bowl for Butter
1 Skimming Dish
1 Streigner
a Cheese Vate
1 Butter Print
1 Milk Pail
5 Milk Pans

All dairy processes required extremely careful management. Fine judgement was needed to ascertain when the milk was right for skimming, how to stop cream becoming 'sleepy' and the exact stage of ripeness in the curd to ensure good sweet cheese. Attention to hygiene was vital. 'First thing, and the most important of all in a Dairy, is Cleanliness,' wrote Thomas Hale in his 1765 *Compleat Body of Husbandry*. 'Not only the vessels and utensils but the very Floor, Walls and Ceiling, everything that is in it and everything that is about it, must thus be managed with the utmost nicety of Cleanness or there will be continual Damage and Loss.' Wooden utensils and earthenware pans were the most reliable; most metals affected the milk adversely. No soap was ever used, but every inch of the pans, scoops and strainers was scoured with salt and very hot water, and then thoroughly rinsed.

A multitude of disasters could befall the delicate processes involved in separating cream, churning butter and making cheeses, and an enormous number of saws and sayings survive to bear witness to the erratic folk wisdom that aided and abetted the dairymaid in her task. Cream that curdled and butter that wouldn't set might well be Satan's work – it was well known that witches had special powers over milk and its by-products. Fairy tales often revolve around such incidents, and the records of witch trials frequently tell of spells cast over dairies and the 'overlooking' of cows. It was therefore a sensible precaution to use a charm as an antidote. A silver sixpence thrown in the churn offered further protection, so too did three white hairs from a black cat's tail. Holed stones and rowan twigs could be fixed over the door of the dairy, and evil-destroying herbs such as clover, dill, betony, St John's wort or vervain might be spread about the benches and the floor.

In the eighteenth century, the increasing enclosure of common land and the growth of towns and cities meant that more and more small households gave up their cows and used a local dairyman. At first he led the cow to each house, and milked her on the spot to prove that the milk was quite fresh and that there had been no adulteration with water; later horse-drawn carts filled with churns toured the neighbourhoods.

But the great houses still prided themselves on their own dairy products. Milk was sent over from the home farm, or provision was made in the stable blocks for a group of stalls for the two or three milch cows which supplied the household. Indeed, dabbling in dairying became a more and more fashionable hobby for the ladies of the house, thanks in part to the intensified prestige of domesticity under the influence of Queen Mary II's Dutch husband, William III. Mary herself had her own model dairy at Hampton Court, and over a hundred years later Jane Austen refers in her letters to a visit to 'a dairy in the Dutch style'.

Another influence on genteel dairying was the apotheosis of the 'natural life' by such prescient Friends of the Earth as the French philosopher Jean-Jacques Rousseau and the ill-fated Marie-Antoinette, who had a delightful little dairy at Le Petit Trianon. There was also a growing medical understanding both of the virtues of milk products and of the dangers of their contamination. It was this understanding of the need for hygiene as much as poetic overtones of milky innocence that led to increased interest in the idea of the mistress overseeing the dairy in person.

The architectural result was 'that pleasant plaything, a Fancy Dairy', picturesquely situated the length of a lady's afternoon stroll from the house, with a practical dairy scullery next door, in which the highly skilled dairymaid went about her business. This social division of function was made the more possible by the fact that a cool, decoratively tiled room with its stained-glass windows was ideal for the simple and physically effortless tasks of separating the milk and setting cream and junkets, and a fully equipped scullery with pumped or piped water, sinks and a cooking range was required to make butter, clotted cream and cheese. 'The dairy is one of the principal decorations of an English park, and stands by itself quite away from the cowhouse,' Prince Pückler-Muskau explained in a letter to his wife in 1832. 'It is generally an elegant pavilion, adorned with fountains, marble walls, and rare and beautiful porcelain; and its vessels large and small filled with the most exquisite milk and its products in all their varieties.'

Just how romantic the dairy could be was made apparent when Sir Harry Featherstonhaugh of Uppark ensured a lifetime's bit of butter on the baronet's slice of bread by marrying his pretty young dairymaid. Sir Harry was something of a reprobate as a young man – abandoning among other doting women Emma Hart, later to become Lady Hamilton and entrance Lord Nelson himself. But he had not married by the age of seventy, in 1824, and he returned to Uppark still restless for company and diversion.

Strolling along the grass terrace which flanked the house and led to the picturesque little dairy, he heard the sound of a girl singing. On his return to the house he apparently asked the housekeeper who it was. 'Not the dairymaid, Sir Harry, she be too old,' replied the housekeeper. It was one of her helpers, a sweet-tempered girl appositely named Mary Ann Bullock. When the dairymaid retired, Mary Ann took over the dairy and Sir Harry's visits to the veranda outside grew more frequent. One day, he presented himself at the door of the dairy, and asked her to marry him. Mary Ann was said to be speechless; in the words of a later dairymaid repeating the tale, 'taken aback like'. 'Don't answer me now,' Sir Harry is reputed to have continued, 'but if you will have me, cut a slice out of the leg of mutton that is coming up for my dinner today.' When the mutton arrived, the slice was cut. Contemporary stories dwell long and lovingly on the rage of the cook.

Mary Ann, just twenty-one, was sent to Paris to be educated, where she learnt to read and write a very good hand, and in September 1825 was married to Sir Harry, exactly fifty years her senior. The footmen tittered, society scoffed. 'I've made a fool of myself,' Sir Harry muttered to his gamekeeper shortly after his marriage, but he lived happily enough with his industrious young wife to the ripe old age of ninety-two. There were no children. Mary Ann of the placid face and neatly coiffed hair lived on in possession of Uppark until 1875; then her sister Frances, also adopted by Sir Harry, took over for another twenty years. It was largely due to the conservatism of this pair of Cinderellas that Uppark stayed so remarkably unchanged during the Victorian era.

The Uppark dairy with its adjoining dairy scullery survives, and is one of the best examples of a decorative dairy in the possession of the Trust. Originally built around

The dairy proper was a cool, peaceful room, often decoratively tiled, where the cream settled in flat pans. At Lanhydrock, Cornwall, the late-nineteenth-century dairy had water channelled along its shelves.

1785, it was redesigned by Humphry Repton between 1810 and 1812. It backs on to, and has direct access to, the home farm. In the tiled room facing the garden, the gentry could supervise the preparation of milk, cheese and butter, sample junkets and flummeries, and generally feel themselves to be in touch with nature in the best Romantic manner. Unusually, it faces south, but a gently domed portico shelters it from the heat of the sun, besides providing a pleasant place to sit and look at the Downs. Stained-glass windows filter the light; there are black and white marble slabs on the floor, and white Wedgwood tiles, edged with a motif of twining ivy, line the walls. Marble-trimmed slate shelves provide cool surfaces for the flat pans in which the milk was left to separate.

The real business of the dairy took place in the next-door scullery. With its pump, fireplace, and vat designed for cheese-making, this is strictly functional and has no window to the south. In it, more cream-setting pans and crocks can be seen and some interesting nineteenth-century dairy machinery. A sloping wooden gutter directed water straight from the pump into the copper for heating purposes – washing utensils, scalding cream or warming milk for cheese-making.

There is another exceptionally attractive dairy at Shugborough. This was originally not a dairy but a banqueting chamber. Designed in the 1760s by James 'Athenian' Stuart on the model of the Tower of the Winds (Horlogion of Androkinos Cyrrhestes) in Athens, it used to be surrounded by a lake, and approached by a bridge. The great flood of 1795 destroyed many of the ornamental buildings in the park and between 1800 and 1806 Viscount Anson, an improving landlord in the Coke of Holkham mould (married, indeed, to Coke's daughter Anne Margaret), transformed what had been an ornamental park into a model agricultural estate. A home farm replaced the old village that had existed close by the Tower of the Winds, and the tower itself was converted by Samuel Wyatt after the draining of the lake. Cows were led along a discreetly sunken track from the home farm, to be milked in open brick stalls in the semi-basement area around the base of the building. It was folk wisdom that the best cream of all was obtained from milk that travelled as little as possible from udder to setting dish.

The dairy itself is on two storeys. The lower is cold and crypt-like, lined with slate and with thick stone shelves and arched vaults. The upper, evidently intended for ladylike junketings with curds and whey, is elegantly tricked out with stained glass and a lining of brown-veined Derbyshire alabaster which the Shugborough accounts record as 'worked into mouldings, arches, bevils and flat slabs' by Richard Brown of Derby. There were once Wedgwood pots in the Egyptian style set in its alcoves, but these have now been removed to the house for safe keeping. On the top floor of the tower the splendid banqueting room remains, its long windows commanding a panorama of the whole estate.

By the nineteenth century more science and less guesswork began to be applied to the management of the dairy. At Berrington Hall in Herefordshire, the dairy arrangements are very much along the lines suggested by Kerr: 'a small apartment, not far from the Kitchen, similar generally to a larder, perfectly cool and well ventilated for summer, and supplied with glass inner windows for cold weather'. The Berrington dairy is an extraordinarily elegant little building, but it is quite evident that very little hard work could have taken place in it. It has recently been restored to show off the exquisite, delicately coloured tiles and beautifully inlaid marble floor. Rather small marble slabs are supported on slim white stands set into niches – in all likelihood there was originally also a circular marble table standing in the centre of the room. Behind the door at the back is the dairy scullery – not now, nor then, for visitors' eyes.

Kerr pointed out that the temperature in the dairy was critical – the ideal situation was to be sheltered from the cold by other buildings and shaded from the summer's heat by trees or a northern aspect. The roof ought to be thatched or otherwise insulated with felt or wood, and thick cavity walls were necessary. Wire window gauze was recommended by Mrs Beeton, so too were calico blinds that could be wetted in hot weather. Cloths soaked in a solution of chloride of lime were another way of ensuring a constantly cool, slightly damp atmosphere. It was important that in winter there was some provision for heating the dairy slightly – the ideal was to achieve a constant temperature of around 55–60°F.

The dairy floor was stone or tiled, sloping towards a drain at one end so that it could be thoroughly flushed out with water at the end of the day. Walls were best tiled or covered with impervious plaster for the same reason. One broad shelf, about two feet wide and made of slate, stone or even marble, usually ran all the way round the room to hold the milk dishes. A central table was a desirable alternative if there was space; it was more accessible and better ventilated. Sometimes the milk dishes were trays built into the shelf or table, and provided with a tap to draw off the milk from under the cream. They might have a hollow compartment around them, containing water to keep them cool, or a groove could be set into the shelf itself, with provision for water to run along it and so keep the shelf chilled.

In the adjoining dairy scullery, there would be a copper, a dresser and benches. Here the vessels were scalded and set to dry, butter was churned and cheese made – if it was made at all; Kerr evidently regarded domestic cheese-making as unusual in 1867. If there was no separate dairy scullery, the scalding of the pans was done in the kitchen scullery, and the butter was churned in the dairy itself. Ideally, the dairy scullery did not connect directly with the dairy, so that none of the heat and steam of the scullery upset the delicate setting processes.

This is well illustrated by the late Victorian domestic arrangements of Lanhydrock,

In the busy dairy scullery, butter was churned and worked, and (in the case of a Cornish house like Lanhydrock) cream brought to clotted perfection on a slow-burning range.

totally rebuilt in the 1880s. Its dairy and adjoining scullery are placed at the end of a short corridor of larders, reasonably close to the kitchen, and as far from the bakehouse as possible. The entrance to the dairy scullery is from the corridor rather than from the dairy itself. Twice a day a pony cart brought churns of milk from the home farm to be delivered to its exterior door. The churns were emptied into pans standing in cold water in the long slate troughs against the left-hand wall. Some whole milk was set aside for household use, and the remainder was used for the making of butter and clotted cream. A scalding range – a peculiarly West Country arrangement – on which to make clotted cream was built on the inner wall of the house and heated to the gentle temperature necessary by hot-water pipes brought direct from the boiler house in the cellar below.

To make Clotted Cream

Take the night's milk and put it into a broad earthenware pan and in the morning set over a slow fire, letting it stand there from morning till night, suffering it not to boil, only heat. Then take off the fire and set it in some place to cool all night and next morning dish off your cream and it will be very thick.

The Lanhydrock dairy is kept cool by an ingenious cooling apparatus. Water brought into the house from a spring in the hillside near by flows in a channel round a marble slab in the middle of the room and round slate slabs on its perimeter. The walls are tiled and the room faces north for coolness.

Butter-making was one of the most skilled of the dairymaid's arts. First of all the milk had to be separated from the cream. This was done by leaving the milk in wide pans for twenty-four hours, or longer in winter, and then skimming off the cream with a skimming dish. After being separated, the cream which was to be used for butter-making was left to ripen for two or three days. Then an agitator was plunged up and down in a tall wooden churn that tapered towards its top, and had a lip to hold the splasher top of the plunger. The process was not dissimilar to that of washing clothes with a dolly stick, and it is quite likely that early butter-making techniques inspired the first crude washing-machines (for these, see Chapter 12).

Once the butter had 'come', it was thoroughly washed. The last of the moisture was removed in a butter-worker, a large shallow wooden tray about three feet long, eighteen inches wide and three inches deep. There is one of these in the attractive farm dairy at Ardress House, County Armagh. Mounted on a four-legged wooden stand, the trough sloped gently towards one end, where there was a bung-hole. A fluted wooden roller was wound across the top of the tray, mashing salt into the butter if salted butter was required, and forcing any remaining liquid out. The butter was constantly dabbed with muslin cloths to take up the excess moisture. Finally, it was patted into shape with grooved wooden batlets about nine inches long known as 'Scotch hands' – the human hand was never supposed to touch the butter while it was being made – and then cut into portions and decorated with a butter stamp, usually hand-carved from wood with a design that identified its maker as surely as the seal on a signet ring.

The whole business of butter-making was to become far more rapid once the cream-separator was invented. One of these can be seen in the model dairy at Wimpole, where there is an excellent collection of nineteenth-century dairy machinery. It worked by centrifugal force, and the small household models could separate six gallons of milk in only thirty minutes. This meant that there was no danger of either the cream or the skimmed milk going sour, a common problem on a warmish day when milk had to be left for long periods.

The simple agitator in a churn was also improved upon. There is an interesting lever churn in the dairy at Ardress. Another variation was the rocker churn, which might well have been adapted from a baby's cradle in the first instance – it was simply a rectangular wooden box which could be rocked vigorously from side to side. One enterprising father set a saddle on top, put his small son to butter-making and sent an announcement of his patent to the *Journal of Domestic Appliances*. More usual, particularly in small households, was the box paddle churn, which had a handle to turn the four-armed dasher inside it. For larger dairies, an end-over-end barrel churn was simple to work and highly efficacious.

Cheese-making on a grand scale was the speciality of particular farms – different areas each using a slightly different technique to produce a type of cheese suited to their cattle, pastures and climate. Stilton cheese was characterized by its high cream content, Cheshire by its marigold flower colouring, Gloucester by the use of the newest milk, Cottenham by 'the fragrant nature of the herbage which the cows feed on in that part of the country'. But the making of several types of small cheeses was part of the dairymaid's repertoire. Cream cheese was made by wrapping thick cream up in a calico cloth and hanging it to drip. After twelve or twenty-four hours it was transferred to an earthenware bowl, stirred up and hung up again to drain for about four days, the cloths changed regularly and becoming progressively more open in weave. Then it was pressed into a tin mould lined with coarse huckaback cloth. The

After the butter had 'come', the watery residue was squeezed out in a butter-worker. Once dry, it was scooped out of the butter-worker and patted into shape with a pair of wooden batlets known as 'Scotch hands'.

popular, and much less rich, Gervais cheese was made from one part cream to two parts milk. Rennet was added, and the resultant curd removed into a scalded cloth after about seven hours. This was then hung and treated in much the same way as the cream cheese, except that a little salt was added.

Hard cheeses were also made when there was an excess of milk in the dairy. For these, rennet was essential. It was made from the inner part of a calf's stomach, cleaned, salted and hung up in paper bags to dry. It was soaked in water the night before use, and the resulting infusion poured into the milk to curdle it. If no rennet was available, various plants could be used, the best known of which were the flowers of the cheese rennet, or lady's bedstraw.

In the nineteenth century, the increase of the population and its concentration in towns led to commercial dairying on a factory scale, although milking cows were kept in London as late as the 1920s. The problem with urban cowhouses was that the animals tended to spend their days in overcrowded yards eating at best hay and such concentrated food as cottonseed or linseed cake, at worst dubious leftovers from local kitchens. The railways revolutionized the dairy trade, and after 1850 the bulk of the milk supply was carried to towns by train. Large dairy and cheese-making farms were established in most rural areas, and even in the country it began to be deemed more efficient to have milk sent up from a farm, or to allow the dairyman to call, than to keep cows for the house.

In our own century, the establishment of connections between tuberculosis and other diseases with contaminated milk has led to legislation which has made home dairy work an unofficial and slightly suspect luxury limited to farmers. The milkman with sterilized glass bottles on his electric cart is a poor substitute for the rosy-cheeked milkmaid swinging her pail as she walked through the buttercups. And even he, the last of that useful band of tradesmen that once delivered so conveniently, is threatened these days.

CHAPTER SIX

BREWHOUSE AND BAKEHOUSE

Brewing is an old craft. The ancient Egyptians had a hieroglyph for it, and to be a brewer under the Ptolemies was to be a man of high social status. The Romans arrived in Britain to find ale-making well established, but they despised it. 'Who made you and of what, by the true Bacchus, I know not,' quipped the Emperor Julian staring at a goblet of British ale. 'He smells of nectar, but you smell of goat.' They attempted, with only partial success, to establish vineyards to make their own wine.

Baking bread is as ancient a skill as brewing ale, and the two were traditionally linked. In small establishments, both processes were carried out in the scullery or back kitchen. In large houses, the purpose-built brewhouse and bakehouse often shared chimney-stacks, fuel stores and grain lofts. They might even be managed by the same person. Neither baking nor brewing was a continuous occupation, and there was some overlap in materials – both required malt and other grains and yeast. However, as a plaintive letter written in 1815 by Sir Henry Harpur of Calke revealed, there could be disadvantages in this. 'As to the Baker, I caution you against any consultation with him. He is the man who has spoiled all my beer for the last three years ... he is neither a good Baker nor a good Brewer ... and I certainly do not mean to continue him.'

THE BREWHOUSE

Many a homely and wholesome draught of liquor is brewed in a kettle over the fire, as well as with every convenience of copper, mash-tub, cooler, etc. Let not, therefore, the smallest family esteem it a concern too high for their attainment, or the highest too low for their attention.

Housekeeper's Receipt Book, 1817

In medieval times, alehouses were as often run by women as men. In this stained-glass window at fifteenth-century Oxburgh Hall, Norfolk, an alewife offers a glass of home-brew to the passing trade.

Medieval and Tudor manuals define brewing as woman's work, as it happened indoors, and public alehouses were as often run by 'ale-wives' as by 'men-maltsters'. Thomas Tusser offers advice on brewing techniques in his *Points of Huswiferie* rather than his *Five Hundred Points of Good Husbandrie*, and Gervase Markham declared that

This office or place of knowledge belongeth particularly to the Housewife; and though we have many excellent Men-maltsters, yet it is properly the work and care of the woman, for it is a house-work, and done altogether within doors, where generally lieth her charge; the man only ought to bring in and to provide the grain and excuse her from portage or too heavy burthens, but for the Art of making the Malt, and the several labours appertaining to the same, even from the Vat to the Kiln, it is only the work of the Housewife, and the Maid servants to her appertaining.

By the eighteenth century, however, the brewer in large country households, where the brewing took place in a special brewhouse, was often a man. Such a brewhouse, large or small, was an important domestic office from the days of the Saxons until the nineteenth century, and, in some cases, even later. In Oxford, Brasenose College owes its name to its site on an ancient brewhouse, and the tradition of brewing at The Queen's College stretched unbroken from its monastic origins until after the Second World War.

Ale, made from malt and barley, rather than beer with its life-enhancing kick of the hop, was the favourite tipple of medieval man. Hops became popular in England in the late fifteenth century, but not without protest – it was argued that they made it possible for brewers to weaken their brew, and that beer was less beneficial to health than ale. In 1542, Andrew Boorde wrote in his *Compendyous Regiment or Dyetary of Health* that beer was 'the natural drynke of a Dutcheman, and nowe of lete dayes it is much used in England to the detryment of many Englysshe people'.

As the inclusion of brewing in Boorde's compendium suggests, there were then sound scientific and sanitary reasons for drinking fermented liquors rather than plain water. Such diseases as cholera and typhoid were transmitted via tainted water supplies. The process of brewing – boiling to incorporate the aromatic principles of hops, and the addition of yeast to ferment the sugar into alcohol – produced a liquor that was not only sterile in itself but also resistant to infection.

A brewhouse was always a feature of a monastery or convent, and the beer produced there was supplied to passing pilgrims and travellers. Monastic hostels were the forerunners of the inns and hotels that became necessary as communications improved and more people sought accommodation on their travels. The small but marvellously complete brewery at Lacock Abbey, in Wiltshire, however, is not monastic. It was built by William Sharington, who bought the former nunnery from Henry VIII in 1539, and it is probably the earliest country-house brewery in existence.

The Lacock brewery is on the north side of a quadrangle of domestic buildings, next door to the bakehouse. Its furnace is fed from the old bakehouse itself, where there would have been wood and coal stores for both brewing furnace and bread ovens. It is possible, indeed, that the bakehouse was once the malthouse. The brewery itself has a high ceiling, to allow the clouds of steam from the boiling copper to be dispelled, and louvred windows to the north. There is a fine paved and cobbled floor, nicely arranged to fit around the brewing vessels. A short flight of steps gives access to the massive copper in which water was boiled up and then allowed to cool until one could see one's face through the steam on the surface of the liquid – a crude measure of the correct heat (around 150°F) in the days before thermometers.

The liquid was then run off into a large barrel known as a mash tun and malt (grist) was added and stirred in with a mash paddle. Mashing took several hours and converted the starch in the grain into sugar, producing a sweet extract called wort. This was drawn off from the barrel in buckets and replaced in the copper, where it was boiled up again with hops and sugar. 'Farnham hops are the cleanest and the best,' claimed Anne Cobbett, 'fresh, of a bright yellow, and highly scented.' The plug cock at the base of the copper was then opened so that the hopped wort (or spree) could run into the shallow rectangular cooling tray below. This was lined with lead and stood on spaced joists, in order to speed up the cooling process. When

A brick-cased copper in which beer has been brewed at Lacock Abbey, Wilts., since the sixteenth century. It is approached by a flight of stone steps. Notice the high ceiling, the lead-lined cooling tray and the ingeniously paved floor.

it was at blood heat (early brewers used the elbow test familiar to old-school nannies at bath-time) it was drained into a broad-based fermenting tun, made of oak staves bound together with iron rings. Here yeast, saved from an earlier brewing, or borrowed from a neighbouring brewery or from the bakehouse, was added.

As the yeast fed on the nutrients in the wort, the mixture fermented and in a few days became beer. Its strength depended on how long it was left in the tun. Finally the yeast was skimmed off the surface, and the beer was strained off into casks. Some was drunk immediately, some was left to mature in the cellars. Beer was made in varying strengths depending on how long it was left to mash. Specially strong brews were often made for important occasions, such as a coming of age or a wedding. At harvest time, Hillman (*Tusser Redivivus*, 1710) recommended the brewing of three sorts of beer:

The first wort or strongest, you may put by for your own use, the second is what is called best beer, whereof each man ought to have a pint in the morning before he goes to work, and as much at night as soon as he comes in. If they work anything extraordinary (as in Norfolk they often do, during the moonshine), their share must be more. Small beer they must also have plenty in the field.

The brewery at Charlecote is on a larger scale than at Lacock. There are two coppers, so that a more continuous chain of work could be carried out. Water was heated in the left-hand copper. It was then drained off into the underbuck to mash, from where the resultant wort could be pumped into the right-hand copper and boiled up with hops and sugar. There are also two coolers at different levels, to speed up the process of cooling. This was as nothing, however, to a plan in Loudon's *Encyclopaedia of Cottage ... and Villa Architecture* which shows a domestic brewery 'fitted up in Mr Vokin's Grecian Villa' with ten cooling trays spiralling around the room in a veritable cascade. At Charlecote, as at Lacock, access to the fires under the coppers was from a neighbouring room, which appears to have been the bakehouse originally, although it was used as a laundry after the kitchens were refitted with a bakehouse scullery in the nineteenth century.

Calke beer was reputed to have been good, although in 1815 Sir Henry Harpur expressed great dissatisfaction with both his brewer and his beer; 'you never see a drop sparkle in the glass and it tastes thick and sweet – what I like is a light fine ale; small beer should be brisk and tart'. The Calke brewhouse is built on a slope so that full barrels could be rolled down it. It still contains a considerable amount of its original equipment.

At Shugborough, as much as 600 gallons could be brewed at a time, and Pamela Sambrook has estimated from the 1819 accounts that the household then consumed about 24 gallons a day. Beer was used as part payment for the staff, including the maids – the head laundrymaid, for example, received half a gallon a day. Pamela has just restored the brewhouse to working order with the help of a retired Yorkshire brewer, and in the process has learnt the hard way about the vagaries of brewing. The first bottled Shugborough beer is now on sale: 'Some people said at the first tasting that it was horrible stuff – but I noticed that they kept on coming back for more!'

Important adjuncts to the brewery were the malt-house and the hop garden. Depending on the local economics and the availability of grain, the malting might be undertaken by a local miller, but large establishments did their own malting. At Cotehele, in Cornwall, early plans for the house show that the malt-house, now used as a film room, stood beside the one-time brewery. At Ingatestone Hall in Essex, detailed records of the brewery survive, and the inclusion of 'rowers ... in which to stir the barley' suggests that they had all the equipment necessary for malting.

Ingatestone Brewhouse c. 1550

Rowers 'in which to stir the barley'
Scavel (spade)
Jets (large ladles)

Sweet wort tun
Copper
Cooler
Chunk (into which the wort ran)
Yealding vat (in which the wort fermented)
Cowls (big water-carrying tubs)
Yeast tubs
Roundlets (yeast casks)
Leaden troughs
Steps (baskets or buckets)
Iron-hooped stuke (handle)
Pulley for loading casks

Malting was a winter task, explained William Harrison in his 1577 *Description of England*. Barley was steeped in water, then spread out to dry on a clean upper floor (the upper storey at Lacock could well have been used for this), and turned four or five times a day for at least twenty-one days until it germinated. It was then spread out on trays and baked in a kiln before being ground. 'The best malt is tried by the hardness and colour for if it look fresh with a yellow hue, and will write like a piece of chalk after you have bitten a kernel asunder – you may assure youself it is dried down.' The malt was coarsely ground and then taken to the brewery.

The quality of the water used to make ale and beer was also important. Soft water was preferred to hard, so standing water was best. Thames water was popular, perhaps for its flavour, and chalk streams were also good. 'Fenny' or 'moorish' water was the worst, and crystal-clean spring water nearly as bad. The strong spring that issues at the foot of the limestone hills around Bradley, in Devon, was highly esteemed; as well as being used in Bradley Manor's own brewhouse, it was piped to a brewery in the town.

Finally, there had to be a reliable source of yeast. This could be obtained from the bakehouse, or preserved from one brewing to the next. It was something of an art to keep yeast well. Some yeasts could be grown in tubs, provided they were kept warm and fed and given small regular doses of air. But most wine and some ale yeasts require continuous fresh oxygen, and this led to the custom of hanging out the besom of twigs which was used to stir the fermenting tun. The sticky yeasts on the twigs remained, well-aired and slightly damp, till they were next required for use. If a brew went flat, the brush could be used to beat it up again, thus refreshing and rewatering the brush itself (hence the maxim, 'good wine needs no bush'). For homely liquors such as mead and metheglin the brush was made of scented shrubs, bog myrtle, rosemary or sweet briar.

It was vital to keep all the equipment of the brewery as clean as possible. New casks had to be seasoned before they were used. One way to do this was to boil two pecks of bran or malt dust in a copper of water, pour it hot into the cask, stop it tight and let it stand for two days before washing it out well and drying the cask. Another method was to fumigate it with a burning canvas strip soaked in brimstone and coriander. All utensils had to be well scoured with brush and scalding water, but no soap was to be used. Anne Cobbett recommended 'a strong ley of wood ashes . . . if there be any apprehension of taint'.

In smaller establishments, brewing, like baking, might be done in the scullery. The laundry copper and the washtubs could do duty as brewing tun and underbucks, but scrupulous standards of cleanliness had to be observed if traces of soap lurking in the wooden tubs were not to spoil the beer. Mr Brassington of Haughton, the son of a Staffordshire farmer, recalls that his father 'brewed once a month, in the old furnace they did the washing in, the copper. It was a small furnace that was in, and he had a larger one put in that'd hold forty gallons. By the time it boiled away, it was down to thirty-six gallons. The barrel was thirty-six – that's how much he brewed at a time.'

Depending on the size of the household, making beer was a seasonal activity until the advent of artificial refrigeration. 'The best months for brewing are considered to be March and October,' advised Merle's *Domestic Dictionary* (1842), 'but good beer may be made in any of the cool months. In very hot weather it is almost impossible to make very strong beer, and in excessive cold the fermentation is languid.' As bottled beer was calculated to last six months or so quite comfortably, this seasonal pattern had a certain logic to it. In larger establishments, however, so much beer and ale was required to satisfy the household that brewing was more frequent, and at Shugborough it took place monthly.

The beer cellar was an important adjunct of the brewhouse. It was where all the business of breeching casks and bottling beer took place. At Erddig in 1833 the inventory records

Ale cellar no 1 and 2: 14 ale barrels, one puncheon [small cask], 7 ale barrels, seven barrels of ale, two barrels of beer and stilledges [stands]
Beer cellar: ten ale barrels, three barrels of beer, puncheon, stilledges, part of a basket of hops, tin can and bucket.

A well-constructed cellar remained at exactly the optimum temperature for keeping beer. Pamela Sambrook discovered that the Shugborough cellar remains at around 60°F, whatever the weather outside. In the capacious beer cellars at Uppark, the leather pipes that carried beer from the brewhouse to be put in casks in the cellars under the house can still be seen, and the racks for the casks remain in position. At Chatsworth the beer was piped from the brewhouse in the stable block to the house.

Sir Henry Dryden, the 'Antiquary', of Canons Ashby, Northants., in the 1880s. He relished old traditions in general and home-brewed beer in particular; he used to dress up as a tramp and invite travellers back to the house to drink his own brand of ale – spiked with bicarbonate of soda 'for extra fizz'.

The pipe ran under the floor of the 'Conservative Wall' of the hothouses, and at least one enterprising gardener tapped the pipe to provide a private supply. Calke Abbey has a tunnel to bring beer from its brewhouse into the long vaulted cellars below the house, where lines of barrel stands are still in position.

The growth of the commercial breweries in the eighteenth century meant the decline of home-brewed ale in inns, and to some extent in the home. In the 1730s the distillery trade was thrown open and taxed lightly. According to G. M. Trevelyan, 'both the rise of the death rate and its subsequent fall have been attributed to the growth and decline of the habit of drinking cheap gin instead of beer'. When the Marchioness of Bath published a manual on *Cottage Domestic Economy* for her tenants in 1829, she reminded them of the good old days of home-brewing, and deplored the debased modern custom of drinking tea or going to public houses for 'brewer's beer'.

Home-brewing underwent a revival when heavier taxation of spirits was introduced, and when rumours of the 'disagreeable filthiness' of the large commercial breweries spread. The *Housekeeper's Receipt Book* made a plea to 'discard the drayman for ever from our cellars', and for 'no family to deny themselves such a wholesome and necessary assistant to domestic comfort as a supply of good home-brewed beer'.

By the end of the century, a brewhouse was, in Muthesius's words, 'something of a special plaything', and he mentions only one contemporary example, at Cloverley Hall, Shropshire, built by W. E. Nesfield.

In rural retreats, beer was made until well into the twentieth century. At Canons Ashby in the 1860s, Henry Dryden, known as 'the Antiquary', used to dress up as a tramp, wander abroad and invite travellers back to the house. He entertained them in the medieval kitchen, 'plying them with his own brand of ale' (it contained bicarbonate of soda for extra fizz) made in the brewhouse next door. Small households also retained the tradition of home-brews. Dorothy Hartley wrote in 1954 that 'in the author's home, the brewing copper was in regular use within the last generation. It was taken for granted that a housewife knew how to brew, just as she could bake bread.'

THE BAKEHOUSE

The earliest bread ovens were portable, a development of the simplest baking method of all: an earthenware pot inverted on a hearth or baking stone. In 2000 BC these were made from a beehive- or tunnel-shaped framework of twigs, covered with clay inside and out. This stone-age design survived until very recently in the form of 'Barnstaple ovens': domed clay pots made in Somerset and still very popular in Wales and the West Country at the beginning of this century. It was again revived to supply bread for the British army during the First World War in the form of the Aldershot oven, made from clay slapped on to a framework of iron wheel rims cut in half. I have seen such ovens, still in use, outside farmhouses in Cyprus and Turkey.

The clay oven, like the much more familiar brick oven which succeeded it, was fired from the inside with a substantial bundle of sticks. Once these had burnt away, the ashes were swept off the oven floor and the loaves of bread slid in with a long-handled flat-bladed wooden instrument known as an oven peel. The mouth of the oven was then stopped with a flat stone or a clay slab, and sealed at the edges with wet clay. Bread baked in clay is said to be sweeter and more wholesome than that made in brick ovens built into the hearth, but there is a fairly long, not always reliable, domestic tradition of claiming the old ways are far superior to the new.

The built-in brick oven, permanently set into the thick wall of the chimney-breast at one side of the hearth, was a skilful construction. Small ovens were almost circular, larger ones more tunnel-shaped. The bricks were symmetrically positioned to form an arched or domed roof, and were fixed into place with fireclay. This dome was an effective way of radiating heat evenly on to the loaves below, giving them a light, spongy top that contrasted agreeably with the flat bottom crust formed by direct contact with the oven floor. Trenchers were flattish loaves that were turned during the baking process so that they had two flat surfaces. Split in half, they were a popular medieval substitute for dinner plates. The floor (sole) of the oven was sometimes made from glazed bricks to make it easier to sweep clean after firing.

The door (frequently in need of replacement and generally missing in surviving ovens) might have been a clay tile or a very thick block of hardwood. There is an exceptionally fine oak door from Chard in Somerset in the Pinto collection in the Birmingham Museum. Carved with a design showing a mermaid combing her hair, it doubled as an ornamental print for impressing on gingerbread. Both types were sealed with fireclay once the oven had been loaded. Later doors were made from iron – attached on hinges, and often beautifully decorated, with a long slim latch to ensure that they stayed firmly shut.

Bread ovens varied in size, though they were usually at least 18 in high. At the top end of the scale was the massive oven in the kitchen of Cotehele, designed to cope with the demands of a large Tudor household – it is 7 ft deep and 3 ft high. The remains of smaller ovens can be seen in almost any open hearth of any antiquity. As domestic quarters became more refined and specialized, the bakehouse was set up as an office in its own right – there is one marked on an early plan of the sixteenth-century courtyard of domestic offices at Felbrigg. Household account books show that the bakehouse of a country house would be in regular use, perhaps twice weekly.

Apart from one or more ovens, an auxiliary fireplace and some source of water (either piped to a sink or available from a nearby pump), the basic equipment of the bakehouse was the wooden trough, pronounced to rhyme with the dough which was mixed in it. Waist-high, of thick wood or slate, it was secured to a thick, short-legged stand. The trough slanted slightly inward to the base, and the inside was smooth, with a sweet yeasty smell. The wood became deeply impregnated with ferments (just as the wooden troughs used for salting bacon and ham became saturated with nitrates), thus encouraging the action of each consecutive rising. When the flour, water and yeast had been thoroughly mixed together, the wooden lid was closed and warm sacks put over the top to help the dough rise. By morning, it would have forced up the lid. Some trough lids had a rim to act as a tray to carry loaves to the oven; the other side could be used as a board to roll out and knead the dough upon.

The trough was never washed, just wiped out with a lump of the dough itself, any odd crumbs being removed with a rough dry cloth. Cloths, baking tins and flour pots could be stored inside it until the next baking day. Sometimes inside the trough you can see 'tally marks' cut to show how much flour was inside, just as a measuring cup is marked today. Stored close to the trough would be sacks of flour –

The massive baking oven at Cotehele in Cornwall. Notice too the boiling copper for vegetables and puddings, the tree-trunk bound into a chopping block, the mortar with its pestle held by an iron bracket and the leather fire-buckets.

grist, with only the bran removed, for ordinary use; fine white flour for soft white bread; and smaller sacks of other grains, malt, rye, and so on, to vary the mixture. If there was a great deal of baking, there might be a flour store next door to the bakehouse or in the attics above.

On a shelf there would be a jug for water, and one for buttermilk, and a jar for yeast with an earthenware base and a glazed top. The earthenware was porous, to keep the yeast at the bottom of the jar cool. A cover was stretched over the top, and a quill inserted to allow gas to escape. A salt-box, kept in a dry place beside the chimney, was essential – there was often a special cupboard let into the wall beside the stove to hold it. A dipper might be used to measure how much water was being put into the flour. Finally, a long knife, to cut the dough and to add the traditional cross on top 'to keep the devil out'.

An alternative to the trough, for kneading smaller quantities of dough, was an earthenware 'panshon' or bowl. This could be set beside the fire to allow the dough to rise – earthenware was better for this purpose than tin as it distributed the heat more evenly to the dough. Once the dough had proved, it could be kneaded with what Eliza Acton unforgettably called 'a happy pawing action, like a contented cat, till the dough is one even mass of soft resilience ... no dry lumps of flour, no damp spots of yeast, but an even texture – with a lovely alive elasticity that seems to spring back against your fists'. Rounded up, it was then put back into the pans, with a deep cross cut in the top, and set to rise again before being put in the oven.

The firing of the brick oven would have started up to two or three hours before, depending on its size and personal idiosyncracies. Faggots of furze and blackthorn, or thin splinters of beech, elm or oak were used, tied in bundles and kept extremely dry, so that they burnt up quickly and intensely. The size of these varied according to that of the oven. One or more were lighted near the mouth and then pushed to the centre of the oven, so that the heat spread as evenly as possible through the brickwork. Sometimes a larger log was added as the bundle of twigs burnt down, to sustain the heat of a big oven.

Before thermometers came into general use, it took experience to know when the right heat had been reached. Pebbles known to change their colour at a certain heat were used in some areas. Another method was to scrape a stick sharply on the bottom of the oven – if sparks flew, or if the carbon it left burnt off instantly, the oven was at the correct temperature. When the oven was hot enough, the remaining embers were drawn out with a long-handled iron hook or shovel, and the bottom of the oven cleaned with a sopping wet mop. This treatment also provided the steamy atmosphere desirable for the baking of bread.

Given the slow and relatively expensive process of firing the oven, it was worth baking in large batches. Once the bread was taken out, the slowly cooling oven could be used for pastry, cakes and puddings, or baked potatoes. Finally it could be used to dry off oatmeal and flour.

Iron cooking ranges with one or two ovens set into them steadily replaced the built-in brick-lined ovens during the nineteenth century. They made more economical use of heat for general cooking purposes, although the mean little ovens set beside the firebox of the standard range were acknowledged to be less efficient at baking. That didn't prevent Jane Carlyle, who was from a thrifty line of north Britons, making her own bread in the basement kitchen of the tall Georgian house in London's Cheyne Row into which she and Thomas moved in 1834. In her former home at Craigenputtock she had if necessary made the bread, churned the butter and scrubbed the kitchen floor. After putting her first loaf into the oven, she records, 'I sat down, feeling like Benvenuto Cellini when his cast of Perseus was thrust into the furnace.' The Carlyles declared the range they found in the rented house when they arrived hopelessly inadequate, and had a large and efficient new one sent down from

Edinburgh. Soon spicy gingercake and fresh bannocks were scenting the otherwise frugally run town house.

Many large houses compromised by closing down their independent bakehouse but installing a baking oven in the scullery. At Charlecote the baking scullery is very complete. The baking oven is tunnel-shaped, with a close-fitting iron door. Just in front of the door there is a convenient gap in the brick shelf through which cinders from the firing could be raked so that they fell directly into an ash tray fitted underneath. Against the walls stand the long shovels for clearing embers out of the deep oven, and a wooden peel. There is also a supplementary Eagle cooking range, with two ovens and hotplates above.

Even as late as 1885, a bakehouse was still felt to be essential for an isolated house such as Lanhydrock. It sports an elaborate oven made by the famous domestic equipment suppliers, Clements, Jeakes and Co., of 51 Great Russell St, Bloomsbury (they held Queen Victoria's warrant and were called upon by houseowners as far apart as Cragside, Uppark and Dunham Massey). The great central oven and its two supplementary ovens took four days to heat up, as it was fired by coal from below rather than internally.

Making bread, like laundry work, brewing and washing, has always been a task which you paid someone else to do for you if you could afford it. In fact, local bakers used to let people bring along a pie or a stew to put into their ovens (as in Beatrix Potter's *The Pie and the Patty Pan*) once a batch of bread had been baked. By the mid nineteenth century, home baking, particularly in southern parts of Britain, was in decline. Mechanized dough-mixers and efficient and economical gas-fired ovens made the commercial production of bread easier on a larger scale. 'Not only are there no ovens in vast numbers of our cottages, but many a small village is entirely without one,' wrote Eliza Acton in 1857. Today the mass-production bakers – the Aerated Bread Company, with its chain of ABC restaurants, was the first – have made traditional bread-making a luxury rather than a necessity. But the fortunate inhabitants of the Devon village of Branscombe, which is owned by the National Trust, experience the real thing. In the old village bakery, Gerald Collier bakes bread from a wood-fired brick-built oven. He gets up at four in the morning to light it, and bakes 120 loaves a day, large and small, using half a sack of flour (140 lbs) and his own well water.

Chapter Seven

Preservation

Here is my larder built with three rooms, one serving for
butter and milk, one for beer and wine and the third to
keep flesh of all kinds, poudered [salted] and unpoudered,
and fowles of all sorts, with convenient hooks to hang
them up from trouble. Here I have no windows to the
South or West, but all to the North and East. Above is a
corn loft, with floor of stone and plaster wall, and an
apple close – these we open and receive light through a
lattice to the North.

Gervase Markham, *The English Huswife*, 1615

Our habits of provisioning have been completely altered in the twentieth century
by new methods of preserving food. Tinned, frozen and, most recently, freeze-dried
and vacuum-packed products are now the staples of every kitchen. Moreover, since
all are easily available a shopping trip's distance from our homes, we can allow the
supermarkets to act as our larders. All the kitchen needs is a refrigerator and perhaps
a cupboard or two to store dry goods.

The larders, ice houses and cellars that were once an essential part of the domestic
economy required careful management. It was not just a question of storage; meat,
fruit and vegetables had to be prepared for preservation, using elemental processes:
salting, smoking, drying and freezing. Root cellars were for vegetables: potatoes in
sacks, carrots embedded in sand, onions plaited into ropes. Apples needed more
ventilation, and were often kept in airy wooden structures standing a little above the
ground on stone 'mushrooms' designed to keep the base of the hut away from the
damp earth and to prevent the ascent of rats and mice. Every apple had to be placed
on its shelf by hand, not touching any of its neighbours. Apples, pears and apricots
were also sliced in rings and dried, to be hung in long garlands up in the gloom of
the rafters. A special cellar was set aside for storing cheeses; others (as we have seen)
were reserved for beer and wine.

LARDERS – POTTING, SALTING AND SMOKING

The *lardarium* took its name from the process by which joints of meat were potted into huge barrels or stoneware tubs and covered with lard. In the neighbouring *salsarium* meat and fish were salted. Because of the scarcity of winter feed for cattle before the agricultural reforms of the eighteenth century, a general slaughtering took place in autumn; the larder was a major storeroom and had to accommodate enough meat to last a household through the winter. At Fynchale in 1311 the larder contained the 'carcases of twenty oxen, and fifteen pigs, of herrings eight thousand, of dograves [a sea fish] seven score, twenty pounds of almonds, thirty of rice, six barrels of lard, enough oatmeal to last till Easter, two quarters of salt'.

In the seventeenth century, the old *salsarium* and *lardarium* were generally known as wet and dry larders respectively. At Dyrham Park in 1710 there was a dry larder, with flour tubs, tables, a 'settle for barrels' and a hanging shelf – to protect stores from vermin. There were also several bird cages: not only blackbirds but larks, plovers, thrushes and even sparrows were netted for pies.

In the 'Wett Larder' were three 'powdring tubs' and a salting stone and trestle. The powdering tub held the mixture of salt and saltpetre which was used to rub into joints of meat, with the combined purpose of flavouring, preserving and colouring it. A salting stone was a shallow sink used for rubbing the salting mixture into the joints of meat.

A two-foot-high raised dais of brick was often built against one wall to support earthenware, slate, wooden or stone troughs for salting meat. In the deepest of these, a pickle of brine was kept; another slightly shallower one was used for lightly salting meat for fairly immediate use. Barrels were also used for soaking meat in brine; the joints hung from a framework of wooden batons.

In the centre of the wet larder there could be a strong wooden dresser, table or chopping block on which meat was cut up. There would also be a balance for weighing meat, and a rack to hold the knives, choppers, bone saws and hatchets. A fish slab was necessary if there was no separate fish larder, and a small ice-box. Kerr also suggested a 'box-sink' set in a window-sill or dresser, for swilling down meat and rinsing hands. On the ceiling would be bearers, with hooks sliding down from them, for hoisting joints up to the ceiling.

The walls were generally whitewashed, and sported iron hooks or holdfasts for hanging uncooked meat. If the larder was sure of staying dry, it could have bacon racks, but if it was damp, these were better arranged in the kitchen or in a separate bacon store. There were eight flitches of bacon and eight hams in the 'meat pantry' at Erddig in 1833, as well as a salting coffer, a marble slab, a stool and stepladder, two colanders and tins, two pewter dishes and earthenware crocks.

A typical recipe for pickle was to mix 4 gallons water with $1\frac{1}{2}$ lb coarse sugar, 4 oz saltpetre, 6 lb bay salt (as in sea, rather than the herb). To preserve meat well was something of an art. Bay salt gave a finer flavour than common salt, but rather more had to be used to give the same degree of saltiness. Saltpetre gave a fine red colour, but also made the meat hard, and always required an equal amount of sugar when used. Sugar made meat tender, but there was a danger of it tasting insipid. It was better not to risk salting and pickling in hot weather, as the slightest trace of taint spoiled the brine. Larders with all the equipment for salting and pickling can still be seen at Tatton Park and Shugborough.

After a week or longer in pickles of various sorts, the joints were smoked. Smoking was originally done out of doors, or by hanging meat high in the rafters above a central hearth. Once fireplaces moved to the wall, smoke holes and bacon shelves were built into chimneys, some of them so capacious that they have been mistaken for priests' holes. In the Cumbrian yeoman's farmhouse of Townend, visitors are invited to stand under the huge chimney and look up to admire the flitches of bacon (plaster casts, alas) that the Browne family smoked to a turn through the centuries. Upstairs, in the corner of the servant's bedroom, a small door leads directly into the chimney-stack to give access to the hams. Smoking cupboards can also be seen in the chimney wall of the kitchen at Shugborough: mysterious doors far too high to reach except with a ladder.

The coal ranges introduced into most kitchens in the nineteenth century were not suitable for smoking meat, and separate smoke-houses fired with wood had to be set up if hams were to be smoked on the premises. Farmhouses continued to take advantage of their capacious chimneys and wood fires until well into the twentieth century, but the gentry ordered hams from their local butcher or sent to Westphalia and Parma.

An excellently planned range of larders survives at Dunham Massey. The wooden bars acting as room dividers are unusual, but would have allowed the free circulation of air. The first room, leading off the kitchen, is in part pastry (see p. 121) and in part a dry larder. A broad wooden dresser shelf runs along one wall, and a cold marble slab is set in the corner to the left of the window. Shelves above the dresser shelf hold crocks for pastry-making ingredients. There is also a wire-mesh meat safe and an ice-box. A door gives direct access to the neighbouring scullery, and through it to the back door. In the next room is equipment for cleaning and salting down meat and fish: shallow slate sinks, slate-topped tables, and a capacious six-foot-high ice-box. Two massive cheese-presses stand beside one wall. Next door is a separate meat larder, with a large rectangular ceiling rack for storing meat of all kinds, fresh, 'powdered', smoked and salted. Through the window the game larder can be seen, just outside the kitchen complex, but not inconveniently distant from it.

Whitewashed walls and hooks for flitches of bacon and hams are a feature of the late-nineteenth-century meat larder at Lanhydrock, Cornwall.

Provision for capacious and specialized larders became less necessary as households relied increasingly on shops for provisions of all sorts. 'The larder is now a store for all kinds of food, cooked and uncooked,' remarked *Our Homes* in 1882. 'The increasing facilities for transport, and other causes, have, by bringing within reach of all large supplies of fresh meat, obviated the necessity for salting down provisions for winter consumption.'

The late-nineteenth-century larder housed all food not kept in the housekeeper's storeroom – meat of all kinds, vegetables, bread, cheese and fruit: everything in fact that we would now keep in a refrigerator. It was generally a square or oblong room near the kitchen, sometimes sunk a step below it, and built to be as cool as possible – preferably on the north side of the house. The windows were opposite to each other, and covered with fine wire mesh rather than glass, so that as much air as possible could circulate. A brick floor with a drain so that it could be easily washed was recommended. Shelves were made from slate and marble slabs several inches thick, and embedded deep into the walls. Fish and vegetables were laid directly on the slabs, with a light cover of muslin over them and perhaps a handful of wet rushes scattered about to cool the atmosphere. These slabs and the wooden larder shelves were scrubbed regularly with chloride of lime to disinfect them.

A useful informal extension to these smaller larders was a large hanging outdoor meat safe, of the type which can be seen at Erddig, in the passage leading into the kitchen court. As Anne Cobbett explains, 'In some places there is no regular larder, but the uncooked meat is kept in a hanging safe in the open air which is drawn up and down by a pulley.'

In remoter areas, however, there was still a habit of self-sufficiency that was slow to die, and a very good set of late-nineteenth-century larders can be seen at Lanhydrock. They are described as meat, fish and dry larders, although the dry larder is far more like the traditional eighteenth-century housekeeper's storeroom than a dry larder in the old sense.

THE GAME LARDER

Some larders sported a circular rack for game, but the unpleasant smell that large quantities of pheasants and the like produced encouraged the development of separate, purpose-built game larders. These tended to be built some distance from the house, both because of the smell associated with them and so that the gamekeeper could conveniently deposit game without disturbing the kitchen staff. It was important that the larder was airy and cool, and the usual way of achieving this was to arrange windows all round the building so that a through draught could be almost guaranteed. Fine mesh kept insects out. Ice was brought from the ice house if an added chill was necessary. Inside, game was hung alternately by head and feet to ensure even ripening of the meat. The size of the larder would depend on the size of the shootings.

One of the most attractive surviving game larders was designed by Repton for Uppark. It is a decorative little building, one of the first that the visitor sees on approaching the house, set back in a small copse of trees. Its pebbled approach path is edged with deer bones. There are large windows, framed at the front end with circular air vents. Inside there are two rooms, the first hexagonal and decoratively paved in contrasting slate and stone slabs; it has a high ceiling rack arranged like the spokes of the wheel and a pendant with four smaller circular racks underneath. This kept the hanging birds clear of each other and used the central space efficiently. Larger carcases were hung from the rails around the walls. Marble shelves in the alcoves provided more cool storage space. The second room was for venison or other large carcases. At one time it probably contained some sort of table and a chopping slab.

An interesting bridge between old-style larders and modern fridge-freezers was described by Dudley Gordon's article on 'An Up-to-date Game Larder' in Laurence Weaver's *The House and its Equipment* (1912). At that time, deep freezing, or 'cold storage', was thought more applicable to commercial rather than domestic use. 'It is not yet realized generally that cold storage can be carried out on quite a small scale perfectly satisfactorily and efficiently, and for this reason most country houses make shift with a box, or chamber, cooled by ice. This has the disadvantage of being messy

The decorative little game larder designed in the early nineteenth century by Humphry Repton for Uppark, Sussex, had two well-ventilated rooms, both furnished with racks for hanging game of different sizes.

and costly by reason of the quantity of ice used.' Gordon asserted that 'a small cooling plant' was a perfectly feasible proposition for 'a sporting estate'; indeed, he predicted, absolutely accurately, 'it is probable that in a few years' time a refrigerating machine will come to be considered just as necessary in a country house as the electric light is today'. The game larder he envisaged had two chambers, one kept at $25°F$ for frozen game, the other at $35°F$ for keeping game for short periods for daily use. A six-inch thickness of cork slabs insulated each chamber, finished with a thin layer of white cement which was washable. Alternative insulating materials were flake charcoal, sawdust, silicate cotton (also known as slag wool) and cow hair. Like an ice house, the larder had two sets of doors to form a lobby, or airlock. The doors were made with a taper, in order to fit tightly when closed, and were as thickly insulated as the walls of the chambers. The mechanics of the cooling plant were a scaled-down version of commercial machines, driven by an electric motor.

ICE HOUSES

Frozen food is not a new idea. Alexander the Great, when on campaign in the fourth century BC, had pits dug and covered with twigs and leaves to store ice and snow through the summer months. Saladin offered 'snow water' to Richard the Lionheart when they met after the siege of Acre in 1192, and Francis Bacon is reputed to have died of a chill caught while he was collecting snow to stuff inside a chicken to preserve it.

Developing methods of keeping ice was obviously a higher priority in hot countries than in temperate ones. Although the French and Italians were taking long-term ice storage for granted by the early seventeenth century, few ice houses were built in Britain until after the Restoration. Perhaps the fashion for them was brought back by returning Royalists who had learnt continental habits while in exile. Certainly John Evelyn, who included a 'conservatorie of Ice and Snow' in his (unexecuted) plan for a royal garden, got his ideas from his continental travels. In 1683, Robert Boyle quoted Evelyn's description of ice houses he had seen in Italy. These were conical pits, about 50 ft deep and 25 ft wide with a wooden trestle fixed at the base 'like a kind of wooden grate' (this allowed water to drain from the ice). The top was shielded from the sun by a thickly thatched wigwam of straw or reeds which had a narrow doorway 'hipped on like the top of a Dormer' and also thatched.

The standard design for an English ice house – a very deep conical pit, brick-lined and at least 12 ft in diameter – was a reflection of the uncertainty of obtaining ice in our temperate climate. In a well-built, well-managed ice house of this sort, ice could be kept for two years or more. Deep in the woods behind Felbrigg Hall, Norfolk, is the oldest ice house owned by the National Trust – one of the bricks is dated 1633.

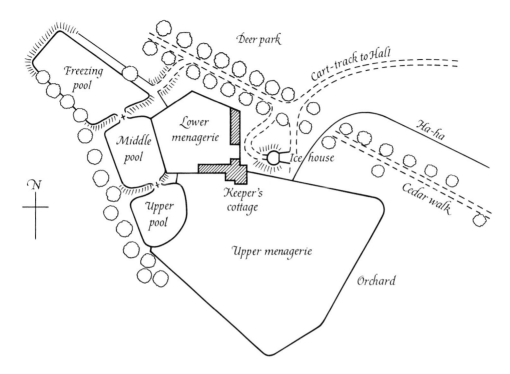

Hanbury Hall, Worcs.: the ice house and freezing ponds in the eighteenth century. When weather conditions were right, sluices would be opened to allow water to flow from the two deep pools into the larger, shallower freezing pool. To improve its efficiency the freezing pool was shaded from the winter sun by evergreens. When ready, the ice would be cut and transported along the cart-track to the hatch above the ice house.

It is some 28 ft deep, and still has an approach tunnel down to it. The charming Gothick facade of blank arches marks it as a place to stroll to and admire – a reflection of its novelty at that period. There is more to see, however, at the very well-preserved ice house at Hanbury Hall, near Worcester. Visitors can walk through its approach tunnel right up to the precipitous drop of the ice-well, and look up to admire the small bricks laid in perfect circles to form the roof. Notice the removable brickwork access trap near the top of the dome. At the beginning of the path to the tunnel, two slabs cover access to the drain which runs from the base of the ice pit.

A great many ice houses survive (Monica Ellis of Southampton University has recorded forty-four in Hampshire alone), although many have become ruined or overgrown. Perhaps the most romantic of all the ice houses that can still be visited is the upstairs dovecote, downstairs ice house set into the wall of the kitchen garden of the palatial ruins of that egregious folly Downhill, in County Londonderry, with its startlingly lovely view of the sea. More complete is the perfectly preserved tower ice house at Penrhyn Castle, which has an interesting room above it that clearly provided for access by the kitchen staff. A bucket could be lowered into the pit through a trapdoor, and there was also a ladder. The actual door to the ice house was outside the gates of the domestic courtyard, suggesting that it was used by outdoor staff to fill the pit with supplies, either of ice or of game to be frozen.

Although there is increased interest in Britain's ice houses, there is still much guesswork about how they were constructed and how they were actually used. Philip Miller's *Gardener's Dictionary* (1768) provides a useful description of how they were built. He recommended bricking the sides of the well to a depth of at least two and a half bricks. At three feet below the surface, arches should begin, carried high enough to admit a semi-sunken doorway with a passage to the outer world. A wooden grate at the base was connected to a laid drain to take the melted water away. Other authorities suggested double doors to improve the insulation of the approach, and an iron grate to prevent rats and other small vermin from getting

One of the best-preserved ice houses in Britain was built in the 1840s, into the basement of this gigantic mock Norman tower at Penrhyn Castle, Gwynedd. Indoor staff collected ice from a room off the domestic courtyard, through a trapdoor in the top of the pit; gardeners filled the pit with ice using a door on the outside of the tower.

inside. The best aspect for the entrance was the south-east, so that early morning sun would dispel the 'pernicious' damps that tended to collect in the porch. Air traps were necessary in the drain that took melted water out at the bottom of the ice pit, because it was air more than anything that made the ice melt. It was critically important that the ice house be free from damp, and ice houses dug in chalky or gravel soils were more successful than those in clay or heavy loam.

John Loudon elaborated on the management of the long approach passage to the ice house, suggesting it be equipped with three sets of doors. Between the first two sets, a thick layer of straw, preferably soft barley straw, was desirable. 'To render the removal of this straw easy, when passing from the outer door to the ice house, it might be put into two or more canvas bags, like immense cushions, which might be hooked to the ceiling and the sides, so as to close up every interstice.' A long article in the *Gardeners' Chronicle* a few years later, in 1842, criticized this use of straw as impractical, suggesting instead leather seals round the doors. However, it is possible that such insulating bags of straw were also used to hang inside the ice house as the ice was removed, in order to prevent the air causing it to thaw. At Penrhyn, there are regularly spaced hooks around the walls of the ice pit which could have been used for this purpose.

Filling the Ice House

Ice to fill the pits at Felbrigg and Blickling would have been readily available from the shallow Norfolk meres, but packed snow was evidently used on some occasions. The steward of Blickling, Robert Copeman, wrote to Lady Buckinghamshire in April 1790, 'There was a great fall of snow this afternoon, as soon as ever it was thick enough I spoke to the Gardeners and had as many Labourers as I could. The ice house is about half full; the men kept at it to between 9 & 10 o'clock.'

The ice house at Blickling was still in use in the 1930s, and remains, although deep in shaggy grass and unkempt coppice, in a reasonable state of preservation. The use of snow is also recorded at Mottisfont Abbey in Hampshire in the 1880s. Shovelled in by the gardeners and grooms and trampled well down, it lasted all summer, and no other source of ice was necessary. Shallow ponds that froze easily could also be useful when it was very cold but no snow fell. If no natural water supply was conveniently available, special provision might be made – in 1842 the *Gardeners' Chronicle* suggested flooding a neighbouring bowling green. At Belton there is a summer-house at one end of a long formal pond; behind it, making an attractive background mound, and conveniently close to the shallow water, is the (now very ruined) ice house. If you plunge into the woods at Wallington, you will find a chain of overgrown fish-ponds. From one of them a sluice gate could be opened when a frost was expected, to divert water along a short canal to fill a very shallow pool,

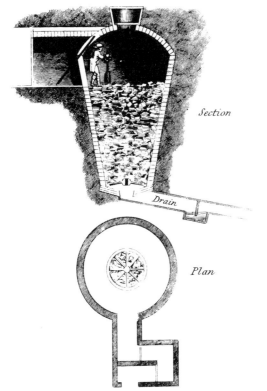

Section

Drain

Plan

Ice house: cross-section and plan. Snow, ice from ponds or specially bought Nordic ice was pounded down into a solid mass in the centre of the ice house. It was removed from the outside of the heap, to ensure that the central core remained as cold as possible. This engraving shows the cartwheel covering the entrance to the drain to prevent ice falling through. The aperture in the dome was for putting small quantities of ice into the pit, and the sloping door acted as a barrier; straw could be laid against it to fill the passage when the ice house was full. There is an air trap in the drain.

The plan shows three angles in the passage with two inner doors to prevent warm air entering the ice house.

again close to the ice house. The outline of a similar chain of ponds can be seen at Hanbury Hall.

If ice was used to fill the ice house, it was broken up into as small pieces as possible – 'resembling salt or sand' according to one authority. It was then thrown in, preferably through the roof or else through the doorway of the ice pit and rammed down systematically using a heavy hand-held rammer. Occasionally water, sometimes boiling hot, was sprinkled on it to make it into as compact a mass as possible.

Ice was a marketable commodity, bought and sold as early as 1726 when 'eighty loads of ice for the Ice House' were delivered to Knole, at a cost of £1 15s 3d. The common street name 'Coldharbour Lane' betrays the former site of a commercial ice house to which ice was delivered by river or canal, carried in barges and wherries from parts of the country where shallow marshes or meres made ice easy to harvest. Ice was also imported from overseas, although the first cargo ever to arrive in Britain, from Norway in 1822, proved something of a wash-out. It took the Customs and Excise so long to decide to classify this novel commodity as dry goods that all 300 tons of it melted away in bond. But by 1830 there was a huge ice repository under London's Haymarket where 1,500 tons of ice could be kept. A ship was constantly kept in transit between London and Norway, and deliveries were effected from the docks using the Regent's Canal. From 1844 ice was also exported to England from the United States by the enterprising Wenham Lake Ice Company. Harvested with enormous steam-driven ice-cutting machines on the Great Lakes, it was prized for its purity. However, when the company found that Norwegian ice could be sold much more cheaply, it bought the rights to harvest ice in a Norwegian lake, renaming it Lake Wenham. From then on, Wenham Lake Ice came from Norway. A passing reference by Thackeray in a *Punch* short story shows how widespread its use had become by 1848: 'Everybody had the same thing in London. You see the same coats, the same dinners, the same boiled fowl and mutton, the same cutlets, fish and cucumbers, the same lumps of Wenham Lake Ice, etc.'

Imported ice was not used only in London. The rapid growth of a countrywide canal network made ice a far easier commodity to transport than it ever had been, and by the end of the century most establishments of any pretensions had some means of storing it. Ice stacks and surface-level ice houses became much commoner when ice began to be imported from abroad and could be obtained all year round. The important thing was to have a sufficiently thick insulating layer of straw, sawdust or charcoal under, around and above the ice. Such a stack was best sited, according to John Loudon, in the shade of a copse of trees, or under a shed roof, closed on the south side and open to the north. William Cobbett gave instructions for a slightly more permanent ice stack in his *Cottage Economy* (1821), but admitted that he had never seen such a thing built. He appears to have had some reservations as to its efficiency: 'There is,' he concluded, 'this comfort, that if the thing fail as an ice house, it will serve all generations to come as a model for a pig-bed.' He was probably not entirely joking: conversions of this sort may have obscured a very widespread incidence of storing ice above ground.

Use of the Ice House

According to Jarrin's *Italian Confectioner,* ice was best removed from the top, at first through the access cover, as it came to hand. Once it had dropped to the level of the doorway, a ladder could be installed, and ice taken from the outside of the mass, leaving the centre to the very end. This 'will be found solid and compact even in the middle of summer; if on the contrary, ice is first taken from the middle, you destroy the body, and the air which will introduce itself will destroy more than you consume'.

Besides providing ice for use in the house, the ice house itself was used to chill or even freeze food. In 1818, John Papworth wrote in *Rural Residences,* his delightfully illustrated book of designs for small country villas, that 'the ice house forms an excellent larder for the preservation of every kind of food that is liable to be injured by heat in summer; thus fish, game and poultry, butter, etc., may be kept for a considerable time: indeed in London they are used for such purposes by persons who deal largely in either fish or venison'.

John Loudon suggested that between the final doors the passage could be widened slightly and shelves set into its sides, providing a useful chilled cabinet for foods not requiring absolute freezing. The Hampshire ice house at Le Court in Greatham has side alcoves of this sort. Loudon also suggested placing a movable shelf or table directly over the ice. Unless this was hung by hooks from the roof, it is difficult to imagine what happened as the ice was removed from beneath it. Perhaps it was only used for short-term freezing. Additional shelves, of course, could easily have been strung around the sides of the ice pit once some of the ice had been removed.

By 1842, Anne Cobbett's *English Housekeeper* took the availability of 'frosted' meat for granted, and gave confident and accurate instructions for thawing it out:

Some cooks will not be persuaded of the necessity for its being completely thawed out before it is put near the fire: yet it neither roasts, boils, nor eats well unless this be done. If slightly frozen, the meat may be recovered by being kept for five or six hours in the kitchen; not near the fire. Another method, and a sure one, is to plunge a joint into a tub of cold water, and let it remain two or three hours, or even longer, and the ice will appear on the outside. Meat should be cooked immediately after once it has been thawed, for it will keep no longer.

ICE CELLARS

In 1845 Jane Loudon described an ice house as 'an important addition to comfort in summer', but she added that 'a more modern invention is a small cellar built adjoining the house, with double walls, the space between the walls being filled with charcoal'. Such a cellar had double doors with a space between, so that one might be shut before the other is opened, 'to prevent the entrance of atmospheric air'. The ice was kept in a sunk part, 'made like a bath, at the farther end of the cellar, furnished with a drain to carry off the superfluous waters', and in the other part of the cellar there were shelves, on which wine or food could be kept cool. 'The old-fashioned ice house was always made in the park at some distance from the house,' she added, 'but the modern ice cellar is very useful for keeping cool water, butter, and other articles of daily consumption; which can be fetched out of it when they are wanted, as easily and expeditiously as they could be out of a common dairy or pantry.'

Stevenson pointed out that small wells could easily be made in the basements or cellars of London houses – it was only the association of the idea of an ice house with the huge stacks stored by confectioners that prevented small households embarking on making such provision. Now that ice was imported on a regular basis from Norway by the Wenham Lake Ice Company, he added, it cost very little.

There is a plan in Kerr's *Gentleman's House* which shows such an ice house attached to the house itself – this appears to have been the arrangement at Castle Coole, where, balancing the bakehouse to the right of the broad tunnel running away from the basement of the house to the courtyard offices beyond, there is an odd neglected space, now chiefly remarkable for a large stone coffer and a pit filled with what appears to be charcoal mixed with gravel.

ICE CHESTS

An easier method of storing ice temporarily was the ice chest. This would have been improvised by lining boxes with hay or straw for the most part, but an 'ice-box' was patented by Thomas Masters in 1844. It was lined with 'orpholite', a substance whose composition Masters kept a secret. He suggested adding small quantities of ice

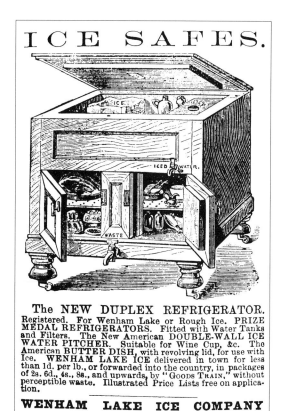

ICE SAFES.

The NEW DUPLEX REFRIGERATOR.
Registered. For Wenham Lake or Rough Ice. PRIZE MEDAL REFRIGERATORS. Fitted with Water Tanks and Filters. The New American DOUBLE-WALL ICE WATER PITCHER. Suitable for Wine Cup, &c. The American BUTTER DISH, with revolving lid, for use with Ice. WENHAM LAKE ICE delivered in town for less than 1d. per lb., or forwarded into the country, in packages of 2s. 6d., 4s., 8s., and upwards, by "GOODS TRAIN," without perceptible waste. Illustrated Price Lists free on application.

WENHAM LAKE ICE COMPANY
125, STRAND, LONDON Corner of Savoy-street).

Ice chests could be handsome pieces of furniture as well as utilitarian larder storage. Notice the taps for supplying iced water and for draining off melted ice. Champagne could be laid on the block of ice itself.

to the box every two days, thus maintaining its low temperature almost indefinitely. A year later Jane Loudon described an 'ice-cooler' which could be brought into the dining-room:

It consists of a double frame of wood with the space between filled with charcoal. The bottles of wine are placed in little tin cases left for them, and ice is put between the cases. Below the ice is a tin grating, through which the melted water runs, and is let off when requisite by a cock. This box is made to hold two bottles of wine on one side, a bottle of water and a glass for butter on the other.

There is an ice-box very similar to this in the kitchen at Baddesley Clinton and another, elegantly veneered, at Wallington. Much larger insulated ice-cupboards survive in the larders of Shugborough and Dunham Massey.

REFRIGERATORS

Mechanical cooling systems were established in commercial use well before they were adapted to the home. Only very large houses could install the cumbersome machinery required for such 'cold storage' as the game larder described above. The first successful domestic refrigerator was developed in the United States. The Domelre (*Domestic Electric Refrigerator*) was marketed in Chicago in 1913. Kelvinator made their first machine in 1916 and Frigidaire, a subsidiary of General Motors, followed quickly in 1917. In 1923, an article in *House and Garden* commented that 'Refrigerators, which are a commonplace in American households, are not sufficiently known or used over here.' The first machine to be mentioned by *Ideal Home* was the Swedish Electrolux in 1926, finished in dark oak or white enamel, and complete with trays of ice-cubes for the newly fashionable cocktails. By the 1930s most substantial kitchens had an electric refrigerator somewhere. Because of the size of their engines, they were made on a heroic scale, with high domed tops and short splayed legs.

CHAPTER EIGHT

THE COOK'S QUARTERS

Man may live without love – what is passion but pining?
But where is the man who can live without dining?
We may live without friends; we may live without books;
But civilized men cannot live without cooks.

Owen Meredith, 'Lucille', c. 1860

In the kitchen, perhaps more than in any of the other domestic offices, the personal stamp of particular families and architects is most evident. 'Peace and Plenty' runs a promising legend engraved in Tatton Park's kitchen: although formal in manner, the Egertons never stinted either their servants or themselves. 'Spare Not, Waste Not', Horace Walpole noted with approval, was a becoming motto for the most perfectly proportioned of all kitchens, the double-cube constructed by Robert Adam at Kedleston. It was changed at a later date, perhaps a little ominously, to that general favourite 'Waste Not, Want Not'. This is also seen at Erddig, where it was observed to the letter by portly Mrs Webster under the appreciative eye of Philip Yorke (she amassed a personal fortune of £1,300), and at Calke Abbey, where it was completely ignored until the advent of the energetic Sir George Crewe. 'Under God's blessing,' he wrote in his memorandum book in 1838, 'after nineteen years of labour, I have at last cleansed the Augean stables of Calke jobs, Calke turkey and Calke extravagance.'

Good cooks were sought-after beings, and it was as well to spoil them. A really grand chef could have his or her own retinue, and take liberties permitted to no other servant. They were also paid more than other servants, including the steward. At Petworth in 1872 the cook was paid £120 a year, the steward £105. Certain perks were customary – for example, all bones, dripping and fat could be sold by the cook. Minions might include a roasting cook (generally male), a confectioner (preferably Italian) and a baker, as well as a bevy of kitchenmaids and a few scullions. Not all chefs were men. In 1824, Mary Elizabeth Lucy wrote from Charlecote: 'We have a most accomplished artist, Sharp, as cook, equal to any man.'

There are fewer affectionate anecdotes about cooks than about either butlers or

Tatton Park, Cheshire. Kitchen mottoes varied. Life under 'Peace and Plenty' was probably a good deal pleasanter than under the commoner 'Waste Not, Want Not'.

housekeepers. More typical are the military metaphors employed by John Earle in his *Micro-cosmographie* (1628):

Colericke he is, not by Nature so much as by his Art, and it is a shrewd temptation that the chopping knife is so neare. His weapons often offensive are a messe of hot broth and scalding water, and woe be to him that comes in his way. In the kitchen he will domineere and rule the Roast in speight of his Master and Curses in the very Dialect of his Calling ... His cunning is not small in Architecture, for he builds strange Fabricks in Paste, Towres and Castles which are offered to the assault of valiant Teeth, and like Darius his Palace, in one Banquet demolisht ...

His best Facultie is at the Dresser, where he seems to have great skill in the Tactikes, ranging his Dishes in order militarie; and placing with discretion in the forefront Meates more strong and hardie, and the more cold and cowardly in the rear; as quaking Tarts and quivering Custards and Milksop Dishes ...

But now the second course is gone up and he downe in the Cellar where he drinks and sleeps till four o'clock in the afternoon and then returns again to his Regiment.

Clearly, unless the cook was, like Mrs Webster at Erddig, also the housekeeper, he or she seems to have been less closely linked with the family, less 'one of us', more feared than loved. Cooks' tantrums were the stuff of novels: in George Moore's realistic backstairs tale of a Victorian servant girl, *Esther Waters* (1894), the whole household trembled at Mrs Latch's approach. On the other hand, Viola Bankes remembers 'tiny, bustling, smiling Mrs Jenks' of Kingston Lacy with great affection.

THE KITCHEN

Social histories of domestic life often give the impression that our ancestors lived in a state of constant party. A common-sense approach to the kitchen will assume that in most households simple, or at least unpretentious, meals were the rule rather than the exception. In Tudor times, it was usual for aristocratic families to keep 'secret house' for several weeks every year. They stayed in one of their smaller, remoter properties with a skeleton staff, and the enormous retinue that ran the great house was sent away on board wages, a fraction of their normal salary. The great hall, buttery and kitchen offices could all be closed down.

Moreover, the enormous hearth typical of medieval and Tudor kitchens appears less profligate when it is understood that it was used after midday dinner and before supper as the source of heat for any trade that might require it – forging, for example, or boiling withies for basket-making; dying cloth and so on. In those days, kitchens were far from being the specialized apartments for cooking that they became in later centuries: they were the heart of the house.

The substantial fortified manor of Compton Castle, Devon, has a good example of such a multi-purpose chamber. It replaced an older kitchen, and is in the base of a tower added in 1520. To make the kitchen separate from the rest of the house was a sensible precaution in case of fire. The focus of the room is the hearth, once centrally placed, but moved to a strengthened end wall in all but the most temporary dwellings by the sixteenth century. It was constructed by the simple expedient of setting a beam across the width of the room and building a double wall. In small houses, a staircase was often built in one side of the space thus enclosed; the other end might hold a bread oven and storage closets. The brickwork behind the fire was usually protected by an iron fireback, more or less elaborately decorated. Essential furniture of the early open hearth were a pair of andirons, or firedogs, used to rest the ends of logs upon, in order to raise them and so encourage a good blaze. The front ends of the andirons were useful supports for roasting spits. Alternatively, a rack hemmed with two vertical rows of hooks to support spits could be leant against the back of the chimney-breast.

The hearth at Compton is large enough to accommodate a baking oven at each side and has three flues, an arrangement that suggests that rather than always lighting one enormous fire, cooks may have lit two or three smaller fires, one under a three-legged cauldron, another using charcoal in a portable stove or within a grate improvised from tiles or stones. The ceiling of the room is very high, to improve ventilation, and vaulted, so that condensation dripped down the walls rather than on to the heads of the cook and his scullions. The windows are high not only because this was a rough age and on occasion the kitchen tower had to be fortified (it was pounded by cannon shot in the Civil War), but because it lessened draughts below and provided the high-level light that was best for the cook.

Furnishings in such a kitchen were minimal. There was no sink, because all work involving water – washing up, meat and vegetable preparation and so on – was carried out in the scullery. Any kitchen furniture was easily movable – a few trestle tables (known as boards, hence 'sideboard') and three-legged stools, a fireside chair or two. A fifteenth-century Lincolnshire inventory listed

> A hen cage, with a shelfe within
> 2 tubs, two sowes [large tubs]
> A great bowl and a lesser bowl
> A hogshead to put in salte
> A market maunde [basket] with a coveringe
> 12 brass pots, kettles, etc., weighing together 167 lbs
> A great iron spit weighing 14 lbs
> A payre of cupboards of iron, weighing 23 lbs
>   [probably similar to the Dutch ovens described on pp. 120–21]
> Other spytts, dropping-pans, frying pans, brandreths etc., weighing 86 lbs

Shelves on the wall would have been filled with pottery and earthenware dishes, wooden bowls and chopping boards, iron and pewter (or in wealthier houses copper and brass) pots and platters.

Not far away at Cotehele, a small Cornish manor-house on the Tamar, there is a much cosier kitchen of a similar period. Although Sir Piers Edgcumbe had built himself a new hall by 1520, probably on the site of the former buttery, he seems to have left the original kitchen untouched, even though this left it unfashionably close to the hall itself. Since Cotehele was not regularly occupied by the Edgcumbe family after 1660 (they preferred their Plymouth seat, Mount Edgcumbe), the house remained unusually primitive, occupied only by a handful of elderly servants pensioned off to act as caretakers. Although the kitchen was somewhat modernized after 1861, when the third earl's widow, Caroline Augusta, decided to move in, the house was again left to caretakers after 1905. In the 1970s the dilapidated Victorian iron range was taken out of the hearth, and a lithograph by Nicholas Condy in 1840 was used to recreate the atmosphere of what is in effect a seventeenth-century kitchen, more typical of a substantial farmhouse than of a gentleman's seat.

Cotehele's kitchen is not especially large as manorial kitchens go – about 20 × 20 ft – but it is typically high, and there are signs that there used to be louvred vents in the roof. There are sturdy wooden pegs everywhere, set along the beams to hold pots and pans, fire buckets, oven peels and spare spits, and also provisions for immediate use: bunches of onions and garlic, flitches of bacon and hams. A slice of tree-trunk bound with iron hoops made a good chopping surface (see illustration on p. 91). Another classic piece of early kitchen equipment to be seen at Cotehele is the massive mortar, mounted in a sturdy wooden stand, with the long handle of its pestle held in a high wall bracket. This made any grinding easy work, whether of salt or sugar from the lump, bones into bone-meal, spices to powder or meat into pastes. It remained an essential tool in any serious kitchen until well into the twentieth century – Lutyens fitted one into the Castle Drogo kitchen in 1927.

There were two hearths on different walls: one for roasting and one for baking – a similar arrangement, although on a much smaller scale, to that of the great monastic kitchens at Glastonbury and Durham. On a high wooden rack hanging from the ceiling more stores were hung, safe from vermin or casual purloiners: joints of meat, previously salted and smoked, as well as sacks of flour, salt, and other provisions. A square hole was traditionally left at the side of the hearth to hold the salt pot, others might hold the tinder-box and the cook's sand-glass – a personal possession, this, often with individual vagaries in estimating minutes.

Some distance up the chimney, a long horizontal bar was fixed. From this, or from smaller brackets set into the stonework, cauldrons, water boilers and stew pots of massive size could be suspended on pot-hooks. The largest of these were probably only rarely removed, one being used as a water boiler, another as a 'pot au feu', added to day after day to use up leftovers of all sorts. Another important part of the ordinary ironmongery of the hearth was the chimney crane. This triangular bracket could be swung out over or close to the fire, and from it, by hooks and chains, pots or kettles were suspended. An idle-back, or lazy susie, was an angled double hook which allowed a heavy kettle to be tilted and poured weightlessly by slipping the upper hook out from the handle. Ingeniously designed levers attached to the diagonal strut of a chimney crane meant that even very heavy cauldrons could be adjusted with the minimum of effort. It is worth looking closely at such devices; they often have very individual features thought out by local blacksmiths. Pots and pans for use on the fire tended to have both handles to hang by and three legs to stand on – more secure than four on the uneven brick floor of the fire. Three-legged pot stands, known as trivets or brandises, could be pushed into the embers to keep pots simmering; three-legged toasting stands with horizontal prongs could grill a chop, or toast a trencher of egg-soaked bread (still nicknamed a 'poor knight').

Lighting a fire was something of a chore before the invention of matches (originally known as 'prometheans' or 'lucifers') in 1831. The hearthside tinder-box had to be kept bone dry, and filled with easily inflammable materials, such as a few fibres of flax (tow) and pieces of dried agaric, a corky tree fungus, soaked in nitre. A sharp flint was struck against a steel to set the tinder burning; then a match tipped with brimstone (sulphur) was lit from it. In the evening a canny cook would preserve the embers until the next morning by covering them with a metal dome with a small gap at one side known as a 'couvre-feu' (curfew). This was also a sensible fire precaution, a legal requirement in Norman times and beyond. Ideally, all the fires in the household were lit by taking glowing coals from the range and carrying them to other hearths on hooded shovels. Bundles of sticks (faggots) were stacked ready to kindle the fire and huge logs kept it going for hours on end. Every kitchen had to have space to store wood. An early engraving of the medieval kitchen of Stanton Harcourt, in Oxfordshire, shows a huge wooden bin piled high with five-foot-long bundles of sticks. Cotehele had a convenient and roomy wood store behind the baking hearth.

Roast meat was prized in England, where the climate made an open fire welcome even in summer. It was sometimes carried to the table on spits, and special silver ones were kept for this purpose. Basket spits had a cage of bars mounted on them to hold small roast meats such as sucking pigs or stuffed fowls. The rows of spits laid across from one firedog to another evolved into a form of a brazier known as a dog grate. A further sophistication was to attach a pulley to one end of the spit in order to turn it by a variety of means. Water power was often used: a small paddle-wheel was set in a nearby stream at Woollas Hall, on Bredon Hill. It could also be a job for a kitchen boy, or even a kitchen dog. In his 1576 treatise on canine types, Dr Caius of Cambridge lists *Canis veruversator*, the turnspit, 'a dog excellent in kitchen service... When any meat is to be roasted, they go into a wheel; which they turn round with the weight of their bodies; and so diligently look to their business, that no drudge nor scullion can do the feat more cunningly.' A dog-wheel which turned five spits is mentioned in the 1710 inventory of the 'Little Kitchen' at Dyrham Park. Visitors to the George Inn at Lacock can see a cage for this purpose set into the wall beside the hearth.

The importance of spit roasting in the kitchen is sometimes exaggerated – an over-reliance on evidence of culinary practice on feast days and in the royal household has infected ordinary daily life with unlikely splendour. In fact medieval menus featured many 'soggy meats' – broths, pottages, ragouts and hashes. Minced meat mixed with crumbs of bread and yolks of egg, boiled up with ginger, sugar, salt and saffron, kept well and was easy to warm through on a small fire. Umble pie, made from the giblets and other internal organs known as umbles, was good everyday fare. A diary entry for November 1622 tells us that Henry Ferrers, seventeenth-century squire of Baddesley Clinton, 'had to dinner a neck of mutton and potage, a piece of powdered biefe [silverside] and cabbage, a leg of goose broyled, a rabbet, a piece of apple tart, cheese apples and peares'. Not a light meal, perhaps, but one that was entirely produced by stewing and baking.

Strict observance of Lent and fast days meant that enormous quantities of fish were eaten, both grilled and baked in pies. Herring pies were rated as delicacies even by royalty. In the reign of Edward I the town of Yarmouth was bound by ancient charter to send a hundred herrings baked in twenty-four pies annually to the king. Early household account books record epicurean prices paid for morsels of whale, porpoise, grampus and seawolf. 'Puddynge of porpoise' was still being served up in the reign of Henry VIII, and a recipe for it survives in a British Museum manuscript. After the Crusaders discovered the delights of the Orient, much of the food was highly seasoned with imported spices and the espicery became an important household office, superintended by an officer known as an epicier. At what point English cooking became as plain as it is traditionally reputed to have been is not altogether clear: certainly Chaucer's Franklin demanded subtlety from his cook:

> Woe was his cooke but that his saucis were
> Poinant and sharpe and redy all his gere.

Charcoal was very widely used for cooking such sauces, simmering stews, boiling preserves and grilling fish and small cuts of meat. Portable braziers which could be used in the open air of the kitchen court are often mentioned in inventories and illustrated in the margins of manuscripts. Chafing dishes, which could either stand

The simple spit across the typically wide medieval hearth is being rotated by a dog running in the wall-mounted treadwheel. The gun was a standard piece of country domestic equipment, kept dry and conveniently to hand above the mantelpiece.

on a trivet over a grate of charcoal or hold coals and support a pan over them, remained a common cooking accessory for hundreds of years. Moreover, the brick baking oven that was almost invariably set in the wall of the hearth (as at Compton Castle) or close by (as at Cotehele) was used not only to bake bread but to cook pies, cakes and biscuits as it cooled down.

Since the main function of the kitchen was cooking, changing fashions in kitchen fireplaces dictated its development. The use of mineral coal made smaller cooking fires possible. In the early eighteenth century kitchen fireplaces were equipped with cradle grates, stout horizontal iron bars on four legs, fixed to the back of the fireplace by tie bars. These were shallow from back to front, but broad and high, an economical way of presenting the maximum amount of heat to the joints being roasted. Such grates had movable sides (cheeks) which could be adjusted to vary the width of the fire. They were wound in or out by a rack and pinion mechanism. The top bar of the grate sometimes folded down to support pots and kettles, and trivets went legless: they were made to hook on to the cheek of the grate and swing over the flames.

As methods of iron production improved, cast-iron grates began to be produced in large numbers. These had substantial side pieces with hobs at each side under which the fire-cheeks could be wound back. Spit hooks were attached to the sides of these grates, and the spit itself could now be turned by a smoke-jack, a tin-plated set of vanes fixed like a windmill in the chimney. The vanes revolved as hot air rose from the fire, and the motion was transmitted to the spit by a series of gears, chains and pulleys. The faster the fire burnt, the more rapidly the spit was turned and the more perfectly the joint was roasted. Benjamin Franklin once toyed with the idea of applying the considerable surplus energy of the smoke-jack to some practical purpose, as did Charles Babbage (inventor of the first computer in 1834), but the tendency of the vanes to clog with soot discouraged what could have been a promising little exercise in alternative technology. Clockwork turnspit mechanisms became increasingly popular in the late eighteenth century; a heavily geared example is still resplendent over the kitchen range at Speke Hall. Smaller 'bottle-jacks' (so-called because they are bottle-shaped) were more flexible, and several might be hooked on a rail running across the mantel of the hearth.

Iron baking ovens began to replace the traditional clay cloamware or brick baking oven set in the wall of the hearth; they had their own small grate underneath to fire them, and a separate flue. In larger establishments, baking ovens were placed in the neighbouring scullery, as at Shugborough and Charlecote, or in a separate bakehouse as at Erddig.

Built-in charcoal ranges were a feature of eighteenth-century kitchens. They were made the more necessary by the disciplining of the ancient wide hearths into carefully designed brickwork chimney-pieces fitted with iron grates. There was no longer room to make little extra messes at the side of the main fire and so permanent auxiliary hotplates and ovens were required. Set in brickwork, built-in charcoal ranges had square iron frames with a rack of bars a few inches below, a shelf below to catch the ash, and space below that in which to store the charcoal. There is a charcoal range in the Calke Abbey kitchen, and others at Felbrigg and Uppark. Three small circles on an 1840 plan of the Cotehele kitchen suggest a small charcoal range once existed to the right of the baking hearth.

The plan for the marvellously orderly kitchen that Robert Adam designed but never built at Saltram shows a ring of fifteen small circles in the great bay window. The gargantuan basement kitchen at Castle Coole also had charcoal ranges set in the window recesses. This was a sensible precaution. Although the gases given off by charcoal were well nigh invisible, they were known to be noxious: Parson Woodforde mentions his niece Nancy being overcome by giddiness while making jam on a charcoal stove, even though she had kept the kitchen door wide open. It was important to ventilate the kitchen properly when charcoal was being used – another reason for the high ceilings insisted upon by all kitchen designers.

The new kitchen built at Saltram in 1780, although not as grand as it might have been if Robert Adam had been allowed his head, is an attractively proportioned room with high coved ceilings and large sash windows. The temporary shelves and trestle-tables that held plates and pots in the medieval kitchen were replaced by permanent and elegantly joined dressers, with drawers and cupboards below. There was probably a large free-standing charcoal range in the middle of the room where the Leamington kitchener installed in 1885 now stands, for Saltram was a sociable seat, visited by George III when he was in the West Country, and enjoying what Frances Parker's brother, the Revd Thomas Talbot, described in 1811 as 'a pretty constant round of visitors' when the family was in residence.

Talbot's letters to his wife give a revealing account of how the Parkers' eating habits varied according to the presence or absence of guests. The 'secret house' tradition of discreet retrenchment seems to have endured. When only the family was at home, all meals were served in the Blue Bow (now the Chinese Bedroom), part of the first-floor quarters into which the family retreated when alone. 'The Mode of Existence here in the absence of Company,' explained Talbot to his wife, 'is the most remote from show or elegance that can be conceived, the whole lower part of the house is abandoned, the library excepted.' Dinner on such an occasion 'consisted generally of a dish of Fish by itself which is handed about the Table, then a made dish and a small roast, etc and 2 enormous covers of Vegetables, then perhaps a Rabbit and a Tart followed on the cloth by 3 or 4 dishes of fruit, bad port wine and Claret . . . his Lordship performing by a Dumb Waiter the whole Ceremony himself'. Presumably all this food had to be carried over from the kitchen, across the east wing

The spacious kitchen at Dunham Massey, Cheshire, was well ventilated by its high windows. In this photograph of c. 1883 a massive Victorian range has replaced the old open fire, but clockwork spits have been retained. On the left-hand side was a large brick charcoal range, later converted to gas.

and up the stairs by the butler, under-butler and the two footmen who were on the domestic staff at that time.

With company present, there was more formality. Breakfast was served in the morning-room at 10.30 a.m., 'or whenever 8 or so of the party have appear'd'. There was 'an Urn and cistern of black tea at one end – do. of green tea at the other and Coffee at the side – the breakfasts and bread by no means good'. This suggested that Mr Howse the cook had little to do with breakfast; it was probably set out by the housekeeper and the still-room maid. For dinner, all the stops were pulled out, and the dining-room was used: 'the table of an immense width with a plateau full of biscuit figures and vases with flowers etc. the whole length, leaving merely room for a dish at each end and a single row of dishes round with 4 Ice vases with Champagne etc at the corners of it'.

'At Dinner we had nothing less than two Earls and a Turtle,' crowed Talbot in a letter to his wife.

Ld Paulett a most profoundly stupid Lord he seems tho' very good-natured – Ld Mt Edgcumbe was extremely amusing and gave us some very excellent imitations and stories . . . We dined in the great Dining Room and had the very best Exertions of Mr Howse the Cook put forth, which he certainly did to some effect, being pronounced the most accomplished Turtle dresser of the Age, which certainly, from under his hands, and accompanied with ice lime Punch cannot be pronounced a very bad sort of diet.

Dunham Massey was rebuilt in the 1730s as part of the alterations made to the house in the lifetime of the notoriously cantankerous second Earl of Warrington, George Booth. He married the wealthy daughter of a London merchant, Mary Oldbury, but though she brought him £40,000 to rebuild his house with, 'they quarrell'd and lived in the same house as absolute strangers to each other at bed and board'. In 1739 Booth published a treatise on the desirability of divorce for incompatibility of temper. I like to think that, while her opinionated and austere husband stripped the Long Gallery and the Great Hall of all their jolly Tudor details and selected a burr-walnut close stool inlaid with his coronet and monogram for his bedroom closet, Lady Mary (a keen rider to hounds) was having her say in the design of the domestic quarters. She was by all accounts a robust, not to say coarse, lady, and certainly the sense of style with which they are designed is quite unique, combining practical usefulness with an extraordinarily attractive atmosphere.

A gallery across one end of the kitchen allowed an interested mistress to watch the cooks and scullions at their work; as it provided the only access to the maids' bedrooms, it also enabled Cook to police their visitors as she sat beside the dying embers of the range over a late-night mug of mulled negus. As well as high windows, which could be opened to ventilate the kitchen, there are ground-level casements giving out a view both to the lake to the north and on to the kitchen courtyard to the south. Under the northern windows runs a wide wooden work surface with drawers hung underneath it. There is a long deal table in the centre of the room, and much copper, pewter and earthenware. The floor is stone, doubtless once softened at each side of the table by strips of matting. On the east wall are three arches, one for a charcoal range, one leading through to the pastry (see below) and larders, and the third leading to the scullery. Opposite, on the west wall, the huge arch of the main range suggests that there was once a very large roasting hearth, hemmed in with hobs and perhaps ovens and hot closets, but still big enough to roast a whole bullock if necessary. The plan of the house shows a gap beside this range that could have been provision for a supplementary oven and hotplate.

As the kitchen became less dominated by the smoke and smuts from the old huge open hearths, it could become a more comfortable and specialized apartment. Rough tasks were carried out in the maze of small sculleries and odd rooms that nestled in its skirts, and the furnishings grew more elaborate. Erddig, with its well-fitted range of dressers, closets and cupboards, its blue-painted walls and red-tiled floor, is a model early-nineteenth-century kitchen. Three great rusticated arches dominate the west wall: the central one for a roasting range and the right-hand one with a small sink (probably a twentieth-century addition); the left-hand one (now shelved) may have held a charcoal range. The 1834 inventory makes it possible to recreate almost exactly what went on in the kitchen at that date. It appears to have been used as a servant's eating and meeting place, since its furniture included a seventeenth-century refectory table and 'long stools', as well as a George III long-case clock, an eighteenth-century 'hall settle' and some leather bootjacks (used for pulling off boots). There were also:

Three copper fish kettles, three copper preserving pans, two copper pots, two brass skillets, twelve copper moulds, four tin moulds, three copper frying-pans, one dish, twenty-four

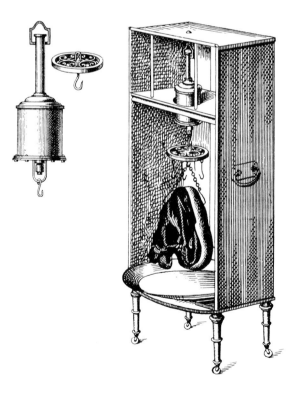

The Dutch oven or 'hastener' reflected heat from the open roasting fire on to the meat. The clockwork bottle-jack unwound slowly, twisting the joint to roast evenly.

copper cups, seven tin ditto, tin pot, twenty-five copper stew pans, grater and two slicers, brassbound bucket, copper fountain, tea kettle, nine bread tins, pair ice moulds, two sieves, twelve block tin dish covers, six pewter water plates, tin pot, still, spice box, dresser and cupboards, beaufet table and five chairs, dripper and hastener, table and tea kettle, cooking table, small do, marble mortar, clock, twine box, three mills, fender and fire irons, earthenware, safe.

Some items may need explanation. The 'beaufet' (buffet) was a stand on which the dessert or any particularly elaborate arrangement of food could be arranged. The 'dripper' was a dripping tray which gathered the fat and meat juices from the joints as they roasted in front of the fire. The hastener, also known as a Dutch oven, was a semicircular screen which was positioned behind the roasting meat, its shiny metal interior reflecting heat on to the joint and so hastening its cooking. The copper fountain was a large water boiler. The brass and copper kitchenware, beloved of housekeepers and cooks, was probably cursed by the maids and scullions who had to keep it polished and bright. The mills were for grinding coffee, nuts and so on.

THE COOK'S ROOM

Kerr declared the cook's room 'a necessary adjunct of the Kitchen when a man cook is kept: it is his official retreat where alone he can reflect upon the mysteries of his art and consult his authorities'. Muthesius described it more pragmatically as 'a little dayroom in which he can do his few reading and writing jobs' (drawing up menus, consulting cookery books, etc.) and emphasized that it was not a bedroom or a sitting-room ('the chef's bedroom is on an upper floor, and he usually joins the upper servants for his meals and free time'). At Calke there is a cook's room of this sort up a small stair above the pastry. The presence of a massive clock mechanism made it useless for sleeping purposes, but it was certainly a convenient place for the cook to withdraw to, with a commanding view of the approach to the back door of the house.

THE PASTRY

A small room adjacent to the kitchen, but well away from the heat of the range, was often arranged as a pastry. Marble slabs for kneading and rolling out the dough might be set into the table itself, or arranged beside a north-facing window. The so-called Cook's Closet at Calke was originally the pastry, but was later fitted out with cupboards as a small store. A more extensive pastry can be seen at Dunham Massey, separated by a thick wall from the kitchen, but open to cool air from the adjacent

In 1910 Waddesdon Manor, Bucks., had a separate kitchen for its pastry chef, seen here with his staff. The gaslight brackets were a great improvement on the oil-lamps which once lit kitchens.

larders. A room on this sort of scale would have been necessary for the exotic creations of seventeenth-century cooks such as Robert May, Sir Kenelm Digby's chef. In later life he blamed the Commonwealth for the decline of culinary innovation and the departure of 'good housekeeping' from England: certainly there are few recent parallels to the little 'diversion' (described by Rose Bradley in her *English Housewife*) which he knocked up for a Twelfth Night supper:

A man-of-war, made of pasteboard, was to be floated in a great charger on a sea of salt in which were to be eggshells full of rose-water. On another large charger was to be a stag made of pasteboard and filled with claret: while on yet a third was to be a pasteboard castle complete with portcullises, gates and drawbridges. The castle and the ship having real trains of gunpowder were to fire at each other while the ladies pelted one another with the eggshells full of rosewater to conceal the smell of the powder. An arrow being withdrawn from the stag, its life-blood in the shape of claret wine would flow freely. On either side of the charger were to be large pies which, if carefully cut [!] would let loose live frogs and live birds respectively, the latter flying at once into the candles and extinguishing the lights. We are told that 'with the flying birds and the skipping frogs, the one above, and other beneath' much pleasure and delight was caused to the whole company.

THE SCULLERY

The scullery was originally the realm of the escullier, or cupbearer, and it was here, rather than in the kitchen itself, that plates, jugs and kitchenware of all sorts were originally kept. The scullery's most important function was washing up and its essential furniture was one or more sinks, so the escullier evidently had to wash up cups as well as to bear them. It was unusual, until the twentieth century, to have a sink of any sort in the kitchen itself. Even in very small dwellings, waterworks were kept strictly separate from the main cooking hearth, and it was a matter of principle to separate the washing of dirty things from the cooking of clean ones.

This was originally a practical measure: the first sinks were basic and leaky, and the floor beneath them was likely to be lethally slippery. Moreover, kitchens with open hearths produced so much dust and heat that anything stored there would have become somewhat grimy. In the small room at the base of the tower which flanks the great kitchen at Compton Castle, there are traces of drains which suggest that it was once a scullery, and at Cotehele a small room with a sink (probably not the original scullery) is tucked away behind the kitchen.

The medieval equivalent to a sink was a wooden bench with tubs on it, or a stone slab set on supports of some kind, hollowed out into a shallow trough with a drain at one end. Tubs would stand in this for washing dishes or clothes; meat and fish could be cleaned in it and knives sharpened on its front edge. Very ancient 'slopstones' of this type survive in many old outhouses, and are often encountered holding alpines in well-tempered gardens. Water might be carried in from a well in the courtyard (as at Chirk Castle) or, as pumping techniques became more sophisticated in the sixteenth century, from a pump just outside the door. Large lead rainwater cisterns fed from roof gutters and drainpipes were part of the ordinary furniture of the kitchen court.

Shallow earthenware sinks began to be mass produced in the Midlands pottery towns after the eighteenth century. But what a sink was made of also depended on the local materials available – slate and granite lasted best; sandstone was kindest to the crockery. Wooden sinks lined with beaten lead or copper were popular though expensive and liable to leaks.

Besides being used for washing up, the scullery was 'the proper place for cleaning and preparing fish, vegetables, etc., and generally for processes in connection with cooking which entail dirt or litter, and should therefore be kept out of the kitchen' (*Our Homes*). Loudon recommended at least two sinks, a board for dirty dishes and plate-rack for drying. 'There might also be a fireplace, a small brick oven and a large oven if the bread be baked there,' he added; 'coppers for heating water for the use of the kitchen maid, dressers and tables, shelves for saucepans, etc.; and it should be well supplied with water.' The floor needed to be easily washable, either stone or tiles, but preferably with a drain at one corner so that it could be swilled down on occasion. If convenient, it should open into the kitchen court so that access could be had to coal, wood and the ash pit. The scullery at Calke has a lead-lined chute through which edible scraps could be thrown into the pigs' mash tub, which was kept outside.

Use of the scullery depended upon the size of the domestic offices as a whole. In a farmhouse like Townend, in which the kitchen was a living-room as well as a place to cook, the scullery, known as the down-house, was used not only for dairy work and laundry but for baking and quite possibly brewing. A similar arrangement was typical of London town houses such as the one lived in by Thomas and Jane Carlyle. There the back kitchen was used for the dirtier tasks, and the front kitchen formed a sitting-room for the maid. Even in a small manor-house like Baddesley Clinton, the scullery was used for a wide range of small tasks. It changed little over the years, and the inventory for 1730 mentions nothing that could not have been there a hundred years before.

> Six copper saucepans and one lid and one tin one
> One pewter colander
> One pewter shaving basin and one pewter porringer
> One tin Dutch oven, one apple roaster; one cheese toaster, one boiler and one tin pudding pan, three frying-pans and one flesh fork.
> One brass frying cover, one tin fish strainer, one plate rack, one dish pail and one chafing dish
> One pail

In a mansion like Dyrham Park, which was rebuilt in the 1690s, the scullery was dignified with the name of 'little kitchen' and kitchen tasks were divided between the two kitchens and a pastry. The 1710 inventory shows that both food preparation and cooking was done in the 'little kitchen', which was in the charge of the 'Skullery House-keeper'. Only a 'copper boiler' and a 'great grate' with a jack and a chimney crane are mentioned in the 'great kitchen'.

Saltram boasts a roomy scullery, built with the new kitchen in the 1780s. Its splendid sinks, one of porcelain, the other of wood with a copper lining hammered over it, probably date from a hundred years or so later on. There are two large coppers, still impressively well-polished, used for boiling vegetables, puddings and hams, with fine tight-fitting copper lids. Hot-water cans are lined up on a shelf, to be filled morning and evening from the hot-water boiler at the back of the kitchen range. A scullery on this scale could be, and evidently often was, used instead of the kitchen when only a small amount of cooking was required, or if the family was absent.

CHAPTER NINE

MRS BEETON'S KITCHEN

The kitchen has the character of a complicated laboratory.

Robert Kerr, *The Gentleman's House*, 1864

The Great Exhibitions of 1851 and 1862 whetted the appetite of thousands of visitors for such potentially revolutionary domestic appliances as gas cookers, food-mincers, washing-machines and dishwashers. But who needed what, and which worked the best? In 1861, arguably the most important date in domestic publishing history, the first edition of Mrs Beeton appeared on the bookstalls. Isabella was only twenty-seven, married to Sam, an enterprising young man who had spotted the need of hundreds of thousands of upwardly mobile 'middling sort of people' for information about the ideal management of their increasingly well-furnished and technologically sophisticated homes.

Sam began a weekly magazine to give such people advice on everything from correct mourning procedures to artistic flower arrangements. Isabella's articles on domestic management were such a success that in 1861 they were printed together as a book – the original *Mrs Beeton's Book of Household Management*. It was an instant bestseller, reprinted and enlarged at regular intervals. Each edition describes the ideal arrangements for a kitchen of the day, and lists the 'kitchen outfits' appropriate to various different sizes of establishments – from 'any mansion' to 'very small houses'. Looked at in succession, they provide a useful rough guide to the general acceptance of such mechanical innovations as the refrigerator or the gas cooker, to say nothing of Mr Spong's tinned-meat mincer or the Frezo! icecream-maker.

It is immediately evident that kitchen design was high on the agenda of the day. The simile used both by Mrs Beeton and the architect Robert Kerr was that of a laboratory, and efficiency was the first consideration. In 1904 Muthesius praised the spaciousness of the kitchen quarters of English houses. 'The continental observer . . . knows the kitchen only from its insignificant status in the continental house and is now confronted by a full-grown domestic organism that amazes him on account not merely of its size but also of its completeness.' He felt, however, that English kitchens usually lacked the 'decorative aspect' prized by German housewives. 'The stress is on the practical instead of on the superficially decorative side.' There was a profound difference between the all-purpose medieval kitchen and this highly specialized and efficient cooking realm. Evidently the kitchen was no longer the heart of the house, but its engine-room.

It is worth bearing in mind that Mrs Beeton's directives were far from universally achieved, and that Muthesius's experience of English architecture was dominated by the completely new houses being built by such architects as Philip Webb, Norman Shaw and their contemporaries. Both glossed over the fact that most houses were modernized piecemeal, if and when their owners could afford to do so. Some, such as Dunster Castle or Lanhydrock, had their domestic quarters totally rebuilt, but others – Canons Ashby, for example – hardly changed at all. It all depended on the state the family intended to keep (if any) and on their personal inclinations. Uppark, once capable of entertaining the Prince of Wales to exotic many-coursed banquets, pulled in its horns domestically at the end of the century, abandoning the extraordinary tunnels to its external pavilions and using a set of basement kitchen offices which were very moderate in extent. The Yorkes of Erddig were similarly conservative, leaving their eighteenth-century domestic quarters almost untouched.

The Victorian kitchen was still ideally a spacious room: 30 × 18 ft was recommended for large houses, for ordinary houses 18 × 20 ft was a suggested minimum. It remained a lofty apartment, often rising through two storeys, so that cooking fumes were less oppressive. Doors were arranged to open with their hinge to the chimney, to avoid disturbing the draught to the fire. High windows are often reviled as evidence of meanness towards servants, but it was received wisdom that kitchens were best lit from above, ideally from a central lantern light, which could also ventilate the room, or else from the north so that heat from the sun would not add to the high temperature produced by the range. No cook stayed long if the kitchen had windows to the west. Muthesius recommended that the range should be situated on the east wall of the kitchen, with light and air entering from the north, because the cook, busy about the stove, generally required light over the left shoulder.

By 1911, improvements in the design of ranges made such precautions less necessary, and Quennell, an innovator with a kindly heart, recommended at least an eastern aspect for the kitchen.

There can be no doubt that this northerly aspect for a kitchen constitutes real cruelty to cooks and deserves the attention of the Humanitarian League. To be condemned to labour in a room into which no gleam of sun shall ever find its way is awful. The kitchen should be planned that some early morning sun can find its way in and give the day's work a cheerful start.

Although the old detached kitchen building lessened both the fire risk and the offensiveness of cooking smells, it was very inconvenient. Planners suggested having the kitchen closer to the dining-room, but with its chimneys and vents arranged separately. If the two rooms were on different floors, a lift was necessary – but care had to be taken 'lest odours should rise up the shaft and conversation sink down'.

Ventilation had to be given careful thought; otherwise, Stevenson warned, 'sickly odours' would find their way all over the house 'notwithstanding all contrivances of closed doors and crooked passages'. It was even more important after the introduction of close ranges with no open chimneys because cooking smells were likely to linger longer. Even the Queen was afflicted. Joshua Bates's diary for 1861 reported an intimate little snatch of conversation between the royal couple and their host during a visit to New Lodge: 'The Queen remarked that you ought to be thankful that in your house you have no smell of dinner, to which Mr van de Weyer observed, it is because I am constantly shutting doors, and so am I, remarked Prince Albert, but I

The kitchen as engine room. The Victorian kitchen at Cragside, Northumberland, faces east and north – an ideal orientation; the lift brings food and dishes up from the scullery on the floor below.

can't prevent it' (quoted by Jill Franklin, in *The Gentleman's Country House and its Plan*, p. 92).

THE KITCHEN RANGE

A major step forward in kitchen fireplace design was the development of the cast-iron range which combined open fire, oven and hot-water boiler. The first patent to combine a kitchen grate with an iron oven was applied for by Thomas Robinson, a London ironmonger, in 1780. Three years later another London ironmonger, Joseph Langmead, improved on Robinson's idea with a grate flanked on one side by an oven and on the other by a boiler for hot water.

The speed with which such ranges spread into general use was remarkable, although they were more quickly adopted in coal-mining districts and in cities than in rural areas. John Farey, writing on Derbyshire in 1813, recorded that 'there is scarce a house without them', and by 1850 even working-class homes of very modest pretensions were equipped with them. In 1845 Jane Loudon recommended

an open grate from four to eight feet wide, having of course a contrivance to make the part intended to contain the fire larger or smaller at pleasure, and the grate should be at least two feet deep, to allow of a boiler behind the fire, communicating with another on the side of the grate, care being taken either to have the boilers fed by a pipe from the cistern, or to fill them every night when the fire is low. It is useful to have an oven on the other side of the grate, not for baking anything, for things never have their proper flavour when cooked in such ovens, but to keep plates and dishes warm.

Poker ovens, which have a long spur of iron running from the hot fireside wall into the centre of the oven, were an early attempt to conduct heat more evenly around the ovens of such ranges, but larger households limited the use of the fireplace oven to plate- and food-warming, and continued to fire a baking oven independently, either using a brick oven in the traditional way with wooden faggots or lighting an independent grate underneath an iron oven built into the wall.

Building a hot-water boiler with a tap at the front into the body of the range left useful space on the hotplates above. Some boilers were filled by pouring water in at the top, but it was better to have cold water piped into the boiler from a cistern controlled by a ballcock. More capacious boilers were developed, the most satisfactory of which was the L-shaped boiler that ran around the back of the fire so that if the fire was made smaller by moving in its movable cheek (generally fitted on the same side as the hot-water boiler), the water would still be heated.

Open ranges of this type, with fires of varying sizes, used a great many trappings of the open hearth – spits, chimney cranes, pot-hooks, trivets and so on. In rural areas, simple ranges of this type remained in use until well into the middle of our own century, and were particularly popular in the 'living-kitchens' of farmhouses and smaller dwellings. At Townend, there is an open range with a chimney crane and a high-level oven at the side, a design typical of the north country.

The 'self-acting' range was a significant improvement on these simple open ranges. It had flues for hot air running from the base of the fire around oven and boiler. These flues could be closed off or opened up by pulling a knob to twist a pivoted iron plate known as a 'damper' across the flue. The dampers could direct hot air to heat either oven or boiler as required, or could be closed completely to increase the heat of the fire itself.

Flues were the clue to the development of what was to become the most common type of Victorian cooking apparatus, the so-called 'close range'. These were not always completely closed: a fire of adjustable size could be seen from the front, and could be used to roast, but it differed from the open range in that all hot air was piped into flues: there was no open chimney above the range at all. The flues, controlled by dampers, directed hot air around the ovens, the hot-water boiler or the hotplate.

The inventor who inspired close ranges is sometimes said to have been the legendary Count Rumford, who certainly understood the principles of heat conduction rather better than most of his contemporaries. 'More fuel is frequently consumed in a kitchen range to boil a tea kettle than with proper management would be sufficient to cook a dinner for fifty men,' he commented in an 'Essay on Heating' written in 1799. Rumford designed ranges with flues running from each separate hotplate up the chimney, but he did not use convected heat to warm ovens, and each hotplate had a separate grate beneath it as well as a separate flue. In fact his heavily insulated stove system was an intelligent improvement on brick-set charcoal stoves rather than a predecessor of the close range. Rumford-style insulation was not followed up seriously until the development of the Aga cooker in the 1920s (below, p. 134).

The first patent for a close range was taken out by George Bodley, an Exeter ironmonger, in 1802. Bodley's range had a small fire with a cover over it, and all the hot air was directed into flues running around the oven and boiler flues. The cover over the fire was a useful hotplate, and Mrs Beeton claimed that the origin of the close range was the Devonian requirements for the slow scalding of clotted cream. Attractive as this idea is, it is an unlikely story and one which ignores the fact that close ranges were far more common in the Midlands than in the West Country. The most successful early maker was William Flavel of Leamington. In the nineteenth century so many firms manufactured iron ranges in the town that the name 'Leamington' became almost synonomous with that of 'kitchener', the snappy name coined by Flavel to indicate the versatility and completeness of his invention.

There is a particularly splendid free-standing Leamington kitchener in the centre of the kitchen at Saltram. It has two very large ovens, for roasting and baking respectively, and a capacious hotplate, approachable from both sides. But such stoves, popular in Germany and other parts of the Continent, were unusual in England, as Muthesius explains:

We infinitely prefer a kitchen stove to be free-standing, at least on two sides; indeed we think the best form is entirely free-standing, accessible from all sides. The English, however, with unshakable obduracy, cling to their practice of wedging it between walls. [They] ... still want to create the impression of a fireside in their kitchens. In the English view the fireplace is the one thing that gives life to the room and makes existence in it tolerable.

By the latter half of the nineteenth century, the close range, set in the hearth with neatly tiled surround and roomy hotplate, was the popular choice for most kitchens. The firebox could be opened or closed, so that it still offered a warm focus for the room. They were made in all shapes and sizes, with up to six ovens and several separate grates. Large kitchens, such as those at Wallington and Shugborough, had two close ranges, set side by side. One would be run at a low heat, and used for heating water, simmering stews and so on, the other could be fired up to roast or bake. At Shugborough, an accomplished and friendly cook bakes scones and other teatime fancies on the kitchen's gleaming close range for the benefit of visitors, and the attraction of the cheerful blaze in its firebox is immediately apparent.

Close stoves have a magnificently competent appearance, but many were imperfectly designed. Although sold on the strength of their supposed economy with fuel, they could actually use more coal than an open range. They were in effect furnaces, burning at a tremendous heat, and careless cooks who left the wrong dampers out could melt fireboxes and crack the boiler. Skilful management was required to make them operate efficiently, and, as the thrifty Mr Lazarus complains in Sabine Baring-Gould's novel of country-house life, *Court Royal* (1886), not many cooks were competent to do so:

[Ranges] are like organs, only to be played upon by one who knows the stops. And where will you find a cook who understands a range? When she wants to bake she pulls out both dampers, one of which is designed to draw the fire away from the oven; and when she wants to boil, she pulls out both dampers, one of which is designed to draw the fire away from the boiler. And when she wants neither to bake or boil she pulls out both dampers, and carries the fire up the chimney, which is just the same as if an organist pulled out stop diapason and hautboy when he wanted pianissimo; and tremolo and dulciano when he wanted forte; and diapason, hautboy, tremolo and dulciano when he wanted nothing in particular.

There were complaints that meat could not be properly roasted in a close range. Whereas baking required a close, medium heat, roasting needed a hot fire, with air

A free-standing Leamington kitchener from the 1880s is the centrepiece of the kitchen at Saltram, Devon. Flues to take away the hot air ran underneath the floor. Saltram retained its old open roasting fire with a smoke-jack turnspit set in the chimney. On the table a fine display of early kitchen implements can be seen.

circulating freely. Houses such as Lanhydrock, Saltram, Charlecote had the best of both worlds, retaining an open fire for roasting and adding a close range as well.

Charcoal ranges were generally removed when these substantial 'kitcheners' were introduced, although kitchens large enough to accommodate them with ease retained them. Others, as S. F. Murphy explains, in *Our Homes*, were converted to gas or steam:

In palatial residences, where the offices for preparing food are necessarily very extensive, there is frequently a series of charcoal stoves, or, if it is the fancy of the *chef de cuisine*, gas stoves, gas either being brought from some public supply, or made on the premises by some of the ingenious modern inventions for the purpose. Then there is the special stove for the immense stockpot which is constantly at work night and day when gas is in use; also the bain-marie pan worked either by fire, gas or steam.

Charlecote, although in outside appearance a Tudor house, boasts very soph-isticated nineteenth-century cooking arrangements. In the main kitchen there is a roomy 'Prize Kitchener', made in Leamington by George William Growes. It has three separate ovens, two for baking and one equipped with a special damper to circulate hot air inside it and so make it suitable for oven roasting. A central fire was normally shielded but could be left open in order to roast small joints.

Next to the kitchener is a classic early-nineteenth-century roasting grate, with a shallow, high fire, two small hobs and an iron ring which could be swung across the fire to support a large pot. A smoke-jack in the chimney operates the spit, and a large dripping tray stands in front of the fire to catch juices from the meat. In front of the dripping tray is a hot cupboard known as a baffle, essential kitchen furniture for large houses with roasting ranges of this type. It is about five feet high and four feet long.

Such a baffle was described as an innovation in the 1847 supplement to Loudon's *Encyclopaedia of Cottage ... and Villa Architecture*. The back is metal, attracting heat from the fire and so keeping warm plates and dishes of food placed inside it from the front. This part of the cupboard, which stays relatively cool, is of polished wood, with sliding doors and smart brass knobs. Each end of the cupboard is insulated, and has a handle attached to it. The whole cupboard is on castors, and when it had fulfilled the useful purpose of protecting the kitchen staff from the heat of the roasting fire it could be pushed along the corridors to the servery. Similar but considerably larger cupboards can be seen at Kedleston and Lanhydrock, and I glimpsed a smaller one tucked away in the flower-arranging cupboard at Mount Stewart, County Down.

Backing on to the roasting grate, in the neighbouring scullery, is another close range with two ovens, and an iron-lined bricked-in bread oven. Water boiled in the

At Lanhydrock, Cornwall, the menu book was written out daily in French until the early 1960s, and menus were placed on the dining table.

back boilers of the ranges was stored in a tank over the door between the kitchen and the scullery. Steam was also led along pipes to the interesting apparatus at the south end of the kitchen. This is a set of lead-lined cupboards heated by steam-filled pipes, one of which ran just under the work surface and was connected to several small outlets in order to provide heat to bain-maries and fish-kettles. Set into the left-hand side of the apparatus was a shallow steel tray, edged with brass, and heated from below in which fish and other food requiring gentle poaching could be simmered. Cooking by steam in this way is mentioned by Loudon as early as 1833.

Lanhydrock, another kitchen with every possible contemporary convenience, has domestic quarters which seem to have been modelled almost exactly on Kerr's principles. Its kitchen is correspondingly businesslike, hygienically tiled and dominated by its technology. It remained in use for eighty years – right up until the end of the family's occupation – and the menu book was written out daily in French by the Hon. Everilda Agar-Robartes, who took over the supervision of the house on her mother's death in 1921.

The Robartes evidently put more emphasis on the roast beef of old England than on fussing about with sauces and sole. There is a fairly modest closed kitchener against the south wall of the kitchen, and a supplementary range for cooking vegetables in the scullery, but the main feature of the room is the spectacular roasting range on the west wall. The jack, operated by a fan in the chimney, has gearing which cannot only turn several horizontal spits at once but can also twist chains from which smaller joints can be hung. There is also a rail for clockwork bottle-jacks.

The roof sports high wooden trusses, in the style of a college hall, with clerestory windows which opened by an interesting system of shafts and gearings connected to handwheels on the end wall. These, and the long windows high in the north wall, make the room very light and airy, although allowing no outlook at eye level for the kitchen maids. Louvres in the wall above the immense roasting fire are connected by a flue to the chimney-stack to lessen the hot air and fumes. In another alcove to the left of the roasting range piped hot water was available at the turn of a tap – with a convenient low shelf underneath on which saucepans or basins could be supported as they were filled.

Lanhydrock has a model Victorian scullery. There is a small close range for the stockpot and for supplementary cooking: boiling vegetables and puddings. The slate sink was used for preparing vegetables and, with the addition of a wooden tub, for washing the kitchen crockery – the china and glass used by the family was dealt with in the butler's pantry and the still-room. Greasy pots could be held under steam jets on the iron draining-board in the corner. There is a coal chest to the left of the range, and a tub for sawdust, which was thrown down on the floor to absorb splashes from the sink, and then swept up. There are roomy plate-racks, and plenty of space to store small kitchen utensils.

GAS AND ELECTRIC STOVES

The introduction of first gas and then electric cooking stoves did not immediately alter the layout of kitchens, but it heralded the end of an era. In the long run it was the compactness, cleanliness and reliability of these stores which made it possible to reduce the size of kitchens, and adapt serveries, butler's pantries or sculleries to the much reduced culinary needs of small twentieth-century families with few if any domestic staff.

Gas ranges began to replace solid fuel in the 1890s. Gas had been used for cooking much earlier than this. James Sharp's wood-encased stove was illustrated on the front page of *The Expositor*, the weekly newspaper produced at the time of the 1851 Great Exhibition in Hyde Park. It has a ring of burners inside, and a permanent water boiler on top. Saucepans, steamers and kettles were heated by small burners set in what appears to be a wooden top. Sharp gave lectures on 'Gas-tronomy' all over the country, but it was many years before fears of explosion subsided and the idea of cooking by gas became acceptable.

Because of the problems of supply, gas stoves were more common in cities than in country areas, but large country houses with their own gas-making plants could install one of the great Cordon Bleu kitcheners designed by the pioneer of gas cooking and lighting, William Sugg. This easily coped with a dinner for twenty people or more. It had a roasting oven with a clockwork turnspit inside, and a double-walled baking oven with sliding shelves. The top had four burners and a grill, with a pilot-light at each outlet. These represented, Sugg explained, 'a great saving of labour and matches, at the cost of a mere penny a day'. They also reduced the danger of explosion, 'which, if it does nothing worse, considerably destroys the equanimity of the cook'.

Dunham Massey installed a private gas-making system in the 1880s and a photograph of the kitchen in 1883 shows a large close range flanked by hot closets and an auxiliary gas stove. The charcoal range on the other side of the kitchen was converted to gas by Jeakes and Co., who also installed the gas-heated hot cupboards in the servery built in 1905.

Dunham Massey still has two smallish gas stoves, one black beauty dating from the 1900s and another enamelled in grey and white from the 1930s. Its close range was replaced in 1929 by the logical next step in the country-house cooking hierarchy, one of the earliest and largest of Aga cookers. The Aga was designed in the early 1920s by a Swedish scientist, Gustav Dalen, who was blinded in a laboratory accident

Gas burners such as these were invented in the 1870s, although (not unfounded) fears of explosions prevented their general adoption until supplies of gas were purified and improved.

and so confined to his own home. He began to reflect on the time and energy wasted in cooking, and designed his superbly efficient stove to save on both.

Thickly insulated, in a manner reminiscent of the early experiments of Count Rumford, the Aga has two ovens heated by coke from an internal firebox. One is very hot, one always cool. There are no convection currents to cause heat loss. The hot oven and hotplate are heated by radiant heat from the firebox itself; the cool oven and warmplate by conduction. Economical in use, the Aga could also be kept in all night, and used to keep a large tank of water constantly hot.

The Dunham Massey Aga is a very unusual one, a caterer's range, almost three times as large as the common two-oven model. It has three very large twin-doored ovens, two huge hotplates, a central simmering plate and plenty of space at the sides for keeping pans warm. More commonly seen are the four-oven Agas such as those at Hardwick and Felbrigg.

Electric cookers were slower to catch on. Rookes Bell Crompton should probably be given credit for making the first viable electrical cooking apparatus in Britain. It took a Crompton saucepan eighteen minutes to boil a pint of water at a cost of just over a farthing. Although enthusiastic exhibitions of 'cookery by Trained Lightning' took place in the 1890s, electricity was not mentioned by Mrs Beeton until 1907, when she declared electric stoves 'quite practicable, if decidedly expensive'. Power was taken from the electric lighting mains, and the current passed through wires coiled on iron or steel plates and embedded in enamel in the sides of ovens and under hotplates and corrugated grills. Saucepans and kettles were heated separately. Mrs Beeton praised its cleanliness and predicted 'rapid development'.

The first electric stoves had a magnificently solid appearance, with gleaming brass switches, swirling metal cables leading from white enamel fuse-boxes into the nether regions of the stove, and red indicator lights. The latter were evidently necessary for servants set in old ways. Adam Gowans Whyte (*The All-Electric Age*, 1922) deplored the 'inertia of the domestic mind' and the 'outrageous misuse of electrical cooking apparatus when the cook is in the habit of switching everything on full to warm the kitchen'.

The well-known Belling company was set up by an ex-Crompton's technician in 1912, and in 1919 its first purpose-built cooker, the Modernette, appeared. Electric cookers increased rapidly in popularity in the 1920s as electricity networks spread all over the country. Although they were better insulated and thermostatically controlled, the early cookers could not compete with the economy, convenience and speed of gas.

However, in the end, of course, it was to be electrification, not just of cookers but of food processors, washing-machines, refrigerators and dishwashers, that transformed the kitchen from the hub of a busy network of household offices to the one-room omnium gatherum that it is today.

FOOD PREPARATION

The inventories already given of the pre-nineteenth-century *batterie de cuisine* list simple, often handmade utensils: lemon squeezers, rolling-pins, wooden and bone spoons, iron ladles and egg whisks. The most vital weapons in the cook's armoury, then as now, were the knives, highly personal tools, honed to a razor-edge on a special stone made of carborundum, or merely wiped briskly across the doorstep or slopstone. They ranged from mighty carving knives to delicate filleters. French chopping knives were specially strong; mincing knives had a firm wooden handle along the blade, to make chopping meat finely for mince easier.

By the time Mrs Beeton was in print, this simple armoury was being supplemented by hundreds of specialized gadgets calculated to make the housewife's life easier. One thing they had in common was the handle that turned them. 'Year by year domestic inventions of every kind are increasing,' declared an article in the *Journal of Domestic Appliances* in 1882:

No matter whether we desire to clean knives or make stockings, peel potatoes, black shoes, make butter, wash clothes, stitch dresses, shell peas or even make our bread, all we have to do is turn a handle ... This is a regular handle-turning age, and we may soon expect to wash and dress ourselves, clean the windows, scrub the floors, lay the table, make our beds, and do every household operation through the same medium. We shall then only require a handle to appease a stormy wife, quiet a screaming baby, and pay the tax collector, and our domestic happiness will have reached perfection.

The hardest part of food preparation was the business of pounding, mashing and grinding. Originally this was done with the pestle and mortar, the most ancient and universal item of culinary equipment. Besides being used for grinding spices, rice or sugar, it could be used for reducing meat to paste or bones to meal. The bigger the pestle, the quicker the job, particularly when its handle was braced in an overhead ring, as at Cotehele and Castle Drogo.

The first machine to alleviate this task was the mincer, through which almost anything could be passed. A special nozzle could convert it into a sausage-maker; changing the internal blades could vary the texture of the substances minced. The largest (definitely for 'any mansion') could cut up 57 lb of meat in twenty-five minutes. The smallest, fitted with a hot-water compartment to keep the contents hot, and known as a 'dinner-mincer' or 'food masticator', was actually screwed on to the dining-table, 'to assist digestion, loss of teeth, etc.'.

The most successful manufacturer of these machines was the London firm of Spong and Company, who were still in business in the 1980s. The 1893 edition of Mrs Beeton recommended the Enterprise Tinned Meat Chopper: 'When cut, the meat is forced out in a perfect cascade of shreds.' Enterprise, an American company, were as enterprising as their name. Their catalogue provided a magnificent summary of the variations on the handle-turning theme, offering beef-shavers, fruit-presses,

Pastry cutters, tin-lined lead moulds, pestle and mortar, colander and assorted ladles were part of the early-nineteenth-century Saltram *batterie de cuisine.*

137

sausage-stuffers, graters, lawn-sprinklers, tongue-pressers, ice-shredders, apple-peelers, -corers and -slicers, coffee-mills, bone-mills, cork-pullers, vegetable-slicers, barrel-jacks, meat-juice extractors, potato-chip cutters and raisin-seeders.

The machine that was to sweep this wonderfully various, but probably nightmarishly cumbersome equipment away at a stroke was the electric food mixer. The earliest I have come across, at the London Science Museum, is an American machine made in 1918 by Landers, Fray and Clark. In 1931, *Ideal Home* featured a machine which 'automatically deals with practically every aspect of the preparation of food'. As well as mixing flour, milk, eggs and dough, it had a chopper attachment to cut up meat, vegetables and fruit. The original Kenwood Chef was introduced in the 1950s, and is still stalwartly thumping away in many kitchens of the 1990s. Whether its lightweight successor, the 'electronic' food processor, will do as well remains to be seen.

THE DISHWASHER

What about that modern saviour of the housewife's sanity, the dishwasher? When household labour costs were low, nobody bothered much about inventing it. The first patent I have discovered, entered in the United States in 1865, was pretty basic. It described a metal cupboard which was to be placed on the draining-board of the sink, and filled from the tap by a pipe. The door was sealed with gutta-percha strips, and metal blades turned by a hand crank forced water against plates stacked at angles in a wire frame. In 1880, Benjamin Howe was making very ambitious claims for an almost identical machine. It 'completes operations in five minutes', he declared, and could be made of 'any size, form or material, to hold from 50 to 1,000 dishes if desired'.

Such machines evidently didn't impress the average houswife much. Hand-cranking was hard work, nor was the randomly sloshing water particularly efficient at cleaning. Hotels and restaurants had more incentive to experiment. In 1885, one of the largest restaurants in Paris was using a spectacular machine, invented by Eugene Daquin. Its large circular tank had two compartments, one for hot and one for cold running water. Eight artificial hands gripped the plates and revolved around a central shaft, driven by a belt attached to a steam engine. After passing through the hot bath 'with an undulating movement' to wash off the grease, the dishes were vigorously brushed by two rotating brushes and dripped into the cold tub. Finally they were removed – by human hands – and placed in a draining rack to dry. 'The use of the machine constitutes no danger whatsoever to either man or dish,' reported *Scientific American* approvingly. The application of electricity made dishwashers much more

The earliest dishwashers were simple metal cabinets with wooden paddles which dashed soapy water against the plates as the handle was turned. This machine was invented by Benjamin Howe, c. 1880.

efficient. In 1906, *La Nature* magazine showed an electrically powered machine of fascinating complexity, again for restaurant use. Wire baskets rolled round an overhead track to plunge into the tubs and out again.

There have been disappointingly few female inventors of domestic appliances, but in the 1890s a Mrs Cockran of Indiana invented a dishwasher which heralded the floor-level models we use today. It was evidently inspired by contemporary washing-machines, and consisted of a wooden tub with a hand-cranked set of plungers to force water over the dishes. It had to be filled by hand and drained by a stopcock, but had some success, particularly when fitted with a small electric motor.

In the 1920s Randall Phillips, an enthusiast for single-handed domestic efficiency, reviewed the household scene a little despondently. 'Many washing-up machines have been devised, but the difficulties of working on a small scale are generally insuperable.' He hoped that the 'Polliwashup' would solve the problem. Water was added from a boiling kettle, a tablet of soap used to make a lather, then a handle was turned six times in each direction.

In 1923 a *House and Garden* article on 'Overcoming the Drudgery of the Dishcloth' spoke more encouragingly about dish-washing machines, although it warned against 'those machines of doubtful value beyond the fascination of their clever machinery, which is more likely to appeal to the man who may have mended them than the women who must cope with their intricacies'. It illustrated what was available. The simplest was just a short length of hose fastened to the hot tap, with a spray nozzle at the end. This contained a soap dispenser, controlled by a thumb lever, so that the user could direct hot water, first soapy, then clear, over the dishes. It was hardly a machine, but at least one could see what was happening.

The only trace of an early 'dishwasher' I found on my explorations of National Trust kitchens was (predictably) at Cragside. Between the kitchen and the china closet at Cragside, there is an interesting metal cupboard with plate-racks in it and a mysterious pipe protruding into its base. It may merely have been a drying closet, but it is possible that a length of hose attached to the taps of the sink could have been used to spray the dishes clean, and that hot air was then directed into the cupboard.

The Blick was described as 'one of the simplest and best of the hand-cranked machines'. The dishes were stacked above the water and sprayed by a central propeller. An electric machine, available from Harrods (of course) was filled from a kettle, and could be converted into a small table when its lid was closed. An extremely sensible feature of these early dishwashers was spare plate-racks, which could be slid out of the washer and mounted on a convenient trolley when full of clean plates, so dispensing with the need to unload the dishwasher.

Electric power was undoubtedly an improvement on hand-cranking, but it wasn't enough to make a successful machine. Ruth Binnie and Julia E. Boxall dismissed the diswasher tersely in their 1926 manual, *Housecraft*, as 'a useless investment'. In his 1928 *How to Plan Your Home*, Martin Briggs advised that the 'bogy of washing-up' was 'more likely to be dispelled by increased simplicity in the nature of our meals than by any mechanical invention applicable to the needs of small homes'.

The 1930s saw some improvements, but more white elephants. One machine was actually built into a mammoth porcelain double-sink unit, with a neatly mounted electric motor underneath. The first squared-off body with single-knob control appeared in 1932, ancestor of the sleekly dignified Kenwood machine of the 1960s, with its flush-fitting lid and convenient chrome towel rail.

Dishwashers were still so much of a suspect luxury that they did not appear in American mail-order catalogues until the 1950s, and by 1951 only one million had been sold in the United States. It was not until the 1970s that the numerous problems associated with dishwashers were reduced enough to make them a generally popular appliance. Now specially developed detergents, salts and rinsing aids, and automatic programming make them efficient enough to be increasingly popular.

THE LAST GREAT KITCHEN

Nikolas Pevsner once offered a memorable distinction between buildings and architecture: 'A bicycle shed is a building, a cathedral is architecture.' Although most kitchens would not claim to be more than buildings, the kitchen created at Castle Drogo by that king of domestic architects, Edwin Lutyens, is undoubtedly architecture. High-ceilinged kitchen, spacious scullery and elegantly octagonal larder follow each other in a rhythm of naked granite facings and arches set in arches. Lutyens was a domestic romantic, as letters to his wife-to-be envisaging the humbler aspects of their London life reveal. He rhapsodized of simple oak tables, linen presses,

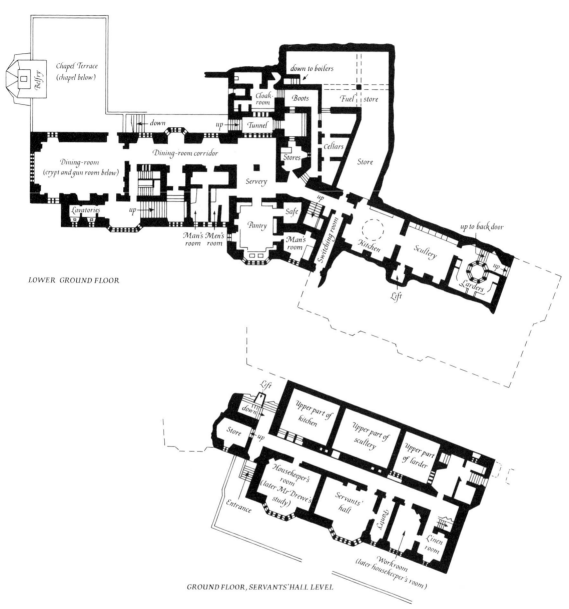

Castle Drogo, Devon: floor plan of the lower ground floor and ground floor, servants' hall level.

brass candlesticks and 'the kitchen, where the pots and range glisten in the light, where the cheery cook turns mountains into molehills and frugal fare into a feast. The bread pan with his father oven open and shut in busy intercourse, the larder restocked from

Inspecting the site of Castle Drogo: Julius Drewe, Sir Edwin Lutyens and John Walker (Mr Drewe's agent).

Smithfield Mart, and the wood washed bins filled with clean fresh vegetables from Covent Garden.'

At Drogo, the vegetables came from the estate's own kitchen garden, left each morning in a specially designed wooden rack beside the back door. Next to this was the larder, arranged in different compartments around a small cupola which provided light without direct sunshine. The adjacent scullery has three stout oak-framed sinks of different sizes, three plate-racks and an octagonal chopping block made out of a solid tree trunk – octagonal shapes are the theme of the kitchen quarters. All these, as well as the nobly proportioned pestle and mortar, were made to Lutyens's specification. The room is lit by lunette windows which open into an internal court not seen from the outside of the castle. In one corner there is a large ice-box. Another range was originally fitted in the recess where a wood-burning stove stands today. Beside it is a service lift to transport food both to the servants' hall immediately above, and to the nurseries two floors above that. The dining-room, however, was on the other side of the kitchen, along a long corridor but at least on the same floor.

In the kitchen proper, a circular beech table reflects the shape of the ceiling cupola, constructed to give the kitchen the height and ventilation traditionally required. It was also the only source of light. Mrs Drewe thought it insufficient 'and suggested that a glint of sun should somehow be contrived. Lutyens disagreed, unwilling no doubt to upset the symmetry of his design. Distemper, he argued, was enough, and, as so often, his views prevailed' (National Trust guide to Castle Drogo).

Pastry and chopping boards were given rounded outer edges to fit the table's edge, and all the kitchen fittings show the attention to detail and common sense that is a hallmark of Lutyens's domestic work. Side-tables are thick-topped and rock solid; their legs are braced with horizontal bars and their drawers slide effortlessly. Carved flourishes finish off the plate-racks, and the panels of the dresser doors are elegantly bevelled. Gleaming copper pans, creamware jugs and white storage jars stand in orderly ranks on the shelves.

This kitchen was used for barely thirty years. Its heyday was in the 1930s, when it was presided over by Mrs Rayner, a cook of some renown. During the war, Castle Drogo was run as a baby home by Mrs Drewe, and in 1945 the two coal ranges in the kitchen were replaced by Aga cookers. In 1960 a new kitchen was constructed on the floor above, and the basement servants' quarters fell into disuse. When the Trust took over, they used the catalogues that had survived from the time the original stoves were ordered to confirm that the two replacement ranges were appropriate.

Drogo was the last of a great line of kitchens. Electricity, the disappearance of domestic staff, and commercial food preparation put an end to the kitchen as the nineteenth century knew it. 'The modern housewife is no longer a cook, she is a can-opener,' wrote Christine Frederick, a prophet of the new age, in 1929. Larders shrank into refrigerators, sculleries to dish-washing machines and copper *batteries de cuisine* into a set of Teflon-coated pans. The lofty kitchens fell cold.

CHAPTER TEN

LIGHT AND HEAT

Electricity meant to the household what the wheel meant
to moving loads.

Siegfried Giedion, *Mechanization Takes Command*, 1949

LIGHT

It is startling to realize that staying up after dark was once a rare event. We are beginning to discover the social implications of longer life spans in the twentieth century, but we have perhaps not yet taken to heart the impetus given by artificially extended day spans to the development of our present inclination to privacy and individually lived lives. The old pattern of working by daylight, gathering around the fire in the evening, and then cuddling up into bed together for warmth was profoundly altered after first cheap candles, then gaslights and finally electric lighting made it possible for everyone to go their own ways all night as well as all day. Electric light was considered in some detail in S. F. Murphy's *Our Homes*, published only two years after the first domestic lights went up in the homes of Lord Kelvin in Glasgow and Sir William Armstrong at Cragside in 1881. The account is a striking reminder of how novel, and suspect, the business of artificial lighting was only a hundred years ago. The writer considers the possibilities of general eyestrain, specific damage to the retina and the unhealthiness of the overheated atmosphere then inseparable from artificial light. Electric light had 'chemical and sanitary' advantages, he conceded, but warned that since plants evidently grew faster 'without their nightly rest' under artificial light, 'continuous exposure to so potent a chemical agent might be expected, in homely terms, to "force the pace" of living' for humans and animals, 'and thus tend to the premature exhaustion of life'. Reactionary rubbish, or a potential explanation for the hyperactivity and neurosis that keeps those newly fashionable occupational groups, psychiatrists and psychotherapists so busy these days? Who knows?

*George Bernard Shaw sitting in the firelight
in his oddly suburban little country house,
Shaw's Corner, in Hertfordshire.*

CANDLES

Rushlights were the simplest form of candle, made by soaking a peeled rush in melted fat. The common soft rush, *Juncus effusus*, was used, at its best if collected in later summer when it was tall but still green. All the peel except for one supporting strip was removed. The reeds, which were about eighteen inches long, were then slowly drawn through a wide shallow pan called a grisset which stood on its own legs above the warm ashes of the fire, filled with melted fat. When completely soaked, they were put out to dry on long pieces of bark, which could be used as crude containers to store them in.

Rushlights were burnt in specially made holders with jaws which gripped the rush about an inch and a half below the end. In country areas they remained in use well into the nineteenth and even twentieth centuries. Rushlight holders can be seen in the hall at Townend and among the extraordinary collection of everyday items at Snowshill Manor: at Moseley Old Hall they are actually lit for parties of visiting schoolchildren. On average a rushlight would burn for fifteen to twenty minutes, but they required constant attention as at regular intervals the rush had to be drawn up through the holder. They were impressively cheap. Gilbert White (*Natural History of Selborne*, 1775) calculated that five hours' worth of light could be produced for less than a farthing. A halfpenny candle, by contrast, lasted only two hours. But rushlights required not only a local supply of rushes but a surplus of fat in the kitchen. In times of hardship, when families ate no meat, they had to rely on candlelight.

Candle-making was such a messy and smelly job that except in the most remote rural areas it was a trade rather than a domestic duty. Chandlers supplied tallow candles in small towns, using beef and mutton fat supplied by the local slaughterhouse; occasionally a farmer might specialize in supplying the neighbourhood. Castle Coole in County Fermanagh has a tallow house (now the ticket office) where the thousands of lights required annually for the vast mansion's extensive servants' quarters were once made.

The tallow was made by boiling up the animal fat in order to separate it from cellular membrane. Wicks were cut from skeins of spun cotton, and then hung over a long rod called a broach. This was lowered into a tub of melted tallow, raised and left to harden, and then re-immersed again and again until the candles were thick enough. Dipping frames, invented in the eighteenth century, made this process less laborious, and machines which slowly revolved with the broaches, keeping them in an upright position, were developed in the nineteenth century.

Moulded candles were being made in France in the fifteenth century, and by the seventeenth century candle moulds were regularly mentioned in English inventories. They used a better quality of tallow, and gave a superior light with less spluttering and smoking. Tallow candles had to be carefully stored, as they went rotten if left in the open air for too long. Cylindrical tin boxes which hung on the wall (out of reach of rats) were used for storage; larger quantities might be buried in tubs of bran.

Beeswax candles were generally used in churches, and by anyone who could afford them. They were far superior to tallow candles, burning with a brighter flame, less smoke and an infinitely pleasanter smell. The wax was melted and strained, then left in long strips in the sun to bleach. A hoop of hanging wicks was suspended over a tub of hot wax, and the wax was poured down the hanging wicks with a ladle. While the wax was still soft, the candles could be rolled to form smooth cylinders, using a hardwood roller, kept damp to prevent the wax sticking.

In the early eighteenth century, spermaceti – an oil taken from the head of sperm whales – was used to make excellent candles which burnt with a bright white flame. They were not much cheaper than wax candles, however. In the 1820s a French chemist called Michel Chevreul analysed tallow and separated it into its component parts of glycerine, stearic acid and oleic acid. He discovered that much better candles could be made by using only the stearine in the tallow. Once a cheap way of producing stearine from vegetable oils was developed (by James Soames in 1829) the way was opened for cheap candlelight. Two tallow merchants bought Soames's patent in 1830 and set up the Price candle company, which was soon to become a domestic byword (and is still in existence). E. Price and Company introduced a new 'snuffless' candle to celebrate Queen Victoria's wedding to Prince Albert in 1840. This had the now-familiar plaited wick, which curls outwards to the edge of the flame so that the ash falls off or is oxidized and the wick does not need to be trimmed with candle scissors, a tedious business but once necessary to keep candles burning brightly. The tax on candles was removed in 1831, and large factories were set up to make the millions of candles required for the round-the-clock working demanded by the industrial revolution. Price's had two London factories, at Vauxhall and Battersea, connected by barge transport down the Thames. They also had coconut palm plantations in Ceylon and were producing a hundred tons of candles a week in 1851, valued at £7,000. In 1857 the first paraffin candles were marketed. Cheap, and offering as bright a light as spermaceti, they were in general use by 1900. But by this time oil-lamps and gaslighting were reducing the demand for candles. Consumption in Britain peaked at 45,000 tons per annum in 1916, and had fallen to 7,000 in 1959.

OIL LIGHTS

The simplest oil-lamps were shallow dishes with a lip on which lay a wick made from rush or twined cotton. The most basic, known as cressets, were merely hollowed-out stones – there are some interesting early examples of these in the kitchen courtyard at Cotehele. Metal lamps, often set on an adjustable stand, were called betty lamps or crusies. A sophistication was a closed metal reservoir with a device to grip a wick upright, and a small handle which could wind up the wick as it burnt away. Animal and vegetable oils were used – colza oil (from rape seed), palm oil and olive oil – but such lamps gave no more light than a single candle.

In 1784 a Frenchman, Ami Argand, invented the first major improvement in lighting, a tubular wick enclosed in a brass cylinder, which improved combustion so much that a single wick could offer ten candlepower of light. A glass chimney protected the flame, and a rack and pinion mechanism raised and lowered the wick. A large oil reservoir was arranged above the wick, so that the thirsty wick could be gravity fed and so burn for several hours without attention. There is a fine Argand reading lamp on the table of the butler's pantry at Uppark. An improvement on this was the French Carcel lamp, developed in 1800, which had a spring pump to supply fuel under pressure from a reservoir below the wick. In 1836 the Moderator was developed, an exceptionally popular style of lamp which had a short length of wire in the central tube to the burner which slowed down the initial flow of oil, but allowed it to speed up as the force of the spring lessened. Both these types of lamp can be recognized by the key necessary to wind them up.

A letter written by Humphry Repton to Sir Harry Featherstonhaugh in 1812 about the lighting for the dining-room at Uppark makes clear both the disadvantages of early lamps and how much thought was put into designing lights to suit their particular settings. Repton had been visiting a London lamp-maker who was evidently the Christopher Wray of the day.

I went first to Hancocks, where I saw nothing but the old dish pendant with two burners betwixt a wire reservoir & the same with one burner is unsymmetrical – (anglice lop sided) – & these are all from 12 to 16 gns each – then I went to (I forget his name) in Bond Street, the grand Luminary (again anglice lamp man) of the Nation – He supplies Uppark with oil – the same kind of lamps I found from 8 to 12 gns. Why this difference between tradesmen – I believe 'em all rogues alike and only differing in the more or the less. Here I saw a kind of lamp with its reservoir under the burner and consequently avoiding the Clumsy vase or Urn above. But when lighted – I found an insuperable objection in the shadow cast from the opake reservoir – this was attempted to be removed by a glass reservoir – but then we see the oil. I then went to an ingenious Lamponist not a Lampoonist . . . I had much conversation and it ended in his convincing me that oil could not be burnt without a reservoir, and that it must be visible and opake and in fact an ugly nuisance. He thought a large wax candle in an openwork socket and spring to keep the flame at a given height would admit of a new design for which I have given him a sketch

Whale oil began to be used extensively in oil-lamps towards the end of the eighteenth century. Sperm oil was the best quality, but was expensive. In the early nineteenth century whale-hunting was on such a scale that the species would probably have been made extinct had not an alternative source of fuel been discovered in 1859 in Pennsylvania: mineral oil, or petroleum. The distillation from mineral oil used in lamps was known as kerosene in the United States and paraffin in Europe. It was very light in weight, and so the cumbersome mechanism of the early oil-lamps was no longer necessary. The flame was practically smokeless and the light clear and bright.

The best-known burner was the Duplex, invented by Hinks in 1865. It had two parallel wicks, with a current of air between them to increase their lighting power; it is still being made today. Paraffin lamps were made in every possible form – elaborate chandeliers for reception rooms, functional 'harp' lamps for kitchens, and tiny pressed tin lamps for servants' quarters and dark passages.

During daylight, oil-lamps were kept in a lamp room, partly because there was a danger they might be knocked over, causing their highly inflammable fuel to leak, partly because they needed to be cleaned out. The smell of lamp oil was so unpleasant that Stevenson suggested a lamp room outside the house, next to the coal cellar perhaps, with a shelf in a window on which to trim the lamps, and storage shelves on the walls to hold them during the day. There was also apparently a risk that uneven expansion in sunlight might cause the glass chimneys to crack. A lamp room survives at Calke because electricity was not introduced there until 1962, and even then only in the principal rooms. When the Duchess of Devonshire visited the house in the mid sixties she remembers it glowing with light from hundreds of candles.

The fuel reservoir of lamps that burned whale oil or colza oil had to be carefully washed out with hot water and dried before being refilled, using a funnel. Room had to be left in the reservoir to allow for the inevitable expansion of the oil when the lamp was taken from the chilly lamp room to the living-rooms of the house, otherwise leaking was inevitable. The wick might need changing or trimming. One wrinkle suggested by Samuel and Sarah Adams was to soak the wick in vinegar and dry it before use – this apparently reduced the chances of it smoking. Any brasswork was rubbed up with oil and rottenstone (decomposed limestone) or coarse corundum (emery powder). Lacquered lamps were cleaned with a dilute solution of soap and water; bronze and enamel with oil and a soft flannel. Glass chimneys were polished with a soft cloth, and cleaned inside with a wash-leather pad mounted on a stick. There is a good display of lamp-cleaning equipment in the servants' hall at Castle Ward.

Lady Maud Baillie, eldest daughter of the 9th Duke and Duchess of Devonshire, was born in 1896 and remembered many details of her early life at Hardwick Hall. 'There was no gas or electricity, and the darkness of the rooms, lit by only a very small lamp or a candle, was terrifying.' Among the manservants was an 'Odd Man', and one of his most important duties was the collection and distribution of oil-lamps. He carried them round the house on trays, fourteen at a time, making sure that there was at least one in every room of the house which was in use. In his autobiography, *From Hall-boy to House-Steward*, William Lanceley commented that dusk was 'sharp work for the servants, who must not take the lamps in too early or leave the rooms in darkness'.

GASLIGHTING

Experiments with gaslights began in the eighteenth century. George Dixon, a Durham collier, illuminated his house by gas in 1780. Gas was produced by heating coals in a tea kettle on the fire, and ran around a system of pipes contrived from the stems of clay tobacco pipes joined together with clay and pierced with holes at intervals. William Murdoch arranged a similar system, but stopped the head of the pipe with a thimble pierced with holes. With his partner, Samuel Clegg, Murdoch pioneered the use of gas for industrial lighting. Burners were placed outside factory windows, a nice echo of daylight, but mainly because the heat they produced would have made working conditions unpleasant. Twenty-six miles of gas pipe had been laid in Westminster by 1816, some of it improvised from the barrels of surplus ordnance from the Napoleonic wars. Staff in the Mansion House worked by the light of 2,062 burners in 1825, but in the Lord Mayor's parlour itself candles were preferred to the heat and smell of gas.

As purifying techniques improved and pressure governors for burners were devised, the use of gas in the home became more attractive. Dunham Massey had a private gasworks on the estate. Gas was introduced to Blickling in 1857; in 1864, Sir Arthur Elton wrote proudly in his *New Handbook of Clevedon*:

There is, however, one feature not consistent with a genuine English village. Gas lamps peep forth here and there amongst the trees and hedgerows. But then gas lamps are associated with increased comfort and safety, advantages, after all, that must not be foregone for the sake of the picturesque. Besides, wait until nightfall and you will admit that gas lamps are not merely useful, but ornamental. The dark valley sparkles with scattered lights and assumes a beauty of another kind.

The family-run gasworks provided gas for the neighbouring towns and villages as well as for the house itself, and gas lingered on at Clevedon Court well into the twentieth century. Sir Ambrose Elton protected his interests as director of Clevedon Gas Company by refusing to install electricity in houses. His apartments were lit by gas until his death in 1951, and the original gas pipes did duty for ninety years.

In the 1880s Baron von Welsbach invented the incandescent gas mantle, which gave a more intense light and used much less gas, cloaking the naked flame in a hood made of a knitted cotton fabric impregnated with thorium and cerium.

ELECTRIC LIGHT

Electric light had originally been created by passing electric current through a circuit including two carbon rods – when the rods were slightly separated the current leapt the gap, creating a reaction that turned the carbon brilliantly incandescent. Such light was fine for lighthouses (the Admiralty installed such a lamp in the South Foreland Light in 1858) but too bright for the home. In 1878, the American Thomas Edison and the Englishman Joseph Swan both invented incandescent carbon-filament lamps suitable for domestic use. In 1881, Lord Kelvin lit up his Glasgow home with a blaze of incandescent electric light fitted to the 106 former gas-burners. In the same year, this letter from the proud owner of Cragside, Sir William Armstrong, was sent to the editor of *The Engineer*, dated 17 January 1881.

Sir, the following particulars of a successful application of SWAN'S ELECTRIC LAMPS to the lighting of a country residence will probaby be of interest to many of your readers, a

A significant moment: Sir William and Lady Armstrong at Cragside, sketched by the Illustrated London News *as they enjoyed their first meal by electric light in 1881.*

neighbouring brook being turned to account for that purpose. The brook, in fact, lights the house, and there is no consumption of any material in the process.

The generator used is one of the Siemen's dynamo-electric machines and the motor is the turbine which gives off 6 horse-power; the distance of the turbine and generator from the house is 1,500 yards; the conducting wire is of copper and its section is that of No. 1 Birmingham wire gauge. A return wire of the same material and section is used, so that the current has to pass through 3,000 yards of this wire to complete the circuit ...

In the passages and stairs the lamps are for the most part used without glass shades and present a very beautiful and starlike appearance, not so bright as to pain the eye in passing, and very efficient in lighting the way ...

The Library, which is a room of 33 feet by 20 feet with a large recess on one side, is well-lighted by eight lamps. Four of these are clustered in one globe of ground glass, suspended from the ceiling of the recess, and the remainder are placed singly and in globes, in various parts of the room, upon vases which were previously used as stands for duplex kerosene lamps. These vases, being enamel on copper, are themselves conductors, and serve for carrying the return current from the incandescent carbon to a metallic case in connection with the main return wire. The entering current is brought by a branch wire to a small insulated mercury cap in the centre of the base, and is carried forward to the lamp by a piece of insulated wire which passes through a hole in the bottom of the vase and thence through the interior to the lamp on the top. The protruding end of this wire is naked, and dips into the mercury cup when the case is set down. Thus the lamp may be extinguished and relighted at pleasure merely by removing the vase from its seat or setting it down again.

The original bare bay-window globe in Cragside library depicted in a contemporary engraving in the *Illustrated London News* has been changed at some point to a less glaring red-fringed hanging light. But the vases with their somehow rather supernatural globes are the same as they were in 1881. Normally, no more than nine of Cragside's forty-five electric lights were switched on at a time, and Armstrong employed a resident electrician, Andrew Richardson.

When the Prince and Princess of Wales and their children visited Cragside in August 1884

ten thousand small glass lamps were hung amongst the rocky hillsides or upon the lines of railing which guard the walks, and an almost equal number of Chinese lanterns were swung across leafy glades, and continued pendant from tree to tree in sinuous lines, miles in extent. For the lighting of all this enormous illumination alone a large staff of men were required, and those employed started on their difficult and lengthy task almost as soon as the Royal guests had sought their apartments in Cragside.

The signal to open the sluices below the lake to start the dynamos working was given by waving a white handkerchief from the windows of the house.

I found a nice sidelight on this technological triumph in a small booklet about Rothbury, the nearest town to Cragside. An army officer stationed there in the Second World War remembered meeting the ex-butler of Cragside, a Mr Crozier. He came to the house as a page-boy aged eleven, and was chosen to switch on the electric light for the first time because he was the youngest in the house and so would be likely to live the longest to tell the tale.

A few months later Hatfield House was proudly lit up for the first time, evidently rather less efficiently. Lord Salisbury and his family threw cushions at the electric sockets when they sparked and a gardener died after receiving an electric shock. Magazines began to warn of the dangers of the new angel in the house, and Hilaire Belloc penned cautionary mock-heroic lines:

> Some random touch – a hand's imprudent slip –
> The Terminals – flash – a sound like 'Zip!'
> A smell of burning fills the startled Air –
> The Electrician is no longer there!

Both Tatton Park and Lanhydrock were electrified early, and splendid original switches and electric lights survive in many of their reception rooms and corridors. The fuse-box at Tatton is dated 1884. In the morning-room at Lanhydrock there is a splendid electrolier, fitted chandelier-style with cut-glass pendants to reflect and intensify the light. All the fittings were reported to be 'in a highly dangerous state' when the house was taken over by the National Trust and rewired for mains electricity in 1970. The interesting electric-light brackets at Wightwick were designed by George Jack, a pupil of the architect Philip Webb, especially for William Morris's furnishings firm.

Castle Drogo, predictably, had its own source of turbine-generated electric power (the turbine house is a little way down in the valley behind the house), and was very well equipped with up-to-date ideas. Frances Drewe recalls that in the dining-room 'they always had a damask cloth, never mats, and my father was very proud of an electric cloth which was put under the damask cloth. They put candlesticks at the four corners which pricked in with little connections into the electric cloth for lighting the table candles.'

Just how cumbersome contriving early electric light was can be appreciated by a visit to Bateman's in Sussex, where Rudyard Kipling harnessed the little river Dudwell beside the old mill (immortalized in rather a different context in *Puck of Pook's Hill*) at the foot of the garden in 1903. Kipling received friendly advice from Sir William Willcocks, who had recently dammed the more formidable waters of the Nile at Aswan. A mighty snake of pipe leads water steeply down from the millpond through a mixed-flow turbine of the type invented by James Thompson, who patented it in 1850 under the description 'Vortex Water Wheel'. It was specifically designed and built for Bateman's by Gilbert Gilkes & Co. of Kendal, West-

The dangers of electricity were legendary at the turn of the century. This is a fin-de-siècle French guide to six easy ways for idiots to electrocute themselves.

An electric-light fitting designed by Philip Webb for Standen, Sussex, a house built and furnished in the 1890s in the spirit of William Morris.

morland. The fifty lead-acid batteries in open glass containers which it charged can still be seen in an outbuilding. When fully charged the batteries could provide ten 60 watt bulbs of electricity for about four hours. On a long winter night, the turbine could be run continuously to provide power for twenty 60 watt bulbs.

In general, however, the development of electricity was considerably impeded by restrictive legislation such as the 1882 and 1888 Lighting Acts. Still smarting from the notorious profits made by the railway, water and gas companies earlier in the century, the government tried to protect the public from exploitation by limiting tenure of plant to twenty-one years and limiting each concession to one municipal area. Not until a National Grid network was set up in the 1920s could electrification of light, heat and power really make an impact all over the country.

HEAT

To an Englishman the idea of a room without a fireplace is quite simply unthinkable. All ideas of domestic comfort, of family happiness, of inward-looking personal life, of spiritual well-being centre around the fireplace. The fire as the symbol of home is to the Englishman the central idea both of the living-room and of the whole house; the fireplace is the domestic altar before which, daily and hourly, he sacrifices to the household gods.

Hermann Muthesius, *The English House*, 1904

Heat is perhaps the most essential element of home comfort. As I explored the well-cared-for public spaces of the houses run by the National Trust, it was easy to forget that to the people who lived in them before this century most of the rooms in them struck dark, damp and chilly most of the time. This was not just a medieval phenomenon. In 1828 Mary Lucy shivered ('so cold, oh so cold') in the Great Hall at Charlecote before belated improvements provided underfloor heating and hot water on tap, and in the 1880s weekends at the Trevelyans' house, Wallington, were as notorious for their lack of physical comfort as they were famous for their stimulating intellectual conversation. According to gossipy Augustus Hare, Lady Trevelyan 'never appears to attend to her house one bit, which is like the great desert with one or two little oases in it, where, by good management you may possibly make yourself comfortable'. When I was looking round Calke Abbey, at that time only half restored, the deep chill of both the basement and the upper storeys made me realize the formidable challenge such great houses presented to those responsible for making them warm and welcoming.

The first domestic heating fuel was wood, supplemented by local supplies of peat and turf. Although coal was taken from surface deposits by the Romans and used to fuel their sophisticated hypocausts, after they left there is very little evidence indeed of its use until the twelfth century. Even then, supplies tended to be limited to the localities in which it was mined, or those which could be visited by the boats which traded from coal-mining districts close to the coast.

Most people kept warm by using wood and charcoal, a much older domestic fuel than coal. It has been made and burnt in Europe for at least 5,500 years. Indeed, one reason why it is very difficult to ascertain exactly how much coal was mined is that before 1500 references to coal generally mean charcoal. Mineral coal used to be called 'sea coal' (it was generally transported by ship) to distinguish it. Besides being used for cooking, portable charcoal braziers provided auxiliary heating for parts of the house or castle where there was no hearth. In medieval times the scholars of Magdalen College, Oxford, were allowed a certain time after meals to 'tarry round the charcoal fire' (Richard Chandler, *Life of Wayneflete*, 1811). All manner of warming-pans and hot-water containers were used to keep the body warm on at least a local basis. 'On Monday night the Housemaid need not sit up to warm the bed for her Master, as she is expected to rise very early the next morning to wash. The Housekeeper can do it while the Mistress is undressing,' directed Susanna Whatman in her *Book of Housekeeping*.

In 1283, no fewer than nine hundred charcoal burners were operating in Edward I's demesne woods of the Forest of Dean alone. By the sixteenth century the rapid destruction of forests for shipbuilding, house building and domestic fuel was causing concern. A law was passed in 1558 prohibiting the felling of trees to make charcoal for iron smelting, but it was largely ignored. In the early seventeenth century the acute shortage of timber encouraged early experiments with the use of coal for both domestic and industrial purposes. The Woburn Abbey accounts in the mid seventeenth century show an average consumption of 200–260 sacks of charcoal a year and 55 chaldron (*c.* 200 quarters) of coal.

Open fires remained far more popular in Britain than they were on the continent. At a time when the Dutch, the Scandinavians, the Russians and the Germans were constructing tiled room-stoves big enough to sleep on and wonderfully efficient against their extreme winters, the Elizabethans were building chimney-pieces like elaborate altarscreens around huge open hearths that required constant attention if they were to put out any sort of constant heat. Muthesius, who pointed out that a mere 14 per cent of the heat from an open fire actually benefited the room, thought the English obsession with open fireplaces extraordinary, but with his infallible appreciation of the importance of matters spiritual, he accepted that 'to remove the fireplace from the English home would be to remove the soul from the body'.

The burning of coal required innovations in the designs of fireplaces and room-heating stoves. Robert Adam was very interested in this subject, and drew elaborate plans for heating appliances at Kedleston. Elegant stoves designed by James Wyatt can also be seen in the upstairs gallery of Castle Coole. The fireplaces in both the hall and the Parnell Room at Castle Ward have interesting circular surrounds, highly polished to reflect heat, and able to hinge out for ease of cleaning. In the White Drawing Room at Arlington Court, the fireplace is similarly highly polished, and there is a very beautiful wall grate in the dining-room, conveniently providing space to keep mulls or dishes warm on hobs at each side.

Attractive as these fireplaces looked, they were not effective room-heaters. Much of the heat was absorbed by the metal, rather than being thrown out into the room.

In an essay published in 1796, 'Of Chimney Fireplaces, with proposals for Improving them to Save Fuel', the enterprising Count Rumford described how his experiments had proved the merits of a small fireplace lined with non-heat-conducting material such as fireclay or brick, and with a tapering neck. It was much more efficient, economic and less inclined to smoke than the straight chimney flue. Rumford flues were angled forward, and then back into the chimney. Rumford's ideas were not widely adopted until the second half of the nineteenth century, when the familiar small fireplaces with ceramic tile surrounds came into general use.

Other technical improvements in the management of the open fire were an ashpan like a drawer underneath the grate and a register plate in the chimney above the grate, both of which could be used to regulate the draught. Doors which could partially or gradually close over the opening can be seen on a fine highly polished fireplace in the bathroom at Blickling. Feeding hoppers could be mounted behind or at the side of some grates; others had back-boilers to provide domestic hot water.

Free-standing room-heating stoves were described admiringly by Loudon in 1833, but he warned that they were extremely likely to be put out of order by servants, 'partly from their extreme ignorance of the nature of the objects to be taken care of, but chiefly, we believe, from their carelessness, and that utter disregard for the interest of their employers, which is the consequence of the great distance at which they are kept, and the manner in which they are treated; evils which can only be cured by the universal diffusion of education and the comparative equalization of wealth'. This sudden digression into social diatribe is interesting. I include it here as a marker: the theme of the effect of new domestic technology on household organization and relations with servants will be taken up in the conclusion.

Closed-in anthracite stoves became increasingly popular after the Smoke Abatement Exhibition of 1882. 'Were the public but to avail themselves of such appliances,' opined the Marquis of Lorne in his speech on opening the exhibition, 'we might one day see roses blooming in Kensington Gardens.' They required much less looking after than open fires, and would even keep in all night given proper management. Felbrigg and Calke Abbey both had such stoves in their main halls.

Paraffin stoves were a quick and effective method of providing portable heat after the 1860s, but were a notorious fire risk. It was gas fires that first significantly alleviated the labour and dirt associated with room-heating, and began the long haul towards the reduction of smoke pollution in cities. A mixture of asbestos and firebrick that could be kept red hot was developed in the 1870s. The fireclay was made in tall fluted columns or rough ball-shaped lumps, not dissimilar to those used today in modern attempts to make gas fires look like coal ones, but white and set behind horizontal bars. The familiar honeycombed columns were introduced in 1925.

How much were these improved methods of heating used? By the turn of the century gas fires were adopted very generally in cities at least, although in 1904 Muthesius (who dealt on the whole with country houses, and large ones at that) declared that 'whole series' of stoves and gas fires might be seen in catalogues of heating appliances, but that 'one can scrutinize a hundred English houses without finding one of these objects'. The English, he concluded, were inseparable from their open hearths.

It is true that here and there, especially in the houses of the small men, the philistines, one sees imitation coal or log fires, constructed of clay and asbestos and made to glow by gas-flames designed to simulate the magic of the fire of the hearth; but cultivated Englishmen with their sound good sense rightly resist this substitute.

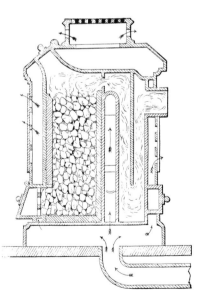

A free-standing room-heating stove in the West Hall of the Argory, Co. Armagh.
The diagram, published in the Book of the Home *in 1905, shows how it worked.*
Although efficient, such stoves were less popular than open fires. There were fears of
fumes escaping and, worse, they were considered 'less cheerful' than an open fire.

CENTRAL HEATING

Central heating was erratically provided from about 1800. The aim was to take the chill off corridors and halls, and to keep houses from becoming damp while empty rather than to provide a substitute for open fires. It is worth remembering that 'sweltering in overheated rooms' was regarded as unhealthy, something that was quite likely to be true given an atmosphere polluted by fumes from candles, gas and open fires. Central heating in bedrooms was regarded as positively depraved. Before pressure governors and thermostats were invented, there were also risks that boilers would burst in wintry weather.

Certainly, the task of warming large houses efficiently was – and is – a daunting one. Plans in Loudon for a medium-sized villa suggest a boiler in the attic to supply hot water and a hot-air stove in the basement 'to heat the whole house'. The Chatsworth library was warmed by hot air from a system of this sort described as 'Price's apparatus', which was fixed partly in the cellar under the Leather Room and partly under the west corridor. The heat was regulated by valves placed at the top and bottom of a bookcase, while an 'air-drain' in the west front of the house allowed for ventilation. The same machinery warmed the west sub-hall, the chapel, and the western end of the north corridor. Charlecote struck 'pleasantly warm' after a similar hot-air heating system was installed by Symonds of Bond Street. It ran under the floors, and its grilles can be seen in the floor of the Great Hall and in the skirting-boards in the dining-room. In 1862 Haden and Jones of Trowbridge installed a 'warming apparatus' in the basement of Blickling.

Cragside was undoubtedly one of the snuggest Victorian mansions. I toured the underfloor-heating system with the administrator, admiring the enormous pipes that snaked everywhere, pouring warm air discreetly through grilles in the skirting-boards and floors. Nothing there is quite what it seems. The enormous marble chimney-piece in the drawing-room is purely decorative. The flue from the open fire takes a sharp right-hand bend, as the room is built right into the cliff behind the house. It joins an eccentric stack of flues from other fireplaces and the central-heating system and emerges discreetly from the ground above and a little to the east of the house.

By 1890, nearly all country houses had central heating of some kind – floor and skirting-board grilles and radiators disguised behind screens in window-seats, or unashamedly fat and hot in hallways and landings. Steam heating was regarded as quicker in effect, but less reliable than hot-water heating. The boiler-house was often put under the care of the gardeners, and had a dual function, providing warmth for the hothouses as well as the house itself. But before the First World War no one considered relying on central heating alone, and open fires were still the norm in bedrooms and reception rooms alike. Central heating undoubtedly increased comfort, but did little to save the labour of laying, lighting, keeping up and cleaning up open fires.

Every house, however small, had to have a coal cellar and a wood store. The business of supplying domestic fuel could become a logistic challenge when hundreds of fireplaces had to be serviced, as at Castle Coole. A cavernous tunnel, wide enough to allow carts bringing coals and turf to pass each other, leads from the two courtyards of servants' offices behind the house to the basement. There are large storage cellars on each side. To keep Mount Stewart warm, coal was constantly in transit by canal and sea from Durham, where the family owned coalmines. It arrived by ship to Strangford Lough, where there was a specially constructed coal quay.

Railways with iron rails running from coal store into the basement were used at Cliveden and Tatton Park. If the housemaids were fortunate, service lifts hoisted it up to different levels. At Harlaxton, near Grantham, coal came in at two levels, on a viaduct which began two miles from the house. It was delivered to the upper storeys and went by chute to the lower floors.

FIRE PRECAUTIONS

May Heaven protect our home from flame
Or hurt or harm of various name
And may no evil luck betide
To any who therein abide

Erddig, legend written on bellboard

Dotted somewhat at random around the household offices of many National Trust properties there is still an extraordinary variety of domestic fire-fighting equipment, a sobering reminder of the greatest threat of all to domestic comfort. Open fires and candlelight seem romantic in retrospect, but they also posed a constant danger. Very few houses of any antiquity have not been scarred by fire at some time in their history; many, of course, were totally destroyed and rebuilt. Fear of fire could reach paranoid proportions in families which had been badly hit. Lanhydrock, completely rebuilt after a catastrophic kitchen-chimney fire gutted the house in 1881, has shiny brass hydrants and neatly coiled hoses at almost every turn of the stairs. Sir Vauncey Harpur Crewe, master of Calke Abbey from 1886 to 1924, imposed a ban on smoking and turned his own daughter Airmyne out of the house for breaking it. He had an

Fire was – and is – an ever-present danger to domestic life, particularly in large country houses. Montbard's 1881 engraving shows Lanhydrock's dramatically rapid devastation.

underground reservoir made in the hillside just above the house, and equipped the whole of Ticknall village with standpipes.

There were some practical precautions which could be taken when a house was built. Siting the kitchen, source of most domestic fires, well away from the main body of the house, as at Compton Castle, was an obvious one. Highly inflammable timber-frame houses, such as Speke Hall and Little Moreton Hall, in Cheshire, have a special fire-resistant infill under floors and between storeys. Lime and ash were worked together until moist, and then rammed down on to a bedding of straw and laths. At Lanhydrock iron girders were used instead of timbers, the floors were made of concrete, and the ceilings of a patent fireproof composition. Six-inch iron pipes were laid from a water source three miles away to a reservoir built on top of a hill above the house, and water was conducted from this directly into the house.

Fire-fighting itself has a long history. In Ancient Rome there were highly organized fire brigades, staffed by slaves using manually operated double-cylinder force pumps. These declined with the Roman Empire, however, and fire-fighting remained crude and ineffective for many hundreds of years. After the Norman Conquest most towns ordered a bell to be rung late at night which required fires to be covered – the *couvre-feu* or curfew. In 1189 the first Lord Mayor of London ruled that houses had to be equipped with a ladder and, during the more risky summer months, with a barrel full of water by the front door.

Fire-fighting equipment was otherwise very crude – primarily leather buckets passed by a human chain. The chain was generally arranged in two lines – men passing full buckets of water from the pump or well towards the blaze, women and children passing the empty buckets back. Ranks of buckets for this purpose can be seen hanging in the servants' quarters at Calke Abbey, Felbrigg and many other great houses. Such buckets were marked with the name of the house to ensure their return if borrowed to fight a fire elsewhere – neighbourhood cooperation was instant and unquestioning in time of fire. The buckets are sturdy objects, specially designed for fire chains: riveted at the base and the sides, with a copper rim and a stout flexible carrying strap. Their deep foot rim could be held firmly while tossing water out. Others were round-bottomed, to prevent their disappearance for any other use, and hung from a rack strategically sited close to a source of water.

Although the leather buckets were almost indestructible and continued to be made well into the twentieth century, new materials were gradually introduced; tin by 1807, canvas by 1834, and, from the 1860s, cast iron, galvanized iron, gutta-percha and indiarubber.

Fire hooks – long poles with iron hooks at the end – were often kept in racks under the eaves of thatched buildings in order to pull off burning thatch or to create fire-breaks. They could be up to twenty feet long, and had rings on their shafts so that chains could be attached to them, and men or even horses harnessed to pull timbers off buildings.

Fire-engines on wheels were made in Germany in the sixteenth century, and imported into Britain – one was used at the head of the Lord Mayor's procession in 1548, where it was being used to force the crowd to get out of the way. They had a large cistern of water and a pump which squirted it out through a long pipe. The first English patent for a fire-engine of this sort was in 1625, but the Great Fire of London made their limitations clear.

Saltram has a very interesting fire-engine, of the type patented by Richard Newsham in 1725. These remained in production for over a hundred years, and were still in use as late as 1940. The Rothbury fire brigade also had one. Water could either be poured into the cistern or drawn in through a suction hose directly from a water source. The pumping levers are long ones, placed alongside the engine so that several men could work it at the same time, so increasing the force of the jet of water produced. A machine of this size was capable of pumping between 90 and 120 gallons of water per minute. Newsham's largest engine could project 170 gallons per minute for a distance of 40 yards. Croft Castle has a wheel-mounted manually pumped fire-engine of a different, and less efficient design, dated 1843. Its handles are placed at each end, and it could only have been worked by two people.

The next major advance was the larger, horse-drawn, manually pumped fire-engine, with long levers hinged at the ends for travelling, so that as many as forty-six pumpers could be accommodated. In 1858 Mr Shand patented a steam-powered fire-engine, and from the 1860s a variety of such machines were produced.

The reason small fire-fighting engines such as Newsham's remained in use was that at a pinch they could be fitted through most doorways to fight a fire inside. But there was also a considerable variety of indoor fire-fighting equipment. Hand pumps in cylinders were popular, and one can be seen in the butler's pantry at Uppark. The best-known makers of such pumps were Merryweather & Sons and Shand Mason

A hand-pumped fire-engine and leather fire-fighting bucket at Croft Castle, Hereford and Worcester. It was small enough to be pulled inside the house if necessary.

& Co. In a large house it was a sensible precaution to stand a Shand Mason corridor fire-engine on each floor – there is still one lurking in the stables at Wallington. The most expensive models could throw 25 gallons per minute to a height of 50 ft. Presumably a bucket chain was at the ready to refill the tank below the pump. Bucket pumps were also useful accessories, portable and flexible.

Fire extinguishers which used chemicals or water expelled under pressure to fight fire were being experimented with as early as the 1760s. Charles Povey patented a wooden barrel filled with water and chemicals with a fuse in the lid which led down a tube to a round pewter bomb full of gunpowder mounted in the centre of the barrel. When a fire broke out, the fuse was lit and the barrel thrown into the burning room in the hope that, when it exploded, the force of the water thrown out would dowse the fire.

Glass 'fire-grenades' of the type that can be seen on the landing outside the servery at Calke Abbey and in the kitchen at Wallington were invented in the USA in 1871. Bulbous, ribbed vessels, they were filled with a solution of sodium bicarbonate or simply salt water. Extravagant claims were made for them, but, although extremely popular for about forty years, they were of very little use.

The first really effective chemical extinguisher was invented by George Manby in 1816. It was a copper vessel filled with permanganate of potash and compressed air, so that if a tap was turned, the potash was forced out through the nozzle. Many other varieties were patented, with resounding names (Philip's Fire Annihilator, Dick's Fire Exterminator) but uncertain efficiency. Foam extinguishers were first developed in the 1930s, and carbon tetrachloride pumping cylinders from 1912.

In cities, official fire-fighting services took over the business of dealing with fires by the middle of the nineteenth century. Hilaire Belloc celebrated 'London's Noble Fire Brigade' in one of his *Cautionary Tales*:

> From Stratford atte Green and Bow
> With courage high and hearts aglow
> They galloped roaring through the town
> 'Matilda's house is burning down.'

But in the shires, fire-fighting remained one of the duties of a country gentleman, many of whom, like Lord Leconfield of Petworth, captained their own fire brigades cf uniformed firemen, and acquired the latest equipment as soon as it came on the market. It was a wise investment. As the recent disaster at Uppark indicated, in remote country houses, fire remains a terrible hazard.

CHAPTER ELEVEN

WATERWORKS

To keep your houses sweet,
Cleanse privie vaults,
To keep your souls as sweet,
Mend privie faults

Sir John Harington, *Metamorphosis of Ajax,* 1596

Because there is limited material evidence of washing facilities in earlier centuries, it has often been assumed that our ancestors' standards of personal hygiene were low. Although it is true to say that many of them would feel our present norms of cleanliness verged on the obsessional (some sort of substitute, perhaps, for the decline of religion and the loss of a more spiritual washing away of sin), it is also true that many of the arrangements for washing in the past were quite as sybaritic and efficacious as modern body-contoured tubs and power showers. Their use varied from place to place and time to time, and although in general it would be true to say the richer the family, the cleaner, it was not invariably so.

An adequate water supply was always essential for any house, large or small. The legendary Roman plumbing expertise was thought to have been utterly lost as the great unwashed poured across the declining empire, but archaeologists are now discovering that piped water supplies in medieval Britain were much more soph-isticated than has been generally assumed. A plan of the monastery at Canterbury made in 1165 shows an extraordinary network of pipes, aqueducts, cisterns, reservoirs and a main water tower. Water was gravity-fed all over the monastery. There was even a fail-safe device: a note on the plan explains the function of a hollow column which stood beside the well and led to the main water pipe: 'If the aqueduct fails, water can be drawn from the well and being poured into the column will be supplied to all the offices.' A similar aqueduct was installed in Theobalds, Sir William Cecil's Elizabethan mansion near Hatfield, and from it water was piped all over the house.

At Bradley Manor, set between the River Lemon and the Bradley Leat, an old mill stream, there was never any danger of running short of water. Indeed, the arms of the Bushels of Bradley were three water bougets, that is, pairs of water skins hanging to form a yoke, and tradition has it that the family was in charge of the drinking water for Duke William's troops in 1066. At Baddesley Clinton, water is led from the nearby river into a moat, a defensive measure (the Forest of Arden was a rough place in those days) but one which solved a great many sanitary problems. Baddesley's numerous privy towers took full advantage of it. A medieval drain runs the length of the house, its floor a little below the level of the moat. Steps leading down to it gave access for cleaning purposes, and there are slots in the roof through which sewage fell from the various privy shafts. At intervals, in order to sweep this drain clean, the moat had to be drained and the sluice gate in the south-west tower opened.

In the seventeenth century the drain was turned into a hide for Catholic priests by Nicholas Owen, the well-known recusant escapologist. The steps and loop windows were blocked, a portcullis made at the exit, escape shafts constructed and the level of the moat raised. All this was done under cover of building a new garde-robe projection. Using the capacious sewers and drains of medieval buildings as hiding-places was commonplace – many so-called secret tunnels were in fact sewers; undoubtedly many more remain to be discovered.

A purer and better-protected source of water was the well. Medieval wells were dug very deep, and many survive in use to this day. The strategically situated well in the courtyard of Chirk is ninety-three feet deep, and has a large underground chamber. It taps an underground stream and ensured that the castle would not run short of water even if under siege. A shaft from the well-head was often built up to the top of the house or castle so that buckets of water could be raised up to any floor of the building. At Newcastle, in the 1170s, water was being raised in wall pipes to all levels of the keep, and at Dover a combination of well water and rainwater was stored in tanks and piped all over the castle. Failing a well, water would be carried in pipes, either of wood or of lead, from a spring in some neighbouring hill. At Trerice (the name means homestead on a slope) in Cornwall, the house was supplied by pipes from a spring in the hillside above and to the north-east of the house.

Rainwater too was systematically stored and highly prized for its special qualities. Capacious lead cisterns, such as the one in the kitchen court at Cotehele, survive in the gardens and courtyards of many old houses, often made by a local plumber and stamped with the family coat of arms to match that on the large square 'heads' at the top of the drainpipes that led water down from the roof gullies. Such designs are as functional as they are ornamental – lead expands and contracts easily, and the thickened areas of the pattern, together with braced corners and heavy rims, prevented the tanks and heads from bulging and possibly leaking. In later centuries, tanks to store water were also built underground, lined with bricks and with a stone access slab. With a pump attached, these were useful auxiliary sources of water for the kitchen quarters.

In his Westminster palace Henry III employed 'Master William the Conduit-maker', who was paid in 1234 for 'repairing the conduit of water which is carried to the king's lavatory and to other places there', as well as 'making a certain conduit through which the refuse from the king's kitchens at Westminster flows into the Thames'. Three hundred years later, Cardinal Wolsey installed an extremely efficient water-supply at Hampton Court. Three conduit houses were built round the springs at Coombe Hill, some three and a half miles away, and water fed into a double set of lead pipes, two and a half inches in diameter. They run from Coombe to Surbiton, under the Hogsmith River and the Thames above Kingston Bridge, and then through Hampton Court Park to the house itself. At intervals there were 'tamkins', small inspection houses where pipes could be plugged off if repairs were necessary. At the same period, water ran five miles through pipes to supply Windsor Castle.

One method of coping with the heavy task of raising or pumping water was to build a rotating machine of some sort, operated either by human or animal power. Such machines were known to the Egyptians in the form of the noria, and to the Romans in the form of the treadwheel. Treadwheels were used in the building trade, metal industries and in mines in Britain in the sixteenth century, and Agricola's *De re metallica* (1556) shows conical horse-wheel houses operating bucket lifts and blowing furnaces. From the seventeenth century, such wheels were often set up at farms (where they could also be used to grind corn and so on) and at great houses which required large quantities of water or had particular problems with supplies. At Elizabethan Hardwick a horse-wheel pumped water from the well to a conduit house which can still be seen on the south side of the mansion. From there a lead conduit took water to the New Hall, perhaps filling, among other things, the two 'sesterns of lead' mentioned in the Low Larder in the 1601 inventory.

In the nineteenth century the gearing of horse-drawn wheels was much improved – the Reading Ironworks exhibited several at the 1851 Exhibition – and even though at that time steam engines could be used to raise water, a horse-wheel was often more economical. Few houses would need to raise water for more than an hour or two a day: easy for a horse to manage, but hardly worth the effort of raising steam. According to Percy Lubbock (*Earlham, Reminiscences of the Author's Early Life*, 1922), 'In one corner, under a sort of brick cloister, was a pump, a great beam that revolved. For half an hour every morning it was dragged round by a white horse with a measured thumping and thudding.' At Felbrigg, in Norfolk, a horse-wheel used to work a two-throw pump to supply water to the house until as recently as 1924. At Castle Coole a pump house was built by the side of the lough, to solve the problem

The massive treadmill operated by a donkey at Greys Court, near Henley.

of getting water up to the house a considerable distance away. The pump was driven by two horses and was still in use up to the middle of this century.

Horse-wheels were operated by a horse walking round in a circle attached to an arm which was geared to the pump or well rope. Donkey-wheels were treadmills, with a huge cage arranged upright inside which the donkey walked. In some cases, especially in prisons and workhouses, such wheels were driven by human power. One of the best preserved donkey wheels can still be seen at Greys Court. The wheel, mounted over a well cut two hundred feet into the chalk, is enormous. As the donkey paced over its elm boards, large buckets were hoisted out of the water and up to a tank in the roof. A hook caught each bucket and emptied it into the tank, and from there water was channelled along wooden gutters into the house itself.

It was only in 1650 that the technique of pumping water up to a height was perfected, an event intimately connected with Uppark. The first effective pump for this purpose was invented by Sir Edward Ford, whose family had owned Uppark and the manor of East Harting for two centuries. It was a reflection of his acknowledged genius that, although he had attempted to defend Arundel Castle against the Roundheads during the Civil War, he was made First Lord of the Works under Oliver Cromwell. After the Restoration he was confirmed in his office by Charles II. Anthony Wood's *Athenae Oxonienses* (1691–2) recorded Ford's hydraulic engineering achievements.

Edward Ford of Uppark was a most ingenious mechanic, and being encouraged by Oliver [Cromwell] and invited by the citizens of London in 1656, he raised the Thames Water into all the highest streets of the city, ninety-three feet high in four eight-inch pipes, to the wonder of all men, and the Honour of the Nation, with a rare engine of his own invention, done in his own charge and in one year's time.

Sir Edward's 'rare engine' was four suction pumps worked by levers attached to a vertical rod, which was geared to a horizontal wheel turned by horses. His grandson, Lord Tankerville, took advantage of this new technology to site his new house at Uppark at an unusual and formerly waterless height. He used his grandfather's pumping engines to conduct water in pipes of lead and iron from St Richard's Spring, a mile or so away from the mansion, and some 350 feet below it. Part of this water-wheel can still be seen in the engine house on the road between Uppark and South Harting. An indicator on the mantelpiece in the Uppark butler's pantry showed the level of the water stored in the house's rooftop tanks, and one of the butler's duties was to watch this gauge. It was regulated by air pressure, which raised or lowered the water level as it compressed or released air pressure in a cylinder in the roof tank.

Changes at the seventeenth-century pump house at Dunham Massey show a history of domestic water pumping in miniature. Below the ground floor there is a sump, or reservoir of water. Above the first floors are two hand-operated wooden-cased suction pumps. Originally two people manned these, in order to pump water up into a wooden cistern at the same level, from which it was gravity-fed to the ground floor of the mansion. Mounted at a higher level in the pump house is another pump, also manually operated, and this lifted water into an upper tank, this time in order to supply water to the first floor of the mansion. Judging from the size of the cisterns and the pumps, water requirements were on a fairly modest scale, although there was probably a separate arrangement to feed water from the mansion's gutters into rainwater tanks.

In 1860 a dramatic improvement was effected by fitting a water-wheel into the pump house. Operated by a crank on its axle is a horizontal force pump with an air vessel to equalize the flow. Water could be pumped continuously from this to a high storage tank in the coach-house block where the carriages were washed. From then on the house could be supplied with unlimited quantities of water. At some time around 1895, the wheel was replaced, possibly by a steam pump, and later the house was connected up to the public water mains.

WASHING FACILITIES

The basin and jug (or ewer) was the most ancient and simple way of washing. Water could be warmed up in a kettle over the fireplace, or brought up from the kitchen quarters if there was no fire in the room. An alternative to the jug and ewer was the fixed basin in the wall. The stone niches which survive in medieval cloisters (at Lacock, for example) and castles often had a portable cistern with a tap on its side fixed above them. This could be removed and warmed over a fire to heat the water inside. A copy of such a cistern from a drawing by Pugin was playfully introduced by Edwin Lutyens in his cosy medieval-style conversion of Lindisfarne Castle, off the Northumberland coast. It can be seen in the upper gallery. Others were provided with piped water, as in the splendid twelfth-century circular 'laver' at Durham, lined with marble and furnished with two dozen or so small lead cisterns, each with its own brass tap.

Simple three-legged stands for a basin became beautiful pieces of furniture in the eighteenth century. They were often triangular in shape, to fit conveniently into the corner of a dressing-room, with holes cut for bowl, jug and soap-dish. By the 1830s marble tops were common, and sets of dishes for washing, known as toiletries, included tooth-glass, sponge bowl, water bottle and even a container for false teeth as well as the inevitable bowl, ewer and covered pail for slops. Everything matched, patterned appropriately: a swathe of begonias for Her, a sharply etched Greek key pattern for Him, the universally popular willow pattern in the nursery and the servants' attics. In Lady Belmore's dressing-room at Blickling a very completely furnished washstand can be seen, with Copeland basin, ewer, slop pail and chamber-pot. Another survives at Arlington Court, where twin pot closets flank the bed.

As nineteenth-century plumbing became more elaborate, many washstands were fitted with taps, and Cragside has some particularly splendid examples of such arrangements. But the vagaries of early heating systems fired by kitchen ranges meant that piped hot water could be slow in coming and lukewarm on arrival. Oscar Wilde scorned the plumbed-in washstand in his room at the Savoy, saying that if he wanted hot water he would ring for it.

PORTABLE BATHS

Early manuscript illustrations show roomy wooden tubs, holding two or more people, and sometimes furnished with a tray to hold food and drink, or even a chessboard. Medieval romances often opened an amorous evening with a shared bath, sprinkled with rose petals or orange-flower water.

Metal tubs began to replace wooden ones in the late eighteenth century. They came in all shapes and sizes: shallow saucers, armchair-style sitz-baths, and long tubs (sometimes with two small wheels at the back to make them easier to take out of the room). The most magnificent of them all was the slipper bath, which looks like a gigantic chukka boot with a tap in its toe. It was very cosy, losing only a minimal amount of heat, and keeping the bather warm in the steam. Moreover the floor of the room around the bath stayed dry. A simple slipper bath can be seen at Wallington, and a more interesting charcoal-heated model at Tatton Park. In this, water was kept hot by a compartment full of red-hot charcoal in the toe, from which a flue led to the chimney of the room. Charcoal stoves known as salamanders – plump spheres with three short legs and a long narrow neck – could also be placed in ordinary open tubs in order to heat up the water inside them.

But heat was not necessarily a prime requirement of the bather. A late-nineteenth-century doctor described a bath of only 98–112°F as 'a powerful stimulant which

A Victorian hand-pumped shower at Erddig, Clwyd. Water was pumped up through one of the supporting columns, to shower down when a chain pulled a plug on the top half of the reservoir tank overhead.

should never be used by persons in a state of perfect health, but is employed only in cases of disease and this should be always under the direction of a medical practitioner'. A cold bath, on the other hand, was judged 'one of the most refreshing comforts and luxuries of life ... calculated to make the whole body rejoice with buoyancy and exhilaration of spirits'.

Showers were an ideal way of administering a short sharp shock of this sort. The simplest sort of shower was merely a matter of tipping water over your own head in bucketfuls, scooping it up from the deep saucer bath in which you stood, and repeating the action. Thomas Carlyle rigged up such a bath in his back kitchen, with which, he wrote to reassure his mother soon after their arrival in London, he was 'diligent', emptying bucket after bucket of cold water over himself as he stood in a tin bath below.

At the 1851 Great Exhibition considerable interest was shown in different types of shower-baths. Many of them were provided with pumps so that water could be raised to the overhead reservoir with ease, rather than carrying it up a stepladder. There is a hand-pumped shower of this type at Erddig. One of the supporting columns is in fact a pipe through which water was pumped up to the top half of the water tank. A chain pull opened a valve in this tank, letting the water through to its sieve-like base, from which water sprayed down on to the bather. When the shower was over, a tap in the piped support could be opened and water pumped up, down and out of the whole contraption.

More sophisticated was a shower described in *Scientific American* in 1878. In this the bather jogged up and down, activating a treadmill which kept the water circulating. It was said to be 'of particular advantage if a hot shower is required, as only a slight degree of heating is necessary'. It is likely that charcoal heaters of the type described above were used to warm up shower water as well as bath water.

Perhaps the ultimate pre-electrical power shower was the Velo-douche, an invention of the 1890s. It combined exercise and ablutions, and consisted of a shallow saucer into which was fitted a framework carrying a bicycle mechanism. When the rider had exercised enough, he could reach backwards and turn a watercock so that water was pumped upwards and out of the sprinkler above his head as he pedalled. The faster he pedalled, the stronger the shower.

STEAM BATHS

Getting clean by sweating was an ancient custom, one of the succession of procedures in a Roman bath, and also popular in Russia and Scandinavia. I suspect it was more widely used in Britain than we realize. Medieval manuscripts show tubs with canopies over them – perhaps for modesty, but quite possibly to keep in steam. 'Vapour' baths

This sketch from the 1905 Book of the Home
shows an improvised vapour face-bath.

were often recommended by doctors, and in 1854 the *Encyclopaedia Britannica*'s article on bathing declared that 'the vapour bath is infinitely superior to the warm bath for all the purposes for which a warm bath can be given. An effective vapour bath may be easily had in any house at little cost or trouble.' The simplest method was to place a brick heated in the oven in a bowl and pour water over it while the bather sat close by, holding a towel over himself and the bowl. A large bag with an inlet for steam produced by a water-heating apparatus was illustrated in *The Mechanic's Magazine* in 1828. The bather sat in this, tightening it around his head. Wooden steam-bath cabinets, the familiar furniture of public 'Turkish' baths in the late nineteenth century, were evidently quite a normal item of domestic furnishings before the advent of the plumbed-in bathroom.

FITTED BATHROOMS

We do not know how much use was made of all these portable methods of keeping clean. Whether or not one took a bath is rarely considered interesting enough to enter in a diary, except that of a hypochondriac. It is easier to find evidence of fixed baths, but, although often architecturally spectacular, they were neither as practical nor as comfortable as the tubs by the fire, movable shower cabinets or impromptu steamings until reliable central-heating systems were developed.

Large communal tubs were part of the ordinary facilities of towns in the sixteenth century. Mrs Pepys has intermittent enthusiasms for attending the public bathhouse, which was, according to Dorothy Hartley (*Water in England*) as popular a seventeenth-century meeting place for women as the coffee-house was for men. They were also taken for granted in country mansions. John Bunyan refers to one quite casually in *The Pilgrim's Progress*:

But the Interpreter would have them tarry awhile, 'for,' said he, 'you must orderly go from hence . . . take them, and have them into the garden to the Bath, and there wash them clean from the soil which they have gathered by travelling' . . . and they came from out of the Bath, not only sweet and clean, but also much enlivened and strengthened in their joints.

The eighteenth century witnessed an upper-class vogue for taking the waters in every way imaginable. Dr Oliver's *Practical Dissertations on the Bath Waters* (1707) recommended dips in cold water, preferably mineral springs, as a remedy for headaches, impotence, the vapours and various other maladies. Bath itself is only the most famous of spas large or small all over the country – even a small sulphur spring

Wimpole Hall, Cambs.: the strikingly graceful plunge bath designed in 1792 by Sir John Soane held 2,199 gallons of water, heated by a boiler in the basement below.

just north of the middle lake at Kedleston attracted would-be bathers from far and wide. Although now in need of repair, the bathhouse they used survives. It was built by Jason Harris, the Curzons' London carpenter, in 1749.

People who took their health seriously built themselves a bathhouse – either in the house itself, usually in the basement or on the ground floor, or in the grounds, where it could form the object of a health-giving excursion. In 1769 Robert Adam designed a new bathhouse at Kedleston, an exceptionally attractive little building on the upper lake which combines a fishing room with two boat-houses and a plunge bath (illustrated on p. 69). At Castle Coole Lord Belmore brought home a genuine ancient marble bath from his tour of Italy and had it fitted in a small room off the basement servery in 1820. There it was conveniently close to the gargantuan kitchen range and basement hot-water boilers.

At Wimpole, the superb plunge bath designed by Sir John Soane is set on the ground floor, on the servants' staircase. It has hot and cold water piped to it. It probably dates from 1792 when Soane designed his Castello d'Acqua in the park – a reservoir (since demolished) which replaced an earlier and much less efficient conduit head. The installation of this wholly new water supply, with larger pipes as well as a greatly increased storage capacity, probably encouraged Lord Hardwicke to invest in the luxury of a plunge bath. Soane rose to the occasion with a design for a skylit chamber that provides grandeur in miniature. A double staircase sweeps round to a central plinth which may once have held a statue of a bathing Venus or Diana. Two further circular flights of steps with curved ends lead down from this to the gracefully shaped tank. When filled, the bath held 2,199 gallons of water, which was heated by a boiler in the basement below. A fireplace in an antechamber kept bathers warm before and after their dip.

Plunge baths should be regarded as roughly the equivalent of the modern domestic swimming-pool – having a bathhouse in the grounds did not preclude having a plumbed-in bath in the house itself. Fixed baths, equipped with hot and cold water, were installed in the Palace of Whitehall in the 1670s and at Chatsworth in the 1690s, while Blenheim and Cannons followed suit in the early eighteenth century. Sometimes it is difficult to tell, in the absence of any evidence, exactly what form the 'bagnio' marked in many house plans actually took. At Dyrham Park it was evidently built on a palatial scale. The 1710 inventory lists 'three turkey work and five cane chairs, a large oval table, a cane couch and a pair of hand irons with large brass heads', in the antechamber to the bagnio.

This antechamber was 'the great outward room to the Bagnio' referred to by William Blathwyt in a letter to his agent and cousin, Charles Watkins, dated 3 July 1703. He told him to have the 'Old Wainscott' in this room 'painted wainscott colour all except the old gilding which should remain as it is till we see what is fitt to be done to refresh that too'. In the bagnio itself were 'a little round stool and twelve leather stools'. This sounds more like a steam bath than anything else, and a sociable one at that. In a letter to Blathwyt in June 1703 Watkins mentions a furnace for the bagnio and that 'Porter has finished his Cornish [cornice] in ye Bagnio and is preparing to set ye Tile.' This 'Tile' was, according to another reference, Dutch, perhaps delftware. But there was also mention of the necessity for soldering sheets of lead so that they would hold water, which suggests there was also some sort of tub or plunge bath.

Usually one room held the warm bath and the shower-bath, and the cold bath would be in an ornamental building on the side of a stream. Ideally the bagnio would be supplied with hot water from the offices, by a pipe connected to the kitchen range or scullery boiler.

There seems to have been very individual and varied approaches to ordinary domestic bathrooms in the nineteenth century. Architectural textbooks show that the technology for plumbed-in bathrooms with hot and cold water was generally available by the 1820s. John Loudon describes a bathroom as 'a cheap and useful luxury, which would be considered by many persons an indispensable requirement', and gives a plan for a villa in which the dressing-room has a bath.

At any moment throughout the year a hot or cold bath may be had without troubling the servants by the following means: there is a cold-water cistern under the roof, and a hot-water cistern at the back of the kitchen fireplace. In this last cistern there is a coil of lead pipes, one end of the pipe communicating with the cold-water cistern above, the other with the bath. By turning a cock in the bathroom, water descends from the cistern in the roof, is heated in passing through the coil of pipes behind the kitchen fire, and ascends by the pressure of the atmosphere on the cistern to the bath. Another cock and pipe, leading directly from the cistern, admit cold water to the bath, so as to temper it at pleasure; and a third pipe serves to convey away the water when done with. The cover of the bath is fitted with a basin, so as to serve as a dressing-table. We have seen this bath filled in the course of a few minutes, and can attest its answering most completely.

Whether or not a house had bathrooms was a matter of personal taste. In 1866 the owners of Calke Abbey actually removed a bathroom fitted in 1833. Only one bathroom was installed at Lanhydrock when it was rebuilt after the 1881 fire, despite the sophisticated hot-water system in the servants' quarters and the fact that water hydrants (in case of another fire) were installed all over the house. At Arlington Court, the traditional bathroom china on a washstand, with hot water brought up in brass jugs from the housemaids' cupboard or even kitchen remained the rule within living memory.

Manuals of domestic etiquette suggest that it was thought polite to allow guests to bathe in their own rooms if they wished. 'There should always be a bath in the

Sumptuously comfortable, the 1860s Lothian bathroom at Blickling Hall, Norfolk, sported a Turkey carpet and an open fireplace with a steel shutter to prevent draughts when the fire was not required. The valve water-closet in the window-seat could be closed away under a slab of mahogany.

room and a bath blanket,' advised Mrs Peel in 1902. 'If there are bathrooms, the visitors may prefer to use them, but the choice should be given.' Another book suggested that the bathroom should be the preserve either of the gentlemen or the ladies – but not both. As late as 1906, there were still no bathrooms at Hardwick, although hot and cold water was piped around the house. The hot water for the main bedroom and the nurseries had to be carried from one tap on the third-floor landing. In 1920, Lady Fry dismissed bathrooms as 'only for servants'.

Blickling's hot-water system was probably put in around the time that William Burn remodelled the domestic quarters. Enormous boilers are still visible in what was once the basement servants' hall. Blickling's 1860s bathroom is one of the best-preserved rooms of its type in a National Trust house. The water-closet is set in a sleek sheet of mahogany in the window alcove, with the pull handle typical of the valve closet. The solid porcelain bath is nicely moulded, the wash-basin capacious. A steel shutter could be closed over the fireplace to prevent draughts when the fire was not in use.

Cragside too exhibits the zenith of Victorian sanitary magnificence. In the Owl Suite, one of the bedrooms has a sunken bath in a corner of the room, and all have plumbed washstands. It was here that the Prince and Princess of Wales slept on their visit in August 1884. Another bathroom cantilevered out beside the northern gatehouse is a later addition, and not especially interesting, but in the basement is a Turkish bath suite, designed by Norman Shaw in the old tradition of the bagnio, and first used on 4 November 1870. It was a masculine preserve, for all the exotic blue tiles in the plunge bath and the pretty changing tent. Bathers first sat or lay down in a somewhat spartan steam room, then plunged. There is also a classically simple wood-cased bath in a separate room.

The decorative wooden casings and heavy brass fittings of Victorian bathrooms were grand temples to Hygeia, but they were also hard to keep clean and bound to harbour damp and insect life. Nor were they always adequately plumbed to the hot-water supply, judging by the reminiscences of Lord Ernest Hamilton (quoted in Aslett's *Last Country Houses*). The 'large iron tanks encased in mahogany, evidently designed to do duty as baths, and – judging from their size – designed to accommodate several people at once' were far from efficient. 'Switching on the hot tap produced a succession of sepulchral rumblings, succeeded by the appearance of a small geyser of rust-coloured water, which stopped after a couple of minutes and was in any case stone cold.'

By the time Lutyens came to design Castle Drogo the mood of the bathroom was teetering between romance and functionalism. The bath there is naked enamelled metal, with five chrome taps (two for the bath, two for the shower and one for an exciting ring of waist-high jets of cold water) boldly mounted on the shower cabinet that rises from one end of it, and with a long internal waste pipe at the other end: easy to clean or unblock. Lutyens could not resist setting the wash-basin in well-fitted elm panelling with a graceful row of columns in front of it, but water stains betray its impracticality. The window seat, again neatly fitted with steps in elm, gives unparalleled views across Dartmoor.

PRIVIES

We do not know enough about the privy habits of our ancestors to do much more than guess at when and where they relieved themselves and how efficiently they coped with the disposal of sewage. Monks, more careful than most of cleanliness, arranged their 'rere-dorters' over running water. Castles too had elaborate provision for privies, sometimes with drains running down to the moat. Compton in Devon was generously equipped with garderobes attached to both the west wing and the towers. When the chute of the first-floor garderobe in the watch tower was cleared in 1945, an unbroken bottle with the crest and arms of Gilbert of Compton was found, apparently dropped in around the middle of the seventeenth century. On the ground floor was the largest garderobe of all, presumably for the male domestic staff. Its constructional details were carefully recorded before the present floor was laid, and it was not dissimilar to the substantial garderobe at Southwell Palace, Nottinghamshire, where seats were arranged round a central shaft so that each occupant was out of sight, if not of hearing, of his neighbour.

Noisome as the poorest villages and the overcrowded cities notoriously were because of untreated sewage, there is evidence that in the statelier homes of England matters were managed fairly competently. At Baddesley Clinton in 1445 Henry Richard and Robert Pole were paid 6d and 4d respectively, 'circa le noggying of le pryvehous'. Nogging was brickwork built up between wooden framing, so this suggests that this was a permanent and substantial outdoor privy. It probably had a 'cloacum' dug beneath it which would be emptied at intervals, just as country cesspits are today. A single-storey projection at the back of the house also contained privies, but its date is uncertain – it may be an early-eighteenth-century improvement.

By the end of the fifteenth century, Little Moreton Hall was well provided with indoor privies, informally known as 'jakes' and politely known as garderobes, rather as we talk of 'the cloakroom' today. The south-wing privy tower has two on each floor, probably emptying into the moat. At Canons Ashby, an early garderobe has recently been discovered in a third-floor chamber, still with its original sixteenth-century wooden lavatory seat. It was automatically sluiced by rainwater, brought by pipes from the roof above. The waste-pipe, buried in the thickness of the wall, descends to the main drains.

At Felbrigg in 1752 William Windham II wrote to his architect James Paine about 'the little house near the bleach' [i.e. the drying ground]:

I think it the best place imaginable. Should not the inside be stuccoed, or how do you do it? how many holes? there must be one for a child; and I would have it as light as possible. There must be a good broad place to set a candle on, and a place to keep paper. I think the holes should be wide and rather oblong, and the seats broad and not quite level, and rather low before, but rising behind. Tho the better the plainer, it should be neat.

Windham's attention to small comforts backs up Lawrence Wright's surmise in his excellent history of the bathroom, *Clean and Decent*, that 'a well-appointed garderobe, wainscoted, matted, perhaps with "paper wallys" and a bookshelf, could have been almost cosy'. He adds that in 'in the Life of St Gregory, this is the retreat recommended for uninterrupted reading'. It is a sobering irony that according to the Tudor antiquary John Leland, books had quite another function in privies after the dissolution of the monasteries. 'A great nombre of them whych purchased those superstycouse mansions reserved of those Librarie bokes, some to serve their jakes, some to scour their candlesticks.'

This sort of privy would have been furnished with a bucket full of dry earth or cinders, to be thrown in after use, and removed at appropriate intervals by the gardeners or 'nightsoil man'. The reason many early privies had more than one hole in their seat was probably less for companionship than to make best use of the space available below.

Undoubtedly the most common indoor resort before the advent of full-scale WC plumbing was to the chamber-pot and the close stool, both of them portable, easily concealed and simple to clean out. Pots can be seen under beds in medieval manuscripts and 'close stools', seats, often elaborately decorated, with a pot concealed underneath a hinged lid, were commonplace by the early sixteenth century, hence the enduring meaning of the word 'stool' as the product rather than the place of evacuation.

At Hardwick, inventories record that most of the bedrooms had chamber-pots and close stools, the latter usually covered with padded leather seats. Bess had her personal close stool in a little room off her bedchamber. It was covered with 'blewe cloth sticht with white, with red and black silk fringe'. The historian of Hardwick Hall, Mark Girouard, points out that there were no backstairs in the house, remarking that 'no amount of silk fringe can have offset the squalor of carting the contents of the emptied close stools down the two great staircases'.

It is possible, however, that investigation might turn up domestic slop chutes in the walls of such houses as Hardwick. These were often built beside chimneys when

Dunham Massey, Cheshire: beautifully veneered close stools made in the 1730s for the cantankerous Earl of Warrington. His own, made of burr walnut, sported his coronet and monogram inlaid into its lid.

a house was constructed, ending in an outdoor outlet about three or four feet from the ground. Here presumably a barrel could be stood and emptied daily once the maids had made a round of the rooms. Useful manure for the knot gardens, perhaps. I have read of such chutes, but only seen one, at Calke Abbey. It emerges at the back of the house, close to the wash-house door, but seems too narrow to have been a laundry chute. Bricked up when adequate water-closets were installed, such chutes would be barely distinguishable from chimney flues, as they were often taken up to the sky to ventilate them and allow rainwater in. Perhaps smooth internal rendering would distinguish them or, of course, analysis of their inner surfaces.

The bedroom commode was often disguised to look like a small cupboard or chest of drawers. In the dining-room of Penrhyn Castle, chamber-pots were housed in sideboard cupboards for the relief of gentlemen at the end of the meal, before they settled down to their port and cigars. Ladies withdrew to use facilities upstairs. For servants, outdoor quarters were provided.

Earth-closets were still popular outdoor sanitary arrangements in the eighteenth century. One survives in the Robert Adam bathhouse at Kedleston. They were also installed as permanent indoor fittings after the Revd Henry Moule invented his 'mechanized' earth-closet in 1860. Many stately mahogany-encased Victorian WCs were originally earth-closets of this sort. Dust-dry earth, carefully riddled and sieved, then baked so that it would pour like water, was stored above the closet. A decent reservoir would hold enough for twenty-five times. When the side handle on the closet was pulled up, an avalanche of earth poured down from behind the seat, sweeping all before it either into a reservoir below, or down a wooden chute which continued down the outside wall of the house. Ashes and cinders from the fire were also used. Anthracite ash was excellent, but not wood ash. Ordinary bituminous coal ash had to be sifted. Portable earth-closets were also popular, although acknowledged to be inferior to the properly installed models.

WATER-CLOSETS

Where natural geography allowed, water had long been used to wash out privies. But it had to be done by hand – by pumping, hauling or carrying water high enough to pour down the privy shafts. Providing an individual cistern which would wash out the lavatory basin each time it was used was the brainchild of Sir John Harington, the merry and glamorous godson of Queen Elizabeth I, and author of the very first treatise on water-closets, the 1596 *Metamorphosis of Ajax*. The title, of course, was a sly pun on the word jakes. Harington envisaged a pipe connecting the cistern with the bowl below, 'to yield water with a pretty strength when you would let it in'.

Drawings accompany his text, complete with pert little fishes in the cistern above. The vault below had to be emptied at noon and night, a cumbersome process which may have been the reason why Harington's water-closets were not widely adopted. At least one was installed in the Thameside Richmond Palace, where water supplies were easily available.

No patents at all were entered for water-closets between 1617, when the patent office opened, and 1775. This does not mean they were unknown, only that the many varieties of the standard pan-closet were not regarded as worth patenting. It had an upper bowl of lead, marble or glazed pottery. Its base was formed by a hinged metal pan similar to the lavatory bowls in aeroplanes today. When a handle was pulled, the pan tilted downwards and emptied its contents into a water-filled waste tank beneath. Then it could be closed 'to cut off the disagreeables'. Such simple pan-closets continued in use all through the nineteenth century; when I visited Dunham Massey in 1989, there was a fine collection of them stacked in the disused meat larder.

Like bathrooms, fixed water-closets seem to have been a matter of individual taste. In the vastness of Kedleston, James Paine installed only one indoor water-closet, but in 1760 Horace Walpole visited Aelia Lailia Chudley's house and was struck by 'the conveniences in every bedchamber: great mahogany projections ... with the holes, with brass handles, and cocks, etc. – I could not help saying, it was the loosest family I ever saw!' At Woburn the Duke of Bedford boasted of four privies, but only one was actually in the house. External 'bog houses' were a sensible arrangement until the invention of more efficient methods of washing out lavatory pans.

After Alexander Cummings, a watchmaker, patented his valve-closet in 1775, matters improved. It had a cistern overhead, a valve at the base of the bowl which was interconnected with the pipe to the cistern and a 'stink trap' – an S-bend in the waste pipe which remained filled with water and so prevented noisome smells from below. A few years later in 1778 Joseph Bramah, a cabinet-maker, improved on the valve of the Cummings closet. The water-closets installed at Blickling in 1791 were probably valve-closets of this type. By 1797 Bramah's firm had made about 6,000 closets and continued to make them until the 1890s. Many National Trust houses still have valve-closets installed, among them Berrington, Castle Drogo, Knightshayes and Blickling.

By 1816, a Mr Phair referred to water-closets as 'in general use ... fitted up in the neatest manner with excellent workmanship'. In 1818 Papworth's plans for a modest little villa showed a water-closet and plumbed-in washstand at one side of the hall, and another tucked under the staircase. In 1825 Adams (*The Complete Servant*) gave directions for lagging pipes in winter with bands of hay and straw and for piercing the pipe leading to the water-closet cistern in winter to prevent it bursting. It was then plugged with a small peg. One of the duties of the manservant was to pump up water to the cistern above the water-closet every morning. Once a week a bucket of clean water was swilled down the bowl to clear any remaining soil.

The 1870s witnessed the invention of two much simpler pans, which dispensed with the complicated metal workings of the valve-closet and relied on the force of water to sweep out the contents of the bowl. The first, the Twyford 'wash-out', deserved its name, according to Samuel Hellyer, most poetical of Victorian plumbers. The flush, he pointed out, had spent most of its force by the time it reached the base of the bowl and was not powerful enough to carry refuse down the trap. The 'wash-down', which is recognizably the ancestor of our own lavatory pans, had an S-bend directly underneath. Water gushed straight down, cleaning the simply shaped bowl, and forcing refuse through the S-bend. With a good head of water at the top of the house, such pans were very efficient. They were made in a wonderful variety of earthenware mouldings, decorated with blue and white transfer patterns.

Until the advent of twentieth-century improvements in the reliability and durability of plumbing systems, water-closets could be a mixed blessing. When it was first built in the 1880s, Newnham College, Cambridge, was fitted with earth-closets because of fears of the ill-effect of 'sewer-gas'. These were also referred to by Stevenson (1880), but he recommends at least three water-closets (for ladies, gents and servants respectively) in any house 'which pretends to convenience and perfection in planning'.

Aristocratic households remained eccentric. At Calke Abbey, only the most basic facilities were installed. When I visited the semi-derelict upper storeys in 1990, the only 'lavatory' was a portable commode in a cupboard in the former owner's dressing-room. Oddest of all was the situation at Welbeck Abbey. In 1879, after the death of the extremely reclusive 5th Duke of Portland, it was discovered that most of the rooms in the house were absolutely bare and empty, except that 'almost every room had a water-closet in the corner, with water laid on and in good working order, but not enclosed or sheltered in any way'. All the rooms, incidentally, were painted the same colour: pink.

CHAPTER TWELVE

LAUNDRY WORK

They that wash on Monday
Have all the week to dry;
They that wash on Tuesday
Are not so much awry;
They that wash on Wednesday
Are not so much to blame;
They that wash on Thursday
Wash for shame;
They that wash on Friday
Wash in need;
And they that wash on Saturday,
Oh! they're sluts indeed.

Robert Hunt, *Popular Romances of the West of England*

The traditional concept of Monday as washday is misleading. Washing was certainly best started on Monday, partly because such a heavy chore required a day of rest before it, partly because with any luck there would be enough cold leftovers from Sunday lunch to avoid the need to cook on a day when every drop of hot water was needed for washing, and partly because unless the process was started early in the week, it would not be completed by the end of the week, when Sunday bests had to be trotted out. Before the introduction of automatic washing-machines, tumble-driers and electric irons, only the poorest of households could complete the laundering process in a single day.

Unlike cooking and house-cleaning, washing was always women's work. In medieval households such as that of the Earl of Warwick, where cooking, cleaning and serving at table were exclusively men's preserves, and household affairs were overseen by a male steward rather than a female housekeeper, a laundrymaid was one of the very few women employed. Styles of washing varied according to each household's needs. Before the days of piped water, laundry was more often than not an outdoor pursuit, affording company and a refreshing change of scene to the housewife. Clothes were beaten clean with wooden bats (hence 'going batty') on the river bank or in the communal washing cistern. How often washing was done was governed partly by the time of year. There would be minimal work in winter, when problems of drying were great, and a flurry of activity in May when sunny days and good drying westerly winds could be hoped for.

Depending on the size of the household, washing might be done by the housewife herself or by a visiting washerwoman, or it might be sent out. In the fourteenth century, the household wash of the Countess of Northumberland was taken in by professional washerwomen in the town. 'Washing is with us this week,' a Norfolk clergyman recorded in his diary for 1799. 'We wash every five weeks. Our present washerwomen, Anne Downing and Anne Richmond, breakfast and dine the Monday and Tuesday and have a shilling each on their going away on Tuesday evening. Washing and ironing generally take us four days.' In the nineteenth century, when cheap cottons led to more washing altogether, laundry was sent out weekly or fortnightly by middling and upper-class city-dwellers; alternatively, a professional washerwoman might come to the house to do the washing once a week.

In Thomas and Jane Carlyle's parsimoniously run house in Chelsea, washing was done in the back kitchen by the maid of all work. There was a built-in copper, which could also be used for cooking processes, a secondary fireplace on which irons could be heated and 'a garden, surrounded with rather dim houses and questionable miscellanea, among other things clothes drying'. Even a substantial yeoman's house such as Townend needed no more washing facilities than a boiling copper in an outhouse.

At the other extreme was the large country house. There the scale of the task of washing is conveyed in part by such inventories of linen as that made at Shugborough in 1792.

Damask tablecloths	85
Damask table napkins	92 dozen
Damask breakfast cloths	23
Damask tea napkins	29 dozen
Diaper [a patterned linen union] tablecloths	67
Diaper table napkins	44 dozen
Bird's-eye [spotted] tablecloths	87
Bird's-eye table napkins	21 dozen
Huckaback towels	32
Diaper towels	5
Holland sheets	17 pairs
Holland pillowcases	17 pairs
Second sheets	19 pairs
Second pillowcases	18 pairs

Servants' sheets	24 pairs
Chintz quilts	2
White quilts	3

But dozens of damask dinner napkins and holland sheets innumerable were only a fraction of the work that could keep four laundrymaids busy for six days a week. Study the family portraits and the servants' group photographs as you wander round the great houses, and reflect on the work involved in maintaining those elaborate wardrobes. There were the family's clothes – men's shirts, women's petticoats and underclothes, children's pinafores and babies' nappies. 'Getting up' the lace frills, the goffered ruffs on widows' caps and the shiny starched evening-shirt fronts provided the laundress with a challenge. There were also the servants' clothes. Housemaids would wear both morning frocks (blue gingham, perhaps, with a large wraparound apron) and black afternoon dresses, with starched white caps and tiny frilled aprons, in which to open the front door to callers and serve tea. At Kingston Lacy in 1910, Mrs Jenks the cook wore 'white ribbed cotton or linen with a white apron, and with an additional white "rubber" or cloth pinned over her bosom and tied behind for cooking'. Heavily soiled clothes might be expected from grooms and gardeners; special finishing techniques were required for the white breeches and starched cravats of the footmen.

Washing on this scale required a full-scale laundry suite. This was often built on the periphery of servants' quarters, perhaps adjoining the stables. One reason for this was the undesirability of allowing the distinctive and pungent smells connected with early washing processes to reach the house itself, another that the laundrymaids needed easy access to the drying and bleaching grounds. However, nineteenth-century country-house planners such as Kerr warned of the dangers of unholy alliances between laundry and stable. Barbara Charlton's memoirs of Hesleyside in Northumberland mention 'scandalous goings-on' in the laundry – 'it was nothing but a brothel until a new entrance was built and gates put up to keep intruders out'. At Pakenham Hall in Ireland, an underground passage was built between the wash-house and the drying green so that the laundrymaids could bypass the temptation of the stables. According to Viola Bankes the laundry at Kingston Lacy was also strategically located:

All the washing of the family's and servants' linen was done, all and every day, by two Irish laundrymaids. The sheets, washed without chemicals and carried in huge heavy baskets to be hung out of sight behind the stables, would emerge beautifully soft and fresh ... We could look down into the two rooms of the laundry from the backstairs landing, or visit them, especially if our mother was away. In one room, kind Julia, who was pitifully thin, and good-natured Ellen, who was enormously fat, washed all the linen in a vast boiler. In the other they did the ironing, heating the flat-irons on a stove and holding them up to their cheeks to see if they were hot.

Before dispatch to the laundry, whether domestic or commercial, an accurate record of the articles sent had to be made. Keeping track of linen on its way to and from the laundry was a nightmare, ultimately the responsibility of the housekeeper. If the establishment was grand enough, a sorting room in the house might be provided for the dirty clothes. 'By preference, this room should be long and narrow, with the light on the long side,' advised Percival Smith in 1883. Kerr recommended that it be fitted up with bins for the classification of different articles. These would be lined with calico bags – naturally requiring regular washing as well – which could be lifted into the large wicker baskets, often sensibly mounted on castors, in which the dirty clothes were taken to the laundry. In well-planned mansions, laundry chutes were installed down which soiled linen could be thrown. The chutes were also lined with canvas, similarly removable for cleaning.

A book in which to record items dispatched was of course vital. Laundry lists have a splendid ancestry – Michael Ventris deciphered the Cretan script Linear B to read of washday in Knossos; hieroglyphs record them in ancient Egypt; from what Pliny tells us, Roman washerwomen were as unreliable in returning entries as listed as those complained of 1600 years or so later on London's Lavender (launderer's) Hill. In his *History of the Hornbook*, Andrew Tuer describes a seventeenth-century washing tally used at Haddon Hall in Derbyshire – an oblong piece of wood, bound with brass and faced with a sheet of transparent horn. The front bears a list of clothes and household linen. In the top row, ruffs, bands, cuffs, handkerchiefs and caps are listed; in the second, sheets, half-shirts, boot-hose, tops and socks, and at the bottom, sheets, pillow-beres [pillowslips], tablecloths, napkins and towels. Beneath each word is a movable disc which could be turned to show the appropriate number, enabling the maid in charge of the counting to compose an accurate list without being able to write.

*Laundry list for family of four and two servants c. 1880: a
fortnight's wash*

2 prs coloured wool stockings	7 silk hanks, 20 white cotton
20 neckcloths and collars	4 frilled collars and tuckers
8 night caps	2 muslins
5 cambric gowns	2 flannel waistcoats
6 flannel petticoats	2 prs white woollen stockings

5 (coloured) calico gowns	10 white shirts
30 shifts	26 prs cotton stockings
8 pinafores	2 coats
2 cotton night caps	2 prs trousers
4 prs drawers	4 fine table cloths
12 table naps	4 tray cloths
4 breakfast cloths	2 prs fine sheets
4 pillow cases fine	20 towels
2 kitchen table cloths	6 glass and 8 kitchen
dusters	cloths
4 knife cloths	4 kitchen hand towels
3 prs common sheets	3 coarse pillow cases

In the well-preserved laundry at Castle Ward, the last laundry book in use is shown to visitors by a most appropriate person: formerly a housemaid, she once made up the list for the laundrywomen herself.

The size of a country-house laundry varied from a single wash-house to a whole suite of rooms containing bleach house, drying room, hot-air closet, mangling room and ironing and folding rooms. Ideally, these were arranged in sequence so that the dirty washing went in one end and came out clean at the other. An average laundry suite required three rooms at least – wash-house proper, drying loft or closets, and the laundry itself where mangling and ironing was carried out. In a plan of the laundry suite at Dyrham Park, drawn up in about 1700 by the head gardener Thomas Hurnall, it is apparent that these three rooms were stacked one above the other.

By the 1860s, piped hot and cold water was a standard specification in the laundry of a new country house. Kerr also suggested a supplementary boiler in the wash-house as well as the coal-fired copper. Fuel was also needed for the laundry stoves and the furnace that heated the drying closets. A large laundry suite had a substantial fuel-store attached to it – in the 1900s, the Erddig laundry used 18 tons of coal a year.

Without experiencing an old-fashioned laundry in action, it is easy to forget the sweltering heat and steamy dampness produced by the boiling coppers, the drying closets and the iron-heating grates or stoves. Some impression of the atmosphere can be had, however, by visiting the laundry at Shugborough, where, thanks to Pamela Sambrook's expert research into how washing really happened, the copper is regularly lit, the clothes scrubbed and the mangle and irons put to use. One of the most delightful aspects of this reconstruction, she told me, is the number of visitors who can still remember the old days of laundering, and who add useful details to her reconstruction of a highly skilled and complex set of operations.

WASHING

The first essential of the laundry's wash-house was a high ceiling, preferably with a louvred ventilator to allow for the free escape of steam. Doors and windows were also large. Floors were originally of stone, later of Portland cement or asphalt. Glazed stoneware channels drained the floor of the wash-house at Shugborough, and standing-boards kept the maids' feet dry. Rainwater was the best form of water supply – its softness gave excellent results, and many domestic courtyards had large rainwater tanks fed from a network of rooftop gutters underneath their paving.

Washing troughs were originally wooden, and capacious enough to accommodate washboards. They were also used for soaking clothes. Erddig had four in its laundry in 1833, but by the early twentieth century large glazed earthenware sinks had replaced these. Besides such sinks – preferably positioned under the windows to give maximum light – the wash-house was furnished with coopered tubs in which large items could be churned about with a number of differently designed wash-sticks. A built-in boiling copper, preferably not of iron, which caused spots of iron-mould on the clothes, was essential. It had to be filled and emptied with buckets and a 'dipper', a shallow metal bowl with a wooden handle. The copper was heated from underneath by its own fire in a highly efficient fashion. A Derbyshire laundress recalled that a few colly-pegs (dried gorse twigs) could boil twenty to forty gallons of water remarkably fast. If coal was used, it was fired up early in the morning by cinders taken from domestic fireplaces that had been kept in overnight.

Before the age of cheap cotton, clothes were washed as little as possible. Originally no cleansing agents were used – dirt was simply bashed out of clothes using batlets and elbow grease. This was harsh on fine fabrics, and the stiffening agents put into poor quality silks to give them body were easily washed out. But dirt, particularly sweat, quickly rotted clothes – as can be seen from the decaying tatters under the arms of many otherwise well-preserved garments. The easiest way to get rid of the greasy dirt that accumulates in household linen is to use an alkali.

Soaking clothes in an alkaline solution known as a lye was the precursor of hot-water washing with soap. Lye was made by collecting fine white ash from furnaces, bread ovens and fireplaces, and placing it in a wooden sieve over a tub. Water was poured over it and stirred, which washed alkaline salts out of the ash and into the water. After being filtered through muslin, the lye was ready for use. Different ashes had different properties – oak was the strongest, apple wood produced the whitest wash, fern ash was a useful substitute in areas where wood was in short supply. Making wash-balls from water and the ashes of half-dried ferns burnt in little pots (hence potash) was a profitable cottage industry, and the seventeenth-century account books of Chirk Castle show regular payments for soap, wash-balls and fern ash.

*Late-eighteenth-century wooden sinks in the wash-house, originally the hen-wife's
room, at The Argory, in Co. Armagh.*

Other substances used as lyes included pigeon or hen dung, bran and urine, all
remarkably efficacious cleansers. Privies often had a small extra hole with a pan under
it in which urine could be collected and used for the wash.

Instead of being rubbed or pounded, linen was loosely folded in a wooden tub
called a 'buck'. (This is why a small tub is called a 'bucket'.) The lye was poured
over the clothes, and drawn off at the base of the buck by a small spigot. The process
was repeated until the lye came through clean. Most clothes would then need nothing
more than rinsing and drying, but some heavily stained linens might be boiled in
the copper.

Lyes were virtually free. Soap, on the other hand, was made from vegetable oils
and animal fats, ingredients that were both costly and much in demand for such
purposes as cooking and candle-making. Soap-making at home was a tedious process,
involving boiling lye with fat and precipitating the mixture to a curd by adding
common salt. Generally rather soft, it was kept in bowls, or small hand-rolled balls.
Soap-making was one of the most ancient of West Country trades. '*Apud Bristollum
nemo est qui non sit vel fuerit saponarius,*' commented the twelfth-century chronicler
Richard of Devizes. It was a seasonal trade, because it made use of the annual glut
of animal fat at the autumn slaughtering of cattle.

In 1633 the first competitive washing commercial took place when the London
Soap Masters rode down to Bristol to test samples of Bristol soaps against the
'accredited brands' of London. Two redoubtable local laundresses, Sara Willys of the

Rose Tavern and Elizabeth Delhay of the Dolphin, publicly washed linen napkins and proved that Bristol soap washed as white and as sweet – 'in good faith rather sweeter' – than those washed with the London brand. Fine Castile soap, made from pure olive oil, was highly rated, but until 1853 substantial excise duties were charged on this and other imported soap. Because it was expensive, soap was carefully husbanded. It was bought by weight and stored in dry cupboards until it hardened. Sharp corners and edges were trimmed off and the shavings dissolved into soap jelly, ideal for laundry work.

The first washing tool to improve on the knobbly knuckles of the experienced washerwoman was a small hand-held wooden instrument which could be rubbed against a ribbed washboard. The next was a hand-held agitator, twisted rhythmically or pumped vigorously up and down in a wooden tub. These 'dollies' – four- or five-legged objects looking like milkmaid's stools with a long central handle – and conical copper 'possers' were to inspire the first washing-machines. There were patents for such machines as early as 1752, but it was not until the 1850s that Mr Harper Twelvetrees produced some of the most satisfactory washing-machines of this sort. Their only drawback was a tendency for clothes to get knotted around the dolly legs. The solution was a reciprocating gearing which was used to effect in the very popular Red Star machines.

Washboards inspired a different style of machine. Inside the Old Faithful washer which can be seen in the Shugborough laundry a curved wooden arm slides over a bed of rollers. Simpler in principle were the extremely successful 'Vowel' machines

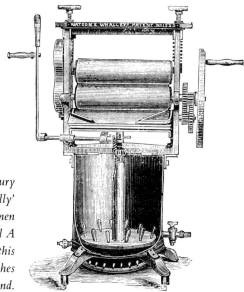

This cross-section of a mid-nineteenth-century washing-machine shows its debt to the old 'dolly' pumped up and down in a washtub by washerwomen in pre-mechanical times. Bradford's Vowel A machines were a considerable improvement on this sort of machine, as there were no stumps for clothes to get caught around.

patented by Mr Bradford of Saltram in 1861. These machines came in five sizes (A, E, I, O and U) and consisted of a hexagonal box which rocked and vibrated around a short axis. The inside was lined with ribs of wood to increase friction on the wash. The 1883 edition of Mrs Beeton praised the Vowel E: 'The machine will wash twelve shirts, or a large blanket or counterpane, and the ease with which the machine is worked is surprising.' Later versions, such as the Vowel I in the Erddig laundry, were improved by better gearing to the turning handle. Such machines were particularly popular in small households. Mrs Haweis's book of tips to newly-weds, *The Art of Housekeeping* (1889), in the course of discussing how much washing money to allow the servants (to pay for a washing-woman to do their washing), suggests that the 'wise bride would at any rate begin by washing at home with one of the easy and economical washing-machines, with which everything except shirts and goods requiring clear-starching can be done in a morning'.

However good the gearing, such machines were tiring to use, and needed constant attendance. The development of small electric motors in the early years of the twentieth century was a vital step forward in making domestic washing-machines viable. The first electric machines to be mass-produced were American, notably those made by Maytag, Hotpoint and Thor. Such machines began to be imported into Britain in the 1920s. Berrington has an interesting early Thor cylinder machine, which the present head of the family, Lord Cawley, remembers in use. It stood beside a sink, so that clothes could be lifted from its tub and put through the motor-driven wringer, draining into the sink. Later Thor machines – remembered by anybody born before 1950 as stalwart supports on washday – had a central agitator on the Red Star principle and could spin clothes dry.

DRYING

Clothes were originally wrung (twisted) dry. If you look carefully around an old wash-house or scullery you may still find the thick blunt 'tenterhook' that was used for this purpose. Once washed, linen was attached to this hook – small garments might be put into a netting sack – and wound round tightly until all water had been squeezed from them. This technique engendered the fashion for tight pleats evident from manuscript illustrations of eleventh-century women, Dresses were twisted tightly when wet, and the long 'rope' that resulted was tied tightly in lines, crossing and recrossing to achieve an intricately creased pattern. Resins from the bark of fruit trees were used to stiffen the pleats and keep them in.

Mechanical wringers that squeezed clothes dry between rollers were a spin-off from the late-eighteenth-century development of mangles (see below). Small wooden wringers could be screwed on to a sink, as at Kingston Lacy; they also became a standard feature of early washing-machines, powered by the same mechanism, switched into operation by slipping a small catch. In 1846 Goodyear patented indiarubber and by 1880 Stevenson's *House Architecture* referred to 'the wringing-machine, a simple and efficient American contrivance, by which water is pressed out of clothes by indiarubber rollers, without the injury to which they used to be subjected by wringing, takes up no space, being fixed to one of the tubs'.

When possible, clothes and linen were dried outside. 'When linen is soiled and discoloured by town washing, or by age, or by lying-by out of use, the best bleaching materials are the natural verdure of the ground, with the dews and winds of Heaven,' declared *A New System of Practical Domestic Economy* (1824). It was advisable not to construct the drying or bleaching green too far from the house, or else items might disappear. In an early picture of Uppark, clothes can be seen spread out flat to bleach in the sunshine on the lawns remarkably close to the house. At Castle Ward, Calke and Dunham Massey there are still walled drying greens close to the laundry offices. Clothes were also dried – and scented – on rosemary and lavender hedges grown for the purpose.

Drying indoors was a last resort, necessary only in wet or wintry weather. In humble dwellings clothes were hung from drying rods (poles or perches) suspended by hooks in the kitchen ceiling. Hooks used for this purpose can easily be distinguished from those for drying meat by their arrangement in parallel lines. Later, if kitchen ceilings were high enough to accommodate them, airing racks were hoisted overhead on pulleys. The wash-house and laundry generally had racks hoisted to the roof, but domestic manuals advise against their use for drying wet clothes; they were really intended for airing. It was regarded as much healthier to have a separate drying loft above the wash-house, as at Kingston Lacy and Dyrham Park. 'Many linens' were stolen from the 'drying chamber' at Baddesley Clinton in 1643.

In the mid nineteenth century, closets for indoor drying were constructed in large institutions and country mansions. They are brick enclosures built over the water-heating furnaces or a special network of hot pipes, and examples can be seen in the laundries of Berrington, Erddig and Kingston Lacy. They hold long movable iron frames which slide out to be loaded with wet clothes. It was important to have smooth, broad drying rails that would not crease the clothes, and for the sliding action to be smooth enough not to shake off the smaller items. A wire grille above the heating pipes was a wise precaution against loss of such small and elusive items as handkerchiefs and socks. Ideally, there was double access to the drying frames. They could be pulled out one way into the wash-house to be loaded, then slid out on the opposite side into the laundry, where the dried linen was taken off.

Such closets were criticized by Stevenson as 'complicated and expensive'. He suggests a simpler system – 'a simple brick chamber through which a stream of hot air is

Drying closets and a small ironing stove in the Victorian laundry at Berrington Hall, Worcs. The frames could be pulled right out of the heated chamber to load and unload with linen and clothes.

passed. It is closed by a door and fitted with bars or horses.' He also warned that unless the stream of air through a drying closet was 'abundant', the clothes would get yellow. 'Even with the most perfect ventilation, they can never, if dried in darkness, have the purity and freshness which is given by the sun and open air of a bleaching green.'

MANGLING AND FINISHING

The room in which clothes were ironed and mangled was often known as the laundry, as distinct from the wash-house. It would have long steady tables, preferably beside the windows. There might also be a folding ironing-board or two, and a small sleeve-board. An interesting item on display in the laundry of Kingston Lacy is a 'breech tree', a board cut in the shape of two flattened legs which was used to stretch riding breeches after cleaning. Dorothy Hartley's *Water in England* gives an eighteenth-century recipe for ensuring that the squire's riding breeches were whiter than white, and stiffer than stiff:

Brush well and damp with clean water. Then apply the mixture all over very thoroughly but lightly. Isinglass half an ounce, Powdered pumice one ounce. White Soap 2 oz. Pipe clay 3 cakes. Starch a large spoonful. Sweet Oil 6 spoonfuls. Mix well with boiling water to a thick cream. Let the breech dry slowly and thoroughly, then dust well with a cane, stretch to proper shape on breech trees and iron with a box iron (take care not to scorch).

The earliest piece of machinery to be used in the laundry was the mangle. It is a fascinating machine, widely misunderstood. In its original form, it was in no sense a wringer, and was not used to squeeze water from wet clothes but to iron sheets, tablecloths and other flat linen. It was invented by combining two very ancient processes – firstly the simple application of screw pressure – such as that used in a cider mill or linen press; secondly the smoothing technique of winding clothes around smooth wooden cylinders, wrapping them in cloths (brattices), and rolling them to and fro, applying considerable pressure from above, with broad cricket-bat-sized instruments. These 'batlets', which had of necessity to be made from well-seasoned wood, were evidently prized household items, often intricately carved on the upper surface.

There are two distinct types of mangle. The spectacular box mangle (illustrated on p. xii of the Preface) was an eighteenth-century invention, developed from the rollers and batlets technique. It was a low wooden table with a frame which extended upwards to support an oblong wooden box weighted with large stones and mounted on runners. Clothes wound on rollers were placed between box and table, and the box was propelled over the rollers by pulling at straps attached to each end. One of the oldest box mangles in the possession of the National Trust is the machine supplied to the Shugborough laundry in 1810 by Baker of London. It remained in use until the 1920s, operated every Wednesday by a handyman.

'The labour of working the box mangle is excessive,' commented a domestic manual of 1861, 'not only on account of the strength required to move it, but from the continual reversing of motion; for scarcely has it been got into motion by great exertion than it becomes necessary to turn it back again.' Later in the century rack and pinion mechanisms and flywheels made box mangles easier to operate because the handle could be turned continuously; the simple box mangles with flywheels at Castle Ward and Dunham Massey can be contrasted with the chain-driven machines at Erddig and Kingston Lacy. The machine at Snowshill (by Eddy, Cate, Oxenham and Eddy), made in about 1860, has a similar reciprocating motion.

The much more familiar upright mangle in a frame was first patented in the late eighteenth century for use in the textile trade. Originally it had three rollers, one octagonal, and heavy weights to apply pressure. By the middle of the nineteenth century, there were generally only two rollers, and springs and adjustable screws provided pressure more efficiently. This made them usefully flexible tools. First clothes could be wrung in them, using old rollers that had cracked or become uneven. Then rollers in perfect condition, ideally made of well-seasoned quarter-cleft maple or a similar hardwood, were fitted, and the linen could be smoothed between well-worn holland mangling brattices to the fine gloss that was the trademark of a skilled laundrymaid. In laundries large enough to boast a box mangle, the upright mangle was only used for wringing, and was therefore generally to be found in the wash-house rather than the laundry.

Once the tablecloths, napkins and sheets were mangled, they were placed under the screws of a linen press before their return to the linen room proper. Other clothes required ironing. Flat-irons were the cheapest and simplest tools of the trade. A good set of flat-irons consisted of pairs of irons in different sizes. A laundress would work with a pair, leaving the one she was not using to reheat on a trivet attached to the bars of the grate. The 1710 Dyrham Park inventory listed '4 smoothing irons, a Grate, and an iron Heater' in the laundrymaid's room.

By the 1850s, special laundry stoves were supplied in a variety of designs: there is a tall octagonal pillar at Dunham Massey and Shugborough, a compact stove at

The magnificent nineteenth-century laundry room at Castle Ward, Co. Down, with a laundry stove capacious enough to hold a dozen or more flat-irons of all sizes, and a kettle for tea besides. On the long table under the window there are cap irons, an Italian iron and a goffering machine.

Kingston Lacy and substantial free-standing, flat-topped stoves at Castle Ward and Beningbrough in Yorkshire. Besides having rests for different sizes of flat-iron, such stoves often made provision for the curved bases of cap irons with a few concave nests. In 1870 an American housewife called Mary Florence Pott patented a double-ended flat-iron with a detachable handle. These 'Mrs Potts irons', as they were universally known, proved extremely popular. They were generally sold in sets of three different sizes, with one handle and a stand. A fine set can be seen in the Castle Ward laundry, which has an imaginative exhibition of the results of using such tools: lace-trimmed night-dresses and children's gowns, pillowcases and shirts, collars, cuffs and tablecloths.

But flat-irons were only the simplest of smoothing tools. Cleaner in use, because it did not have to go near the fire at all, was the box iron – an Erddig inventory of 1726 mentions four box irons and eight 'heaters', possibly a reference to the slugs of metal which were heated on the fire and then placed inside the iron. A pair would be required for each iron, so that a constant heat could be maintained by changing them around. Erddig now displays an exceptionally fine collection of irons, but they do not all belong there – they are part of the Best Collection of domestic utensils, which is on loan to the house. It includes a charcoal iron, loaded from the back with slow-burning charcoal. Irons like this are very efficient, and are still in use in such parts of the world as India and Czechoslovakia, where power is unreliable and expensive in rural areas. There is also a set of goffering tongs, which were used to crimp ruffs, and a small frame holding a stack of rods round which ribbons were wound. A later development was the little goffering machine with fluted brass rollers, like a miniature mangle, which could be screwed on to the tabletop. The first patent for them was taken out in the United States by Susan Knox in 1866.

From the 1890s paraffin, oil and even petrol irons were also popular – they are alarming-looking appliances, with large spherical reservoirs perched behind the handles, but they were very efficient in the hands of an experienced laundrymaid. If gas was available, a gas iron was easily the best type of pre-electric iron. There were two types: one had a burner fixed inside the body of the iron; the other, much less disagreeable in use, consisted of a hollow iron slotted over a stand in which a burner was incorporated.

The earliest electric iron was patented by H. W. Seely of New Jersey in 1882. It was heated by means of an electric arc between two adjustable carbon electrodes. A similar French iron, patented a few years later, was described in use as 'a handful of blinding light, flying sparks and weird noises'. In 1895 Crompton's London electrical firm advertised a massive, 14 lb electric iron which embodied an electrical resistance heating element basically similar to that of a modern iron. Lighter irons were advertised in the Army and Navy Stores catalogue of 1907, but their general use had to wait until the widespread introduction of electricity in the late 1920s and early 1930s.

Immaculately finished, aired and folded, the clean wash was put into baskets and carried back to the main house. The ladies' maids, the gentlemen's gentlemen and the nursemaids took in the clothes for their respective departments. The housekeeper checked the linen against her list, and put it away, spiked with fragrant lavender faggots, in the cupboards of the linen room. Finally the laundrymaids would return to the laundry to finish the week's work by cleaning and scrubbing out the wash-house, the ironing and mangling room and the drying loft ready for the next load – the next day.

Despite the efficiency and method of a country-house laundry suite, Stevenson regarded home laundering as 'hardly economical' in the 1870s. Commercial laundries, with washing-machines and mangles driven by steam or hydraulic power multiplied rapidly, and the 1911 census showed a sharp decline in the numbers of private laundrymaids. Motor transport meant that laundry could be collected and delivered quickly and efficiently from any nearby town, and the laundry as a domestic office in its own right disappeared.

In small households which did their own washing, three factors reduced the amount of labour involved enormously: changes in fashion, the invention of easy-care man-made fibres and the development of the electric washing-machine. But it is worth reflecting on the fact that a chore once removed from all but the poorest homes has now returned. Washing may be lighter work than it ever was, but it is still the least popular of household chores.

CONCLUSION

Houses rise and fall, crumble, are extended,
Are removed, destroyed, restored . . .

T. S. Eliot, 'East Coker'

A woman should not be less careful in her domestic
management because the spirit of the age gives her greater
scope for her activities.

Mrs Beeton's Book of Household Management, 1907

It will be evident, from the frequency with which I have lingered over details of the domestic arrangements at Castle Drogo, that I find it a uniquely interesting house, a *summa domestica*, epitome of the 'high housekeeping'. But Drogo, perhaps the most comfortably equipped castle in the world, was outdated even while it was being built. Edwin Lutyens was aware that it was an anachronism. 'I do wish he didn't want a Castle, but just a delicious lovable house, with plenty of good large rooms in it,' he wrote of Julius Drewe's original commission. Drewe died the year after Drogo was completed. Its highly organized luxury was contingent not just on technology but on a large and efficient staff, and the sudden revolution in the availability and quality of domestic servants during and after the First World War was a death-blow to his dreams.

Why did servants leave? In the twentieth century, they were well treated on the whole, but still tended to be discontented. Their social status *vis-à-vis* their peers was low, an aspect perhaps of the fact that their duties were increasingly servile – brushing riding habits, ironing newspapers, painting the lines on tennis courts – and less and less productive. As William Lanceley put it, 'The thorn lies in the fact that a man is reduced to a kind of degraded sycophance' (*Hall-boy to House-Steward*). Once there were alternative occupations – as dashing young 'typewriters', shop assistants or assembly-line workers – in the new 'light' industries, servants quitted in droves.

Household manuals such as Lily Frazer's *First Aid to the Servantless* (1913) reflected the sense of injury experienced by employers, although despair was interestingly combined with elation at no longer having to cope with the endless difficulties of engaging, training and disciplining staff. 'The wealthy woman of today does not desire a place; she prefers a service flat somewhere in W1,' declared P. A. Barron's *The House Desirable* (1906 – quoted in Clive Aslet's excellent and elegiac *The Last Country Houses*). Mansion flats, with communal laundries, piped vacuum-cleaner services and rubbish disposal, and the ability to send 'dainty dinners' up from central kitchens were also Lily Frazer's ultimate solution to domestic management.

But large numbers of rural romantics remained loyal to the countryside, even though today a combination of high property values and death duties have made the great houses that were once showpieces of the best of British domestic traditions a liability that few can afford. Many families found it difficult to adjust to the new

Mrs Jones, housekeeper, and Mr Jones (unrelated), gardener and handyman, in 1911; they were the last of the small army of much-cherished servants who once looked after the Yorkes of Erddig, Clwyd.

order – or rather, absence of order. The Yorkes of Erddig and the Harpur Crewes of Calke lived on eccentrically in the gathering dust, finally making over their houses to the National Trust in a state of decay which earlier generations would have regarded as unthinkable and immoral. Other once-great families have become in effect servants themselves, caretakers and stewards of a heritage they haven't the heart to desert. Living, significantly, in the servants' quarters, they have arranged their former homes as museums of a way of life that is no longer possible. Such mansions are no longer marvellously organized machines for living in, but white elephants. These days, home comfort is bought, not made. Only the very rich enjoy it without effort.

What of the average middle-class family? How did Mrs Pooter cope without her 'general' or Virginia Woolf without her daily char? In her 1913 articles on *Housekeeping with Efficiency*, the American Christine Frederick offered seductive visions of cutting down domestic staff by applying industrial method to the home. The old weekly routines, 'regular as clockwork', were forced on mistress as much as on maid. Brand-new Hoovers in hand, such women abandoned genteel self-fulfilment and voluntary work among the deserving poor, and took up arms against a sea of dust, chanting the modish battle-cry of the time-and-motion experts: 'Use your head to save your steps.'

They may have overdone things. Research on domestic time-use in the 1960s suggested that women as a whole were doing as much if not more housework than they did in the 1920s. Theorists shook their heads over this, muttering 'hygiene obsessionals', 'gluttons for punishment', 'service slaves of patriarchy' or 'innate conservatism' as the mood took them. But a new breakdown of statistics by the economist J. Gershuny separating by class has shown that it was in fact the huge increase in hours spent by *middle-class* women on housework when their maids left them in the lurch that created this apparent increase. Working-class women are actually finding domestic life lighter and pleasanter than ever before.

There are hopeful implications here. We could soon have time on the run. Information technologists are already talking about 'smart houses' that take over most of the tedious, time-consuming chores. Perhaps we can begin to graduate from hand-to-mouth domestic mop-up operations and think seriously about how proper organization could improve the quality of household life for all of us. First, there is much worth retaining from the past. In many ways home life, although more strenuous and exhausting, was more productive, and therefore more satisfying, than it is today. It is significant that many women – and indeed men – like to use the leisure gained by modern technology to make housework a hobby: baking bread, making jam, spinning wool and sewing, just because of the satisfying sense of personal creation such occupations give them. Hundreds of years of social conditioning cannot vanish at the click of a switch.

Moreover, after one has looked at the history of housekeeping from a practical point of view, it is impossible to avoid noticing the striking contrast between the isolation and individualism of modern domestic life and the varied social interactions and interdependencies of households in previous centuries. The domestic contract which used to be summed up by the words 'hus(house)band' and 'house(hus)wife' has altered out of all recognition. 'Good husband without, it is needful there be/Good huswife within as needful as he,' wrote Thomas Tusser, neatly dividing indoor and outdoor domestic labour. Now most husbands are far away from home all day and wives have had to accustom themselves to solitary confinement. Children too use the home more as a hotel, a springboard to individual futures, than as an intrinsic part of their lives.

Without the technological revolution of the last hundred years, women would certainly not have their present freedom to consider full-time working outside the home. But most of them shoulder a double burden in order to do so. Housekeeping, once a demanding and skilful full-time occupation which was accorded considerable social status, is now a nuisance: something to be fitted into odd moments or neglected until extremes of chaos make a blitz necessary. Electricity has transformed the sheer labour of housework, but it does little to assist in its organization.

Have we missed an opportunity? Good housekeeping was once a genuine science, handed down from mother to daughter and even taught in schools. It was crossed off the school curriculum with egalitarian enthusiasm because it was seen as committing girls to domestic slavery. But ignorance and inexperience make housework more, rather than less, enslaving. It is time that we had a new domestic contract for the family, something that involves all its members. Skills in cooking, cleaning and renovating the home should be taught in schools to boys and girls alike. As for homework, what could be more appropriate than using it to do just that: work for the home?

The alternative is to continue the present commitment to individual achievement at the expense of the family group. Nothing could be less like the complicated structures upholding the domesticity of Castle Drogo than the organization of one of the smallest houses owned by the National Trust, a tiny Dorset cottage called Cloud's Hill. At the time that Julius Drewe was planning his luxurious fortress, this was T. E. Lawrence's personal hideaway. It was a place to unwind, to be himself, to be 'at home' in a way he could not possibly be in the nearby army barracks where he lived as Private Ross. Although it has a spartan bathroom, there is no kitchen at all – hot food was sent over from the nearest obliging pub. Upstairs was simply a music room and a small dressing-room with a bunk for the odd visitor. Yet its heart was, in the traditional manner, its hearth: a huge open fireplace in the book-lined bedsitting-room downstairs. There Lawrence could perch on the padded fender and boil a kettle, mull wine, make toast, before lounging on the leather-covered divan beside the window to think and to write. It is a singleton's paradise. Is it the domestic future?

GAZETTEER

This is an annotated list of the National Trust houses which I think have most to offer those interested in domestic arrangements. It is necessarily selective – to list every kitchen, bathroom and dovecote on show in a National Trust house would make this part of the book disproportionately large. By no means all the houses mentioned in the text are included here, only those which have a great deal on show in the way of domestic quarters, or have one quite outstanding item, such as the ice tower/dovecote at Downhill, or the donkey wheel at Grey's Court. For a complete list of all properties, fuller general descriptions and details of times of opening and facilities, you will need the *National Trust Handbook*.

Ardress House, Portadown, Co. Armagh
Seventeenth-century Ardress is a 'family house' with no pretensions to grandeur but a great deal of atmosphere. The poultry yard is still occupied, and the dairy has some unusual early machinery.

The Argory, Dungannon, Co. Tyrone
Substantial Victorian well-being permeates this well-upholstered and comfortable middle-class house. Lights, hall stove and the acetylene gas plant in the one-time laundry yard are of special note.

Baddesley Clinton, Knowle, Warwickshire
A moated fourteenth-century manor with privy tower and chain of fish-ponds. The underground drainage system can be viewed through glass windows in the floor.

Belton House, Grantham, Lincolnshire
Although the household offices themselves are not actually on view, externally Belton offers a satisfying complete late-seventeenth-century domestic layout, with wings containing offices leading towards the coach-house and stable block.

Blickling Hall, Aylsham, Norfolk
Long wings of domestic offices flank the approach to Blickling; underground passages from the former kitchen can be seen as you cross a small bridge to the front door. The bathroom and water-closet are particularly splendid, and there is an ice house (somewhat dilapidated) in the grounds.

Calke Abbey, Ticknall, Derbyshire
One day Calke will be a five-star cornucopia of domestic interest, but it is still in process of restoration. Even in their present state, the brewery, laundry, kitchen quarters, with cellars, scullery and cook's room, and strings of specialized offices off the long corridors between kitchen and servery, are illuminating.

Carlyle's House, Chelsea, London
Domestic life in a four-storey Georgian town-house was cabin'd and confined: the Carlyles' maid had a fourposter bed in the front kitchen; a lead cistern in the back kitchen provided all domestic water. Interesting for those who live in such houses today to see how servants' quarters were originally arranged. Read Thea Holme's evocative *The Carlyles at Home* before visiting.

Castle Coole, Enniskillen, Co. Fermanagh
Potentially the most spectacular museum of domesticity in the world, Castle Coole boasts two enormous separate quadrangles of domestic offices. They are on the point of collapse at the moment, but there are plans to save them. There is also an underground tunnel to the house in which two coaches could pass each other with ease, with adjacent storage cellars and airy basement kitchens, housekeeper's room and other offices. Very little of this, unfortunately, is on view to the public, but it can be glimpsed and guessed at.

Castle Drogo, Drewsteignton, Devon
Designed by that doyen of home comfort, Sir Edwin Lutyens, Drogo is quite simply the most stylishly comfortable castle in the world. Sculleries, larders, bathrooms and pantries are all finished with a rare degree of attention to detail.

Castle Ward, Strangford, Co. Down
A 'his and her' house, half classical, half Gothick, Castle Ward has secret doors in the library and a nice line in bell-pulls. Perhaps the single most evocative sight there is the flight of stone stairs into the basement worn down diagonally by the hurrying feet of servants. There is an excellent laundry and well-reconstructed housekeeper's room and wine cellar.

Charlecote Park, Wellesbourne, Warwickshire

The kitchens at Tudor Charlecote date from the mid nineteenth century, with both open hearth and closed ranges, and an unusual steam-heated work surface. There is also a good bakehouse and brewhouse, and an eel trap.

Cotehele, St Dominick, Cornwall

Cotehele's remote position has protected it from the passage of time. The dumpy, red-tiled medieval dovecote is exceptionally attractive, so too are the rambling outbuildings. The kitchen, restored to early simplicity, has an enormous hearth, baking oven and copper, and is well-furnished with utensils of the period.

Cragside, Rothbury, Northumberland

A temple to high Victorian technology, Cragside can boast not only the first country-house electricity in the world, but a system of hydraulic power that operated the kitchen spits, lifts and even rotating orange pots in the greenhouses. Plumbed washstands and sunken baths, an early gas stove and underfloor hot-air heating are just a few of its many innovatory domestic conveniences.

Downhill Castle, Castlerock, Co. Londonderry

Ruins sometimes have more atmosphere than careful reconstructions. The vast skeleton of the Earl-Bishop of Derry's great folly beetling over the northernmost cliffs of Ulster is like a great floor plan spread open underfoot. Worth a visit for the atmosphere, and the combined ice house and dovecote, almost the only part of Downhill which remains undamaged.

Dunham Massey, Altrincham, Cheshire

The servery, butler's pantry, kitchens and very complete range of larders and sculleries are Dunham Massey's chief domestic glory. The unusual brick gas range seems to have been converted from a charcoal one, and a six-oven Aga has supplanted the old range with its varied ovens and roasting fire. But there is much more – a deer barn, a pump house, laundry and other service rooms, an excellent housemaid's closet, and evidence of telephone systems and early electric fittings.

Dunster Castle, Dunster, Somerset

Although there is not much domestically on show at Dunster, the wine cellars in the crypt are well-equipped, and the servery next door to the dining-room is very fine. In the Tenants' Hall, an interesting exploded drawing shows the extent of the subterranean Victorian service wing.

Erddig, Wrexham, Clwyd

The eccentic Yorke family had a close and fond relationship with their domestic staff: portraits, poems and photographs vividly record hundreds of years of faithful service. The eighteenth-century household offices were never dramatically altered, and they include laundry, bakehouse, carpenter's shop, dovecote, kitchen, still-room, pantries, etc.

Felbrigg Hall, Cromer, Norfolk

Felbrigg's domestic quadrangle is not all open to the public, but enough can be seen to appreciate its neat convenience. There is an ice house in the grounds and a fine seventeenth-century dovecote in the beautifully restored walled kitchen garden.

Florence Court, Enniskillen, Co. Fermanagh

Two wings of domestic offices, one a kitchen and laundry courtyard, one a home farm, and a long line of basement service rooms support the long graceful eighteenth-century façade of Florence Court. Their original functions are delightfully illustrated by a scale-model of the domestic quarters which is on display in the estate office. There is an ice house in the grounds.

Greys Court, Rotherfield Greys, Oxfordshire

The treadmill donkey wheel at Greys Court is a spectacular survival of the age when all water had to be pumped, lifted or carried by human or animal power. Some 40 ft in diameter, it is mounted over a well dug 200 ft into chalk.

Ham House, Richmond, Surrey

An outstanding Stuart house, with fine kitchen quarters, recently restored. The 'gentlemen's dining-room' and 'back parlour' were for the use of the upper servants. The ice house has a beautifully built dome of bricks – it was used as an air-raid shelter in the Second World War.

Hardwick Hall, Doe Lea, Derbyshire

Although Hardwick's sixteenth-century kitchen and still-room are occupied by the restaurant, they are still well-equipped with domestic fittings. Mark Girouard's *Hardwick Hall* is a useful guide to reconstructing how its original occupant, dashing Bess Talbot, led her daily life. No bathrooms, and an elaborately padded close stool. The herb garden, orchard and nuttery have been restored.

Kedleston Hall, Derby, Derbyshire

A monumental Robert Adam mansion, interesting in its 'rational' layout. The domestic pavilion in the east wing balances one for the family's private use to the west, and has a lofty double-cube kitchen and a fringe of outbuildings around its palatial skirts. The fishing pavilion has a cold-water plunge pool.

Kingston Lacy, Wimborne Minster, Dorset

A satisfyingly graceful range of domestic outbuildings flank this Dorset treasure house. The laundry has been restored, and has drying closets, a fine box mangle, and interesting machines in its wash-house. Viola Bankes's *A Dorset Childhood* gives a vivid picture of family life there at the turn of the century.

Lacock Abbey, Chippenham, Wiltshire

The medieval parts of Lacock illustrate the spartan simplicity of convent life – laver and warming room, and a great tank which may or may not have been a communal bath. The brewery dates from the sixteenth century: portly vats with fat copper taps and an ingeniously constructed stone and cobbled floor.

Lanhydrock, Bodmin, Cornwall

Rebuilt after being gutted by fire in 1881, Lanhydrock servants' quarters are complete and quite unchanged. There is a well-equipped dairy, bakehouse, a full range of larders, kitchens and scullery. Fire hydrants are a prominent feature of its interior.

Lindisfarne Castle, Holy Island, Lindisfarne

Lutyens again, but this time turning a Tudor block fort into a romantic Edwardian home. Lindisfarne's kitchen is farmhouse style, with a high-backed settle tailored to its sloping floor. In the scullery the ungainly boiler dominates; the bedrooms have pretty blue and white china plumbed-in washstands.

Penrhyn, Bangor, Gwynedd

This enormous neo-Norman castle had all the high Victorian domestic comforts. Elaborate central-heating systems, an unusual ice house in the foot of a tall tower and a rabbit warren of household offices. Many are not open to the public, but their original functions can be seen in fascinating detail on the plans of the house displayed in the scullery.

Saltram, Plympton, Devon

Saltram's domestic quarters narrowly missed the chance of being converted to Robert Adam's inspired specifications. Even so, its Great Kitchen is impressive, with a central, free-standing Leamington kitchener and a splendid copper *batterie de cuisine*. The Green Dressing-room upstairs is furnished with a hip bath and hot water cans.

Shaw's Corner, Ayot St Lawrence, Hertfordshire

The simple life was favoured by George Bernard Shaw, who wore woollen 'jaegers' and ergonomic knickerbockers. His bathroom and kitchen in this unostentatious Chiltern house have a wholesome, not to say spartan, atmosphere.

Shugborough, Milford, Staffordshire

Perhaps the most outstanding of all the houses I have visited in the variety of its domestic offices and outbuildings, Shugborough has the added bonus of 'action replays' of such processes as laundrywork, baking and brewing, and a very well-arranged museum of everyday life. Cheese is made and flour milled on the Home Farm; there is a beautifully tiled dairy in the basement of the Tower of the Winds.

Speke Hall, Liverpool, Merseyside

Speke is one of those houses which were little touched by time because their owners rarely occupied them. It was also fortunate to be in the hands of William Morris enthusiasts in the nineteenth century; as a result it was sensitively modernized and conveys an intensely fifteenth-century atmosphere. The kitchen and adjacent offices form part of the single central courtyard which was the hub of domestic life for master and servants alike.

Springhill, Moneymore, Co. Londonderry

A charming seventeenth-century manor-house with a full set of external domestic offices and an interesting range of basement rooms which clearly divide menservants' quarters from maidservants' – not, unfortunately, yet open to the public. There is also a good range of stables and farm buildings, and a fine tower dovecote.

Tatton Park, Knutsford, Cheshire

Tatton is second only to Shugborough in the completeness of its reconstruction of below-stairs life. Basement railway, wet and dry larders, still-rooms and kitchens, linen closet and housekeeper's room and a varied range of cellars. There is also an interesting home farm with rare breeds.

Townend, Troutbeck, Cumbria

Townend, a substantial seventeenth-century yeoman's house, has the earliest and most complete of 'fitted kitchens'. Grandfather clock, bread cupboard, even the spice drawers, are neatly joined together. Smoking racks can be seen in the huge chimney, and there are servants' bedrooms above.

Uppark, South Harting, Sussex

Seventeenth-century Uppark has separate pavilions for brewery, dairy and home farm, and kitchen, bakehouse and laundry, linked to the house by underground passages. The whole of its basement offices have been restored and arranged in appropriate style: beer cellar and wine cellar, butler's pantry and strongroom, still-room, and a secondary kitchen, housekeeper's room and larder.

Wimpole Hall, Arrington, Cambridgeshire

Wimpole's nineteenth-century domestic offices have been removed, but its eighteenth-century basement is gradually being opened up and restored. The home farm, designed by Sir John Soane, is occupied by rare breeds, and has an interesting Victorian dairy, full of equipment.

BIBLIOGRAPHY

The most useful direct sources for this book were the National Trust guides to individual properties, which usually have short bibliographies of their own. I also found the Shire Albums series of specialist booklets, well-illustrated and well-referenced, on esoteric topics, such as *Dairy Bygones* and *Dovecotes, Old Poultry Breeds* and *Charcoal-burning*, invaluable. Books with substantial and relevant domestic bibliographies are asterisked.

A Book about Beer, by 'A Drinker', London, Cape, 1934

Adams, S. and S., *The Complete Servant*, London, Knight & Lacey, 1825

Airs, Malcolm, *Making of the English Country House, 1500–1640*, London, Architectural Press, 1975

Allsop, F., *Telephones, Their Construction and Fitting*, London, Spon, 1909

★Aslet, Clive, *The Last Country Houses*, New Haven, Yale, 1982

Aslet, Clive, and Powers, Alan, *The National Trust Book of the English House*, London, Viking, in association with the National Trust, 1985; Penguin Books, 1986

Baillie, Lady Grisell, *Household Book*, Scottish History Society (series 2, vol. 1), 1911

Bankes, Viola, *A Dorset Heritage, The Story of Kingston Lacy*, London, Anthony Mott, 1986

and Watkin, Pamela, *A Kingston Lacy Childhood, Reminiscences Collected by Pamela Watkin*, Wimborne, Dorset, Dovecote Press, 1986

Baring-Gould, Sabine, *Court Royal*, 1886

Bayne-Powell, R., *Housekeeping in the Eighteenth Century*, London, John Murray, 1956

Beauman, Sylvia, P., and Roaf, Susan, *The Icehouses of Britain*, London, Routledge, 1990

Beeton, Isabella Mary, *Mrs Beeton's Book of Household Management*, London, 1861 and later editions

Bradley, Rose, *The English Housewife in the Seventeenth and Eighteenth Centuries*, London, Edward Arnold, 1912

Braidwood, James, *On the Construction of Fire Engines*, Edinburgh, 1830

Briggs, R. A., *The Essentials of a Country House*, London, Batsford, 1911

Brown, Bernard M., *The Brewer's Art*, London, Whitbread, 1948

Brown, Sanborn C., *Benjamin Thompson, Count Rumford*, Cambridge, Mass., 1979

Brunner, Hugo, and Major, Kenneth, 'Water Raising by Animal Power', *Industrial Archaeology*, vol. 9, no. 2, May 1972

Byrne, M. St Clare, *The Elizabethan Home Discovered in Two Dialogues by Claudius Hollyband and Peter Erondell*, London, Cobden Sanderson, 1930

Charlton, L. E. O., ed., *Recollections of a Northumbrian Lady, 1815–66*, London, Cape, 1949

Clifford, D. J. H., *The Diaries of Lady Anne Clifford*, Stroud, Glos., Alan Sutton, 1990

Cobbett, Anne *The English Housekeeper*, London, 1842

Colvin, Howard, *Calke Abbey, Derbyshire: A Hidden House Revealed*, George Philip, in association with the National Trust, 1985

Cook, Olive, *The English House through Seven Centuries*, London, Nelson, 1968

Cooke, A. O., *A Book of Dovecotes*, London, Foulis, 1920

Cooper, Charles, *Town and Country, or Forty Years in Service with the Aristocracy*, London, Lovat Dickson, 1937

Cooper, Lady Diana, *The Rainbow Comes and Goes*, London, Rupert Hart-Davis, 1958

The Country House: A Collection of Useful Information and Recipes Adapted to the Country Gentleman and his Household, and of the Greatest Utility to the Housekeeper Generally, 2nd ed., edited by I.E.B.C., London, Horace Cox, 1867

Crook, J. Mordaunt, *William Burges and the High Victorian Dream*, London, 1981

Cullwick, Hannah, *Diaries of Hannah Cullwick, Victorian Maidservant*, ed. Liz Stanley, London, Virago, 1984

David, Elizabeth, *English Bread and Yeast Cookery*, London, Allen Lane, 1977; Penguin Books, 1979

★Davidson, Caroline, *A Woman's Work is Never Done: A History of Housework in the British Isles 1650–1950*, London, Chatto & Windus, 1982

Defoe, *Complete English Gentleman* (1728), ed. Karl D. Buhlbring, London, 1890

Disraeli, Benjamin, *Henrietta Temple*, London, Longmans, 1880

Dring, T, *Treatise on Husbandry*, London, 1681

Drury, Elizabeth, *The Butler's Pantry Book*, London, A. & C. Black, 1981

Earle, John, *Micro-cosmographie*, 1628

Eckford, E. Stoddart, and Fitzgerald, M. S., *Household Management*, London, 1915

Edwards, F., *Our Domestic Fireplaces*, London, 1865

Ellis, Monica, *Ice and Icehouses through the Ages with a Gazetteer for Hampshire*, Southampton, University of Southampton Industrial Archaeology Group, 1982

Emmerson, Andrew, *Old Telephones*, Princes Risborough, Bucks., Shire Publications (Shire Album 161), 1986

Eveliegh, David J., *Old Cooking Utensils*, Princes Risborough, Bucks., Shire Publications (Shire Album 177), 1986

Family Economiser, London, Houlston, 1865

Fedden, Robin, and Joekes, Rosemary, *The National Trust Guide*, 4th ed. rev. L. Greeves and M. Trinick, London, National Trust, 1989

Fell, Sarah, *Book of Household Accounts*, ed. N. Penny, 1920

Fiennes, Celia, *Through England on a Side-saddle in the Time of William and Mary*, 1888

★Franklin, Jill, *The Gentleman's Country House and its Plan, 1835–1914*, London, Routledge & Kegan Paul, 1981

Frederick, Christine, *Housekeeping with Efficiency*, London, 1913

Friedman, Alice T., *House and Household in Elizabethan England: Wollaton Hall and the Willoughby Family*, Chicago, University of Chicago Press, 1989

Gandy, Joseph, *The Rural Architect*, 1805

Gill, Richard, *Happy Rural Seat: The English Country House and the Literary Imagination*, New Haven, Yale, 1967

★Girouard, Mark, *The Country House Companion*, London, Century, 1987

'Cragside I and II,' *Country Life*, 18 and 25 December, 1969

Life in the English Country House, New Haven, Yale, 1978; Penguin Books, 1980

Godfrey, Elizabeth, *Home Life Under the Stuarts 1603–1649*, London, Grant Richards, 1903

Hams, Fred, *Old Poultry Breeds*, Princes Risborough, Bucks., Shire Publications (Shire Album 35), 1978

Hansell, Peter and Jean, *Dovecotes*, Princes Risborough, Bucks., Shire Publications (Shire Album 213), 1988

★Hardyment, Christina, *Mangle to Microwave*, Oxford, Polity, 1989

Hare, Augustus, *In My Solitary Life*, London, Allen & Unwin, 1953 (an abridgement of the last three volumes of *My Solitary Life*)

Hartcup, Adeline, *Below Stairs in the Great Country Houses*, London, Sidgwick & Jackson, 1980

Hartley, Dorothy, *Food in England*, London, Macdonald, 1954

Water in England, London, Macdonald, 1964

Hellyer, Samuel Stevens, *The Plumber and Sanitary Houses*, London, 1877

Hickman, Peggy, *A Jane Austen Household Book*, Newton Abbot, David & Charles, 1978

Holme, Thea, *The Carlyles at Home*, London, Oxford University Press, 1965

Horn, Pamela, *The Rise and Fall of the Victorian Servant*, Dublin, Gill & Macmillan, 1975

Horne, Eric, *What the Butler Winked at*, 1930

Hussey, Christopher, *English Country Houses*, 3 vols., London, Country Life, 1955–8

   Life of Sir Edwin Lutyens, London, Country Life, 1950

Inskip, Peter, 'The Compromise of Drogo', *Architectural Review*, 1979

Irving, Washington, *Bracebridge Hall*, London, 1822

Jackson-Stops, Gervase, *Country Houses in Perspective*, London, Pavilion Books, in association with the National Trust, 1990

Jarrin, G. A., *The Italian Confectioner*, London, 1827

Jekyll, Gertrude, *Old English Household Life*, London, Batsford, 1939

Judges, A. V. ed., *A Health to the Gentlemanly Profession of Serving-Men, by I. M.*, 1598

Keith, Edward, *Memoirs of Wallington*, privately printed, 1939

*Kenny, Virginia C., *The Country-house Ethos in English Literature 1688–1750: Themes of Personal Retreat and National Expansion*, Hemel Hempstead, Herts., Harvester Press, 1984

Kerr, Robert, *The Gentleman's House*, London, 1864

Ketton-Cremer, R. W., *Felbrigg, The Story of a House*, Ipswich, Boydell Press, 1962; London, Century (National Trust Classics), 1986

King, F. A., *Beer Has a History*, London, Hutchinson, 1947

Kitchiner, William, *The Housekeeper's Oracle*, London, 1829

Lambton, Lucinda, *Beastly Buildings*, London, Cape, in association with the National Trust, 1985

Lancaster, Maud, *Electric Cooking, Heating, Etc.*, London, 1914

Lancelly, William, *Hall-boy to House Steward*, London, Edward Arnold, 1925

Laslett, Peter, ed., *Household and Family in Past Time*, Cambridge, Cambridge University Press, 1972

Lawrence, John, *A Practical Treatise on breeding, rearing and fattening all kinds of Domestic Poultry, Pheasants, Pigeons, and Rabbits, with an Account of the Egyptian Method of Hatching Eggs by Artificial Heat, Second Edition, with Additions on the Breeding and Feeding of Swine from Memorandum Made During Forty Years' Practice*, London, Sherwood Neely & Jones, 1816

Lewis, Lesley, *Private Life of a Country House, 1912–39*, Newton Abbot, David & Charles, 1980

Lightholer, Timothy, *Gentleman's and Farmer's Architect*, London, 1762

Loudon, J. C., *An Encyclopaedia of Cottage, Family and Villa Architecture*, London, 1833

Loudon, Jane, *The Lady's Country Companion, or How to Enjoy a Country Life Rationally*, London, 1845

Lovett, Maurice, *Brewing and Breweries*, Princes Risborough, Bucks., Shire Publications (Shire Album 72), 1982

Lucy, Brian Fairfax- and Pearce, Philippa, *Children of the House*, London, Longmans, 1968; new ed., *Children of Charlecote*, London Gollancz, in association with the National Trust, 1989

Lucy, Mary, *Mistress of Charlecote, Memoirs*, ed. Lady Alice Fairfax-Lucy, London, Gollancz, 1983

★Lummis, Trevor, and Marsh, Jan, *The Woman's Domain: Women and the English Country House*, London, Viking, in association with the National Trust, 1990

Markham, Gervase, *Country Contentments*, Book II, *The English Housewife*, 1615

Masters, Thomas, *The Ice Book*, London, 1844

Meade-Featherstonehaugh, M. and Warner, O., *Uppark and its People*, London, Century (National Trust Classics), 1988

Megson, B., *English Homes and Housekeeping 1700–1960*, London, Routledge & Kegan Paul, 1968

Mellor, Hugh, *Castle Drogo*, National Trust Guide

Merle, Gibbons, *Domestic Dictionary*, 1842

Molloy, E., *House Telephones, Bells and Signalling Systems*, London, Newnes, 1940

Moore, G., *Esther Waters*, London, 1894 (OUP World's Classics, 1964)

Moss, Fletcher, *Pilgrimages to Old Houses*, 1906

Muller, H. G., *Baking and Bakeries*, Princes Risborough, Bucks., Shire Publications (Shire Album 156), 1986

Murphy, Sir Shirley Forster, *Our Homes*, London, Cassell, 1883

Muthesius, Hermann, *The English House*, Abingdon, Oxon, Professional Books, 1990 (first published 1904)

Parkes, Mrs William, *Domestic Duties*, London, 1825

Phillips, R. Randall, *The Servantless Home*, 1920

Plaw, John, *Ferme Ornée*, 1795 (pattern book)

Powys, Mrs Lybbe, *Diaries*, ed. E. J. Climenso, London, Longmans, 1896

Pückler-Muskau, Prince, *Tour of England, 1826–8*, ed. E. M. Butler, London, Collins, 1957.

The Queen's Closet Open'd, by 'W. M.', London, 1696

★Robinson, John Martin, *The English Country Estate*, London, Century, in association with the National Trust, 1988

Georgian Model Farms: A Study of Decorative and Model Farm Buildings in the Age of Improvement, 1700–1846, Oxford, Clarendon Press, 1983

Roper, William, *Life of Sir Thomas More*, London, Dent (Everyman's Library), 1908

Rumford, Benjamin Thompson, Count, *The Complete Works of Count Rumford*, London, Oxford University Press, 1968–70

Rybczynski, Witold, *Home, A Short History of an Ideal*, London, Viking, 1986

Sackville-West, Vita, *Knole and The Sackvilles*, London, The National Trust, 1991 (first published 1922)

Sambrook, Pamela, *Laundry Bygones*, Princes Risborough, Bucks., Shire Publications (Shire Album 107), 1988

Servants' Guide and Family Manual, 1830

Servants' Magazine, 1868

Servants' Practical Guide, London, 1880

Seymour, John, *Forgotten Household Crafts*, London, Dorling Kindersley, in association with the National Trust, 1986

Soane, Sir John, *Pattern Book*, London, 1778

Stevenson, J. J., *Small Country Houses of Today*, London, 1873
  House Architecture, London, Macmillan, 1880

Sturgis, Julian, *Comedy of a Country House*, London, John Murray, 1889

Sugg, Marie Jenny, *The Art of Cooking By Gas*, London, Cassell, 1890

Sylvestor, Charles, *Philosophy of Domestic Economy*, Nottingham, 1819

Taylor, Robert, *Swan's Electric Light at Cragside*, Sotheby Parke Bernet (National Trust Studies), 1981

Thomson, Gladys Scott, *Life in a Noble Household 1641–1700*, London, Cape, 1937

Tinniswood, Adrian, *Historic Houses of the National Trust*, London, National Trust, 1991

Tredgold, Thomas, *Principles of Warming and Ventilating Public Buildings, Dwellings, Manufactories, Hospitals, Hot-houses, Conservatories*, London, 1824

Tuer, Andrew, *History of the Horn-Book*, 2 vols., 1896

Tusser, Thomas, *Five Hundred Points of Good Husbandry*, London, Oxford University Press, 1984 (first published 1573)

Verney, Lady Mary, ed., *Verney Letters of the Eighteenth Century*, London, 1930

Waldstein, *Diary of Baron Waldstein, a Traveller in Elizabethan England*, translated and annotated by G. W. Groos, London, Thames & Hudson, 1981

Walton, Karen M., 'Housekeeping in the Eighteenth and Nineteenth Centuries', *National Trust Yearbook 1977–8*, ed. Gervase Jackson-Stops, London, Europa Publications, 1977

Waterson, Merlin, *The Servants' Hall: Domestic History of a Country House*, new ed., London, National Trust, 1990

Weaver, Laurence, *The House and its Equipment*, London, 1912

Wells, H. G., *Experiment in Autobiography*, 2 vols., London, Gollancz, 1934
  Tono-Bungay, London, Macmillan, 1909

Whatman, Susanna, *The Housekeeping Book of Susanna Whatman*, ed. Christina Hardyment, London, Century (National Trust Classics), 1987

White, David, *The History of the Art of Baking in all Ages and All Countries*, Dunbar, 1824

Wolley, Hannah, *The Gentlewoman's Companion*, 1675

Wood, Margaret, *The English Mediaeval House*, London, Phoenix House, 1965

Wright, Lawrence, *Clean and Decent: The Fascinating History of the Bathroom and WC*, London, Routledge & Kegan Paul, 1960

Wright, Thomas, *The Universal Architect*, London, 1758

Yarwood, Doreen, *Five Hundred Years of Technology in the Home*, London, Batsford, 1983

INDEX

Figures in *italics* refer to captions.